Defying Autism:

Keeping Your Sanity and Taking Control

Stephanie B. Lockshin

Jennifer M. Gillis

Raymond G. Romanczyk

Institute for Child Development
State University of New York at Binghamton

Published by: DRL Books, Inc.
                12 West 18 Street
                New York, New York 10011
                Phone: 212 604 9637
                         800 857 1057
                Fax: 212 206 9329
                www.drlbooks.com

Editor: Kimberly Fusco
Book Design: John Eng
Cover Art: Judy Law

Library of Congress Control Number: 2004108821
ISBN: 0-9755859-0-8

Defying Autism:
Keeping Your Sanity and Taking Control

Table of Contents

Dedication

To our families and all the families we have been privileged to serve.

Introduction

Autism Spectrum Disorders (ASD) happens to families; it's just a fact of life. Some families experience the emergence of symptoms of ASD soon after the birth of their child while others learn about the symptoms during the course of early development. Whether it is the lack of eye contact, irritable temperament (i.e., difficult to console), resistance to being picked up and held, delayed or unusual use of speech, unusual patterns of behavior or any of the other ASD symptoms that initially alert parents to the fact that something is "amiss", it is not long before a pattern of atypical development is recognized. Struggling with questions about the need for concern (i.e., "Is this just a blip on a pattern of normative development?", "Will this go away?", "Should we get an evaluation?", "What's happening to my child?", "Am I overreacting?") introduces additional stress. Then comes the stress associated with referral for diagnosis, diagnosis, the diagnostic process, decision-making related to early intervention, and the continuing expression of ASD symptomatology.

Collectively, we have 70 plus years of experience working with children diagnosed with ASD and their families. During this time, we have learned much from our families. Perhaps the most impressive quality they display, is that regardless of individual differences in the family's educational background, socioeconomic status, family size, etc., they want to help their ASD-diagnosed child at virtually "all costs". This is a change from the prevailing views of the not too distant past, where parents were more passive recipients of treatments chosen by professionals. The inspiring book, Let Me Hear Your Voice, by Catherine Maurice (1993), solidified and widely disseminated the contemporary view of parents as active participants in treatment choice and implementation. Ten years later it serves as a continuing source of strength and hope for families, and has certainly influenced us in our work with families.

This book was written to provide you with a step-by-step guide to identifying specific goals for skills that you would like to teach your child and guidelines for helping you develop teaching programs that outline how you will teach new skills. Importantly, the approach we outline for goal selection is focused not only on the needs of your child who has been diagnosed with ASD, but is focused on the needs of your family. This family focused model was generated from our knowledge of the professional literature that documents family stressors associated with ASD and our professional experience that indicates that adding stress to a fragile family system can have negative outcomes.

Our family focused model begins with assessment of family stressors that are associated with ASD. Using these stressors as a starting point serves as a springboard for thinking about child-centered goals that will contribute to the reduction of stress in the family. Thus, family members are encouraged to identify specific, child-centered goals that will improve the child's skills or social emotional functioning that will in turn, positively effect family functioning.

Many of the parents that we have worked with initially expressed reluctance when asked to consider their own needs during planning meeting to devise home intervention. This is largely because they were focused solely on helping their child grow and develop. However, many have changed their perspective when they began to see the benefits of goal planning within the family context especially when, for the first time, they were able to successfully manage sharing time amongst siblings, decrease supervision needs by keeping their child productively busy at home, and go on family outings without incident (e.g., bowling and to the movies).

Simply put, the primary goals of our family focused model are two-fold: to teach the ASD-diagnosed child new and adaptive behaviors, and to simultaneously reduce family stress. We believe that thinking and planning with these two, inter-related goals in mind, results in the best outcomes for both the child and the family.

The model encourages everyone in the family to participate in the process of behavior change and it utilizes information provided by all family members as a starting point for goal selection. We refer to our model as the Family Individual Enhancement Plan.

Our thinking about the F.I.E.P. model was shaped by two major forces – research documenting effective intervention strategies and lessons learned by working cooperatively with families, i.e., listening, problem solving, rejoicing in successes, and trying to understand our failures and using new insights to modify our teaching strategies. Imagine the joy experienced by families whose children are becoming more independent with activities of daily living, parents who are now able to leave their children with caregiver so they can enjoy a night out, dine out with the entire family, parents who feel better able to balance each child's need for parental attention, and children who are eager to help with family chores to create more time for leisure activities. What's more, the reinforcement for participating in these family activities derives directly from the family: being a participating member of the family.

▶ How is this Book Different?

Our book, written in the genre of a self-help resource for parents, is unique in that it highlights a family focus in the development of home interventions for children who have been diagnosed with ASD. This book targets two groups, namely, parents who are continuously searching for new resources that improve their ability to affect positive behavior change and parents who have limited access to professional resources. For both groups, the book may be used to help generate home goals and implement home teaching programs. However, due to many of the challenges related to treating children with autism spectrum disorders, the book will contain information about the risks of "flying solo" as well as warning signs to indicate when professional consultation is needed. Thus, when there are sufficient resources in your community for treating the symptoms of ASD and associated problems, it may be prudent to consult with professional and use this book to stimulate ideas. While this book is written primarily for parents of children with autism spectrum disorders, it may also be used by professionals and professionals "in training" (i.e., graduate students) to assist them in their work with families.

A substantial portion of the book is devoted to parent assessment of child needs, the status of the family's current working relationship, goal identification (both child and family), and prioritization of goals for individual family members and for the family unit. Emphasis is also placed on self-assessment of the family's readiness to adopt this approach. Numerous worksheets are provided to guide parents through the assessment and decision making process. It is important to note that this book does not attempt to address the full range of family and developmental issues, but rather focuses on issues that frequently arise within families of children with ASD.

► What Will I Learn?

After reading the book, you will be able to identify both short and long- term child and family goals, prioritize child and family goals, evaluate your resources, and differentiate between goals that you can manage on your own and those for which professional consultation will be needed. You will also be able to begin the process of effecting behavior change that will have a positive impact on the entire family. While many of our readers may not feel ready to tackle complex or multi-program interventions, everyone should be able to at least identify a specific goal, design a teaching program, implement the program, and monitor the effectiveness of the program.

It is important to remember that interventions for families and children with ASD need to be highly individualized as each child and family presents with unique needs. Therefore, the book does not prescribe specific home programs (i.e. a one size fits all approach). Instead, it outlines a process for identifying goals that will specifically help your child and your family.

Yes, this is a major undertaking and you may feel intimidated and may even doubt your ability to accomplish such a complex task. However, we provide you with numerous examples at each step of the way to provide you with help to individualize programs to fit your family's unique circumstances.

► Chapter Contents

Chapter 1 provides an up-to-date overview of ASD and best practices in the treatment of ASD while Chapter 2 provides a rationale for adopting a family focused approach to treatment planning. Specific topics included in Chapter 2 include validation of the perception of heightened parenting stress often reported by parents of children with autism, contemporary views on the role of parents in the treatment of autism, and discussion of how specific characteristics of autism may disrupt family life and impede the family's ability to progress through normative stages of family development and to successfully resolve developmental issues and challenges. Chapter 2 also introduces the concept of the family as a microcosm within which to address difficulties related to community integration. Within the family, children with ASD need to learn and practice skills that enable them to communicate effectively with others, care for their own needs, get along with others (i.e., sharing, waiting, taking turns, playing, etc.), and contribute in a meaningful way. These are all necessary ingredients for success in school, independent living, the workplace, and the community at large.

Moreover, family focused interventions assist families in addressing the ASD-related symptoms that interfere with each family member's ability to gratify personal needs (i.e., socialization, belonging, acceptance, autonomy) as well as overall family functioning. The chapter will outline the benefits that can be achieved through thoughtful goal planning that focuses on both child and family needs. Among these are a sense of empowerment and an increased sense of unity as family members begin to address mutual goals. Related outcomes may also include improvement in communication and cooperation. These are all ingredients for healthy family functioning.

The remaining chapters focus on pragmatics in that they contain specific information about "how to" develop a family focused intervention program. Each chapter contains worksheets to assist parents in making choices and examples to guide them through the process.

In Chapter 3, Getting a G.R.I.P. (Growth, Relationships, Independence, and Participation) on the challenges, we present lists of child and family needs, namely, our "Top 10 Child Needs" and the "Top 10 Family Needs". These are provided to stimulate thinking about the selection of child-centered and family-focused goals. We then walk you through application of the G.R.I.P. format as a starting point for goal selection. The G.R.I.P. format originated within the context of the development of the Individualized Goal Selection Curriculum (Romanczyk, Lockshin, and Matey, 2000) and is now widely used as a starting point for goal selection for children with ASD. Given the research supporting the relationship between "readiness" for change and outcome, this chapter discusses issues associated with readiness, identify possible impediments to change, and to provide families with tools to assess their readiness for behavior change.

Two other very important topics are included in this chapter, namely, the psychological/psychiatric issues requiring professional consultation and assessment of resources needed to effect change. The discussion begins by highlighting the complex nature of the task that the family is about to undertake and to stress the importance of routinely monitoring the psychological well-being of family members during this process and identification of potential psychological issues that might either interfere with the success of family-focused intervention or become exacerbated by the demand for changes within the existing family structure. This topic is especially relevant to families outside of large population centers where limited resources are available. The chapter therefore includes brief checklists to help families screen for these types of problems and advise them about when to seek out professional consultation.

The final topic included in this chapter focuses on guidelines for assessing the resources needed for implementation of family-focused interventions. Everyone in education and mental health has been feeling the "crunch" of budget cuts and the evaporation of already limited resources. Therefore, skillful use of existing resources such as schools, neighborhoods, local agencies, and service organizations is discussed.

Chapter 4 introduces the A.I.M.M. model (Assess, Intervene, Measure, and Modify) which we refer to as the "Nuts and Bolts" of treatment. Use of this model is particularly important since time is valuable and parents need a method for insuring that their efforts are producing changes in the desired direction. The A.I.M.M. model is intended to provide a safety net for detecting impediments to progress on goals.

The introduction to Chapter 4 provides a brief overview of the importance of assessment both prior to and during the course of intervention. Assessment before intervention starts is important because it pinpoints the skills to be taught, refined, or simply used more frequently. Discussion also focuses on how the A.I.M.M. model is designed to assist parents with determining the child's current ability on specific skills, measuring the effectiveness of the teaching strategy (i.e., progress), and knowing when the child has mastered goals. More specific information specifying the details of assessment and measurement is included in Chapter 5 and Chapter 7.

The next section of the chapter provides an overview of interventions that have the support of well-controlled research. The intent of this section is not to promote any one particular strategy, but rather to provide you with an understanding of treatment strategies to help make decisions about which strategies will work for your child and family. Importantly, only those treatment strategies with research support are included in this section. Pharmacotherapy will be among the treatment options discussed. Within this section, we focus on the following topics: the pros and cons of medication, accessing information, decision-making, and monitoring effectiveness.

In Chapter 5 the issue of assessment is revisited with a focus on how to measure skills and behavior and the variety of formats that serve this function, e.g., measurement of child ability relative to same-aged peers, mastery of goals selected, skills and problem behaviors prior to intervention, measurement of progress during the teaching process, and measurement of broad outcomes.

You will be taught how to measure your child's ability on skills prior to intervention (i.e., to aid in goal selection). The other main focus in Chapter 5 is standardized assessment. This topic is included here because many parents find this process confusing, frustrating, and anxiety provoking. In this section we outline the importance of and the limits of standardized assessment, what should be included in a comprehensive assessment, and we address the issue of provider qualifications, that is, "who" is qualified to do "what".

Chapter 6 addresses the complex topic of intervention. This chapter is designed to assist you with identifying which goals to choose, when to address different goals, and the development of teaching strategies. While these are mind-bending topics, they are critical ones for success. One of the most important areas of intervention is prioritization of goals for both the child and the family. In the discussion of prioritization, the chapter will focus on the benefits of using a curriculum guide and will discuss the relevant instructional areas for intervention. We focus on the process of child and family change, and we'll provide step-by-step guidelines for devising well-conceptualized intervention programs. The major theme that pervades the content of this chapter is the importance of investing time in developing a road map of how to get from Point A to Point B and how to maximize benefits through thoughtful organization and implementation of goals.

Within this chapter, we describe the process of utilizing G.R.I.P. information and available assessment information as a starting point for selecting appropriate target behaviors and will discuss the benefits of using a curriculum guide for goal selection (i.e., having a reference tool that provides examples of skills that can be taught and logical sequences for skill development). Emphasis is placed on developmental issues and functional skill sequences (i.e., those that result in clinically relevant changes in function) within domains that are likely to rise to the top of the priority list (i.e., communication, socialization, and leisure skills).

Since the book addresses family skill development as well as child skill development, this chapter focuses on family intervention with an emphasis on time management, coping, and relationship building. The content in this section of the chapter is on strategies for reorganizing the family's schedule to decrease stress, improving communication among family members, strategies for productive family problem solving, family negotiation, compromise, judicious division of labor, and joint selection of target behaviors that will benefit the family at large.

While these sections of the chapter focus on global goal identification, the next section focus on providing families with guidelines on specific goal selection. Issues addressed include making decisions about how many goals to address at one time and suggestions on how to coordinate and sequence goals to maximize benefits without exhausting family resources. Prioritization of skills that deliver "big payoffs" for both the child and the family are emphasized (e.g., toileting training as mastery of this skill increases opportunities for inclusion within school programs and community activities and at the same time decreases the workload associated with incontinence).

Thoughtful and systematic development of teaching programs is addressed next. This section includes a discussion of the basic elements that need to be considered (i.e., specification of the skill to be taught, outlining the teaching methodology, setting the criteria for success, and addressing motivational issues). Worksheets provide practice with these skills and sample programs (including sample data recording sheets) are also included.

In many ways measurement is the keystone to effective intervention. Even though it plays such a critical role, it is often misunderstood and ignored. Important decisions about a child are then made using simple subjective evaluations that are known to be of very limited use, especially in the context of treating ASD. Given the content of this chapter, it could "stand alone" and be used by parents as a resource to help them evaluate child progress in any educational or therapeutic program.

Chapter 7 explains why ongoing measurement is necessary and how it can assist you in improving services you receive from schools and other providers, and how it empowers you to be an active part of decision making, rather than a passive consumer. In a very real sense, measurement of child behavior and family behavior 'levels the playing field' between parent and professional as it permits unambiguous evaluation of what is occurring.

Step by step instructions and numerous forms that can easily be used at home are provided. In contrast to Chapter 5, the emphasis here is on the daily process of measurement of specific skills and problems that are being addressed, as opposed to the assessment of child characteristics using formal standardized instruments. Focus is on individualizing the measurement process for a specific child and set of circumstances. Examples of goals, alternative measurement strategies, and interpretation of information is provided as well as hypothetical situations for practicing application of knowledge accrued. Instruction is guided by the use of "parent-friendly" monitoring sheets that have been developed especially for home intervention. Tips on how to collect samples of child behavior within the home are provided so that the measurement aspects of treatment can be easily managed.

Chapter 8 provides you with a model of how the "measurement" information collected is directly linked to modification of ongoing specific teaching programs or the overall intervention plan. In essence, this chapter completes the A.I.M.M. cycle and illustrates that the treatment process (i.e., A.I.M.M.) is dynamic and continually adjusted based on feedback from ongoing measurement. The important point here is that the development of effective programs is a process and that the model is designed to provide us with feedback about program effectiveness: Are we getting close to achieving the goal? Lack of progress or slow progress is not interpreted as failure, but rather, as a problem to be solved via application of the model. You are provided with guidelines for conceptualizing how programs can be changed to improve progress. The remainder of the chapter will take you through the modification step and back to the assessment or measurement phase.

Chapter 9 provides examples of family friendly home programs that have been successfully implemented by families affiliated with our school. Each of these will be presented as a case history and will adopt the following format: presenting problem, use of assessment information, conceptualization of the intervention, implementation, results, and discussion. In some cases, discussion of the modifications needed for success will be included.

Chapter 10 is designed as a summary of the information presented in the book. In essence, its function is to serve as an abbreviated resource for parents as they proceed with the development and implementation of their home interventions. Specific locations where they may find the unabridged text will be provided for ease of use.

The final chapter, Chapter 11 provides you with resources that may be helpful in answering a variety of questions that may arise as you read this book or as you are faced with choice points in the decision making process.

▶ How to Use this Book

Each chapter in this book focuses on a specific set of concepts that relate to formulating a home program. The information provided will give you a rationale about why this step is important and how it is related to other steps in the process. Completed worksheets accompany the text to show you how they are to be used. When relevant, we will include questions to guide you to consider important topics and to help you make decisions when confronted with choice points. Blank worksheets are located in the Appendix of the book and it is highly recommended that you complete these as you work through each chapter. However, you may not want to complete the worksheets immediately after reading the chapter for the first time as it is important to invest some time thinking about the topics and choice points and discussing these with your collaborators. Where applicable, suggestions will be provided for recruiting input from other family members, professionals, etc.

▶ Materials You Will Need

- A binder for storing completed worksheets.

- A curriculum guide that provides you with a listing of relevant goals

- Highlighters in several different colors to accentuate current goals, goals that have been completed, and to highlight key components for program implementation.

- Several packets of Post It notes to help you collate information during the goal identification process.

- Binder dividers with the following topic headings:

  — Family concerns

  — Priorities for intervention

  — Goal lists. A listing of goals that you intend to address should be included so that you can keep track of when goals have been addressed and when they have been completed. A working goal list also reminds you of the course and sequence of the goals you have selected.

  — Specific programs that are in progress and measurement of progress toward goal completion.

1

Autism: Myths and Best Practices

▶ Arming Yourself with Accurate Information

There is no substitute for knowledge when confronting a complex problem. The information available about autism spectrum disorders is enormous, but most of it is simply opinion, often presented as if it were fact. We strongly feel that an objective, science based approach provides a powerful method to help us address important human needs. Caring and compassion are the basis for helping others, but they are only the first part. Knowledge is the essential partner, without which caring and compassion too often result in the opposite of good intentions. Providing for the well-being of your child with ASD, yourself, and your family is certainly a complex problem. Although you may want to believe that all service providers are knowledgeable and objective, this is not the case. You must be an active participant in all decision-making and must be an informed consumer. The alternative is to rely on good faith and hope all turns out okay. We urge the former approach. As Michael Shermer (2002), writes "For those lacking a fundamental comprehension of how science works, the siren song of pseudoscience becomes too alluring to resist, no matter how smart you are". We have addressed this problem of how one evaluates claims and determines the accuracy of information in detail elsewhere (Romanczyk, Arnstein, Soorya, & Gillis, 2002; Romanczyk and Gillis, 2004), and because it is so important, this topic is the first chapter. So brace yourself – here's where the self help begins. This part is a little technical, but you must be able to speak the same dialect as service providers as you take charge of your child's development.

▶ Autism Spectrum Disorders

Perhaps one of the most confusing issues a parent must face when the diagnosis of autism spectrum disorder is made, is understanding the specifics of the diagnosis with respect to your child. Because we refer to this as a spectrum, it clearly indicates that there is a wide range of how the disorder can affect the individual child. It is best not to think of autism as a "thing" that a child has, but rather it is a somewhat imprecise way of describing the cluster of symptoms that the child displays.

Autism Spectrum disorder is a term used by both professionals and the lay public to describe the specific psychiatric diagnoses of pervasive developmental disabilities (PDD). The source for the diagnostic definitions in United States is the fourth edition of the Diagnostic and Statistical Manual of the American Psychiatric Association (DSM-IV, TR, 2000). This manual presents a series of symptoms in various categories that are used to determine the diagnoses. There are five disorders within the broad category of PDD. The ones most relevant for our purposes are autistic disorder, Aspergers disorder and pervasive developmental disorder – not otherwise specified (PDD-NOS). Notice that the various names of categories and disorders are similar and can be quite confusing. The symptoms for these three disorders are in many ways quite similar. The primary impairment across these disorders is the impairment of social functioning. Each disorder also emphasizes other characteristics to a lesser or greater extent, such as degree of communication impairment. Often there will be further descriptors used, with or without a formal diagnosis, such as " mild autism", "autistic like", "low functioning autism", etc. It is important to understand that such terms do not have precise, generally agreed upon, definitions or implications. This is an important issue when discussing prognosis. To date, we do not have reliable measures that predict the long-term outcome except for the very general factor of intellectual development being a positive prognostic indicator. But even with this indicator, there is a wide range of possible outcomes, and one should not assume that a child with initially slow or limited intellectual development will necessarily have a poor outcome and vice versa. Outcomes are very dependent upon the type and duration of services that the child receives.

▶ Beware of the "treatment du jour"

A major source of confusion and distress for parents is the "treatment du jour" phenomenon, or as some call it the "cure du jour". That is, there are constant reports in the media and on the internet of new and breakthrough treatments for autism spectrum disorders. Sadly most of these reports have more to do with their supposed newsworthiness from a human interest perspective rather than accurate and objective reports about well conducted research. This problem is now also a growing one in the general field of medicine, where news reports and advertising in the media often go far beyond what is actually known through scientific study.

Thus, in order to protect yourself and your child, it is sadly the case that you must become a very critical and knowledgeable consumer. Ironically, most of the popular and common treatment approaches are actually experimental in nature, even though they are presented as mainstream, and approaches that are often mistakenly criticized as experimental are in fact well validated and not experimental. It is very difficult to separate what is accurate from hype, from self-serving, from philosophizing, from proselytizing, from ideologue, from just ignorant (no matter how sincere or well-intentioned). This means that your source of information becomes quite important. Information is available from friends, colleagues, professionals, schools, the news media, the popular press, support groups, and, of course, the Internet. Unfortunately, there are no standards for these types of information sources as to how claims are evaluated and placed in circulation. Certainly the old advice of "caveat emptor" (let the buyer beware) is still a very sound strategy. In our emphasis on this topic, we wish to stress that it is important to be open-minded about new developments, but this must be done with critical evaluation as the implications for your child are so profound. Claims by individuals can be made in the spirit of good intentions, personal beliefs, misinterpretation of fact, and in the worst case, fraud and misrepresentation. Most of the time proponents are sincere and are concerned for children's well being. Sadly, such intent provides no protection from being wrong. The best protection from misinformation is good common sense and applying the general skepticism of being a good consumer. Here are a few thoughts and signs to watch for in claims of treatment success:

- If it sounds too good to be true it probably isn't true.

- It's easy and it's quick and it takes no effort - there are few things in life where this is true.

- The treatment is supposedly a "breakthrough" that is rejected by the establishment.

- You must believe in the therapy for it to work. Thus if it doesn't work it was simply because one didn't believe strongly enough. This is one of the worst as the places blame on the parent and never on the failure of the treatment.

- Proponents of the treatment say they don't need research because the results are so positive.

- The rationale for use of the treatment is "In my many years of professional experience I have found this to be effective." Opinion (even when sincere) and demonstrated effectiveness are not the same.

- The kids just love this treatment. Beware, pleasure and effectiveness are not the same. Having fun should be part of everyone's day.

- The outcome is evaluated by a teacher or caregiver using subjective ratings and descriptions rather than objective standardized measurement (most supposed 'research' projects are done this way).

- The proponents of a treatment speak more about how they're not like other treatments than they speak about the form and substance and evidence for their treatment.

- The treatment is only available from a specific person or guru and it usually costs lots of money.

Related to the above issues about being a good consumer, there is the more difficult question of combining treatments. Some propose that doing a little bit of everything is a good strategy. That is, rather than focus upon a particular treatment approach, one uses a number of different approaches in the hope that there is synergy (that is, an additive effect). Unfortunately, this often results in not spending enough time and effort with any one approach and therefore the individual is receiving diluted treatment. You can think of this in the same way as the dosage for a medication. Typically medication will have an effect for a particular illness only if delivered in the proper dosage over a certain length of time. This is why many prescription bottles often have a warning label on them to make sure that you continue with the medication until all of it is gone rather than stop as soon as your feeling better. Thus, more is not always better if the impact is to lower the dosage of specific treatment approaches that have been shown to be effective. It is important to remember that when we say a treatment is effective, that statement is only accurate in the context of using the specific procedures that were tested, implemented by trained individuals, and for specific numbers of sessions or hours. What might be seen as 'minor' alterations of the treatment procedures may have profound negative impact.

▶ Style of Approach

Everyone has personal styles that they use when it comes to making complex decisions. In another book (Romanczyk and Gillis, 2004) we describe the decision-making styles and the process parents go through in identifying effective treatment, and we excerpt here some of the styles that we have observed. We feel it is important to point these out and urge self-examination. Understanding the complex forces that influence your decision-making is necessary in order to make truly informed choices. Here they are:

▌ "They know what's best"

Place trust in a service provider to choose the intervention procedures (pediatrician, school district, case manager, etc.). Trust may be based upon reputation, personal likable qualities, willingness to spend time with parents, promises of effectiveness, minimizing child's deficits and offering good prognosis, etc.

▌ "Hedge your bets"

Do a little bit of everything in the belief that it can't hurt, and that a diverse 'package' will be of help even if some of the individual treatment approaches are not really effective. Also known as the 'everything but the kitchen sink' approach. This approach assumes that all components are compatible with one another and that the balance and sequence between approaches is not important and that the amount (or dosage) of an intervention approach is not critical.

▌"Fanatical focus"

Pursue a single course with overwhelming intensity and focus that goes beyond the typical recommendations. The essence of this strategy comes from two sources: the false belief that if a specific 'dosage' is good, then increasing it is better, and emotional comfort that comes from putting all of one's energy into a loved one's care. Such extreme focus is often based on a lack of understanding of the empirical literature and lack of appropriate child centered assessment and evaluation information. This approach has the additional risk of placing great strain and emotional drain on the family.

▌"Hope for the best"

Forgo formal treatment and participate in typical activities that are available. Often influenced by family members who don't 'trust' professionals, have examples of family members or knowledge of other families where someone was slow to develop and ultimately 'turned out fine'. This approach can also stem from denial of the problem due to emotional conflict and fear and can be associated with anger directed at a professional who is responsible for making the initial diagnosis.

▌"Cure du jour"

Pursue each new treatment as they appear and drop the current program. This approach stems from the 'new is better' philosophy and often reflects being overly influenced by marketing, 'breakthrough' announcements in the media, and the simple repetition of history. Approaches found to be inadequate tend to come back in cycles as the information about the approach is forgotten or the approach is now described in different terms.

▎"A friend told me"

Do what seemed to work for the child of someone you know or have read about. Because autism spectrum disorders encompass a heterogeneity of specific child characteristics and expression of severity, this approach is as ill advised as sharing medication for an illness you have with a friend who 'has the same problem'.

▎"Guru selection"

Following and believing in a single, specific 'expert' – similar to "fanatical focus" in that information is used selectively and the decision is strongly emotionally based because the approach is packaged in the context of the 'expert' having made 'breakthroughs', is outside the 'establishment', requires 'loyalty' by not challenging information presented, is disparaging of other professionals, often at a personal level, and uses seemingly impressive case studies to prove the approach works. Guru promotion is often accompanied by statements that the person is concerned about helping people, and not in doing research. Effects are claimed to be 'obvious'.

► Efficacious Treatments

There are well over 100 different treatment approaches that have been popularized for the treatment of autism. Sadly most are not effective and some can be dangerous. It is important to utilize the information that has been obtained from well conducted formal treatment outcomes research to evaluate whether a treatment is appropriate for your child. We see this as the same issue regarding use of a medication. Most individuals would want to use medication approved by the FDA rather than a medication that someone simply made up and claims to be effective. Certainly one can argue that having such an approval process does slow down the availability of new medication that could help people in need. However it is also clearly the case, and we have many tragic examples, that medication not properly tested can have devastating negative effects.

It is not necessary to become a scientist or statistician in order to utilize the information obtained from a good sound scientific study. There are many sources you can access to obtain the objective information about the current state of scientific knowledge. In general, it is not wise to obtain an opinion about the adequacy of the scientific support from a service provider as your primary source. Clearly a service provider has already made a judgment in terms of offering specific treatment approaches and may or may not be aware of or sensitive to the full range of information available. They may have their own biases and also a lack of formal training in certain approaches.

It can be very confusing when the term 'research' is used. Virtually every form of therapy claims that 'research has shown …". It is interesting that from a marketing point of view, advertisers have learned that most individuals feel more comfortable if the product has been tested in some way. Unfortunately, this is where the meaning of research is often distorted. Some use the term research in the form of "I have done research on this treatment for many years". All too often this phrase means simply the person has done reading on the topic and thought about the various components and their experiences. This is similar to when a college student "researches" a term paper. In other instances, research is used to describe a process where measurements are taken before and after a treatment to show effectiveness. In general, such information gathering is not actually research, but rather simply case studies or anecdotal report, that are subject to many interpretation problems that are not always obvious to the consumer.

The essence of research is that one controls for possible alternative explanations of change, so that one can conclude that the specific treatment was the cause of the improvement, and not some other factor that was actually producing the change that the researcher may or may not have been aware of. There are formal rules to guide research, often referred to as experimental design or experimental methodology. The bottom line is that poor research is easy to do and good research is very hard to do. Thus it is critical that one not accept research results as simply who has more, as in a baseball game where whoever has the most runs wins. Rather it is the quality of the research that counts – one well conducted research project is much better than dozens of poorly conducted research studies. Just because something is published in what sounds like a 'scientific' journal, doesn't mean it has passed the test of sound research methodology. All journals are not equal in their scientific credibility and rigor.

New information and research are constantly appearing, as one would expect. There is always a tendency to believe that newer is better, but this is not always true. There is much to be said for the tried and true versus the 'promising' new development. Such judgments are very difficult and require a large set of specialized skills and specialized knowledge. Such people are often referred to as scientists, but more correctly they are research methodologists. These are individuals who do not have a vested interest in the research outcome, but rather are simply concerned with the quality of the research procedures. It would be extremely difficult for an individual family to access such expertise to help in their decision making. Fortunately there is an alternative that is freely available, and this is the reports prepared by various independent review boards commissioned by objective government or professional groups. Such reports are not the same as position papers or opinion papers (no matter what they are titled) that are produced by service providers, or proponents of a particular philosophy or treatment. Such reports can be criticized as being inherently self-serving and not truly objective. In contrast, empirically based review committees, of the type we recommend, use a formal methodology to evaluate the quality of research, not just the conclusions, and use the resulting high quality research to form recommendations.

Because the process is complex and it is often difficult to compare the recommendations of "a panel of experts", fortunately there is an objective and consistent way of evaluating treatments (Noyes-Grosser, Holland, Lyons, Romanczyk, Gillis &, in press). The U.S. Agency for Health Care Policy and Research (AHCPR) initially developed 19 evidence-based clinical practice guidelines in the early to mid 90's, and in the process formalized the processes, procedures, and criteria for evaluating research and preparing clinical guidelines for consumers and service providers. Currently named the U.S. Agency for Healthcare Research and Quality (AHRQ), it is part of the United States Public Health Service (Holland, 1995). Sometimes guidelines using this methodology are referred to as best practice guidelines. The AHCPR clinical practice guideline methodology in turn uses principles recommended by the U.S. Institute of Medicine. This

AHCPR methodology, is the accepted standard for developing evidence-based clinical practice guidelines (Eddy, 1995; Holland, 1995; Schriger, 1995; Woolf, 1991; Woolf, 1995).

The New York State Department of Health (NYSDOH) Early Intervention Program selected the AHCPR methodology and developed evidence-based clinical practice guidelines focused on identification, assessment, and intervention for young children with developmental problems (autism spectrum disorders, communication disorders, Down syndrome, vision impairment, hearing loss, and motor disorders). The stated goal of the project was to provide families and service providers with recommendations based on scientific evidence.

More than 8,000 research reports were reviewed and evaluated using the AHCPR methodology. These guidelines are available in their entirety from NYSDOH (http://www.albany.edu/psy/autism/doh_gid.html) and should be standard reading for every parent and professional who seeks to help children with ASD.

Even when rigorous methodology and cross checks are used in producing such guidelines, it is a longstanding tenet of good scientific methodology that one must be able to replicate results. That is, another person or group, other than the original person or group, must be able to follow the same procedures and obtain the same results. In other words, it is necessary to be able to reproduce results by other independent individuals. It is the same for establishing guidelines. If the process is objective and well-defined, it should be possible to duplicate the results and conclusions, because they are not based on mere opinion.

In this context, several other objective treatment reviews have been produced recently. One is "Educating Children with Autism", authored by the Committee on Educational Interventions for Children with Autism, Division of Behavioral and Social Sciences and Education, of the National Research Council, published by the National Academies Press. The report was commissioned by the U.S. Department of Education's Office of Special Education Programs to "consider the state of the scientific evidence of the effects and features of early educational intervention on young children with autism spectrum disorders," (p. 2). The committee takes a similar approach to the NYSDOH process and cites it as a reference. They state that: "To achieve a systematic and rigorous assessment of research studies, the committee established guidelines for evaluating areas of strength, limitations, and the overall quality of the research ..." (p. 14). This report does not offer specific treatment recommendations based upon conclusions drawn from the research as does the NYSDOH guidelines, but does provide evaluative statements, such as, in the context of sensory integration therapy that: "These interventions have also not yet been supported by empirical studies." (p. 99). Another example is the statement that "By far, the bulk of autistic spectrum disorders intervention research has been conducted from the perspective of applied behavior analysis." (p. 148).

The recent Report of the Surgeon General (1999) concerning mental health in the US is a third important objective source. It is quite specific. In the section on children, specific reference to autism is made. The report states:

"Because autism is a severe, chronic developmental disorder, which results in significant lifelong disability, the goal of treatment is to promote the child's social and language development and minimize behaviors that interfere with the child's functioning and learning. Intensive, sustained special education programs and behavior therapy early in life can increase the ability of the child with autism to acquire language and ability to learn. Special education programs in highly structured environments appear to help the child acquire self-care, social, and job skills. Only in the past decade have studies shown positive outcomes for very young children with autism. Given the severity of the impairment, high intensity of service needs, and costs (both human and financial), there has been an ongoing search for effective treatment.

Thirty years of research demonstrated the efficacy of applied behavioral methods in reducing inappropriate behavior and in increasing communication, learning, and appropriate social behavior."

(http://www.surgeongeneral.gov/library/mentalhealth/chapter3/sec6.html#autism)

▶ Some Issues to Consider

As we have said, evaluating treatment approaches is a difficult technical task. Because of the work done by others (above), fortunately you do not have to start from scratch. Here's a brief checklist of issues to help structure your deliberations.

- ✓ Evidence-based
- ✓ Comprehensiveness of approach
- ✓ Family involvement required
- ✓ Theory of approach
- ✓ Availability
- ✓ Cost
- ✓ Intensity of approach
- ✓ Philosophy of approach

▶ The End of the Beginning

Such homework as gathering information, especially from the above sources, prepares you for the 'big' choices – what type of treatment approach and how much of it. This then is just the starting point, because no treatment is 100% effective for everyone who receives it. On-going modification of treatment programs is the norm. Such modification should be based on the same type of systematic evaluation used in evaluating research. This is a focus of this book, an approach that we describe as the AIMM Model. It is a set of very powerful tools that parents can use to take control of their child's and family's well-being.

                               ℘ ✠ ℘

2

Family-Focused Intervention – A Good Fit Model

▶ Beliefs and Assumptions

In our work with families who have children diagnosed with ASD, we often encounter parents who have adopted a set of assumptions that define their parenting role. In large part, these assumptions reflect the parents' response to ASD. The assumptions serve to help parents to meet the needs of their disabled child (e.g., minimize the child's distress), cope with their child's atypical response to more typical parenting interactions, and preserve daily routines and activities. It is easy to see how these assumptions can transform into beliefs and standards that shape parenting interactions and family life.

These beliefs may result in standards that are highly demanding and unrealistic. Initially, these beliefs may reduce some of the stress that can accompany ASD and related behavioral and emotional issues (i.e., we all function better when our roles are well-defined and we have a plan of action). However, acceptance of these unrealistic standards and erroneous beliefs, will contribute to increased stress in the future.

Although not all-inclusive, the table below presents examples of distorted beliefs that can set up a vicious cycle of failure and self-doubt. We refer to these erroneous assumptions and beliefs as "parenting myths."

Parenting Myths
Parents must be perfect in all their decisions and actions. "Perfect" parents do not have children who are unhappy or in distress.
Parents are the only ones who can adequately care for their child with ASD.
It is essential to always put the needs of the child with ASD first.
All other family members must sacrifice their own needs to provide adequate care for a child with ASD.
Families of children with ASD can never approach normative functioning.
Superman (woman) lives at your address and you are playing the role.

A brief look at the "myths" may leave you feeling overwhelmed or angry because you ascribe to these beliefs and do not think that these are myths, or feeling relieved to hear that these are excessive expectations. Feeling overwhelmed would not be surprising because the demands inherent in these assumptions reflect unrealistic and inappropriate goals for parenting under any conditions. Another potential problem associated with these myths is that they may become incorporated into your belief system and may generate additional, faulty beliefs (i.e. beliefs that have little basis in reality) that can have a strong influence on your behavior.

Which myths influence your behavior and your family's interactions? The example in the table below is intended to stimulate your thinking.

The "Big" Parenting Myth	Examples of Erroneous Assumptions
It is essential to always put the needs of children with ASD first.	• If we give Johnny what he wants, he will be happier. • We should sacrifice to make him happy. After all, he has a serious handicapping condition. • Johnny has so few interests. If he wants to play with his siblings' toys, the other children will just have to put up with it. • My husband and I don't ever go out because it is so hard to find a baby sitter that Johnny likes. Going to the movies or out to dinner isn't really that important, is it?

As in the example myth above, all myths and self-imposed limitations are associated with erroneous assumptions. We would be remiss if we did not present you with the "realities" as counterpart to some of these common myths.

Myth	Reality
Parents must be perfect.	Children build tolerance and develop coping skills when their needs are not immediately met.
Parents are the only ones who can care for a child with ASD.	Children can and need to learn to adapt to others.
It is essential to always put the needs of children with ASD first.	Well-adjusted families balance the needs of all individuals in the family unit. Not all needs get met all of the time.
All other family members must sacrifice their own needs to provide adequate care for a child with ASD.	All family members, including the identified child, must compromise to ensure that all family members experience need fulfillment.
Families can never approach normative functioning.	Despite the untoward emotional, physical, and at times, financial stressors associated with having a family member with a lifelong disability, families can and should strive for normative family life.
Superman (Superwoman) lives at your address.	He (she) doesn't.

If your find yourself believing in any of the myths, you may be wondering, "Where do these erroneous beliefs come from?"; "Why do they persist?"; and "How can I alter these perceptions?" Some of the answers to these questions are found in the family therapy literature that we summarize briefly, below.

▶ Families and Family Functioning

As defined by Goldenberg & Goldenberg (2000), families are complex organized systems in which members share an intense bond (i.e., strong and robust, reciprocal emotional attachments and loyalties that span across generations and that persist over time, distance, physical separation, and hardship). This bond develops from a shared history, collective perceptions and assumptions about the world, and common goals. In addition, Goldenberg & Goldenberg (2000) have conceptualized the family unit as a natural social system in that each family possesses an organized power structure, specific governing rules, designated roles for its members, and characteristic methods for negotiating and solving problems that enable the family and its individual members to effectively accomplish important tasks.

In order to function as a cohesive unit, families implicitly and explicitly generate rules that delineate and distribute roles and functions to family members and establish parameters for acceptable and unacceptable behavior. Over time, these rules influence interactions among family members and develop into stable and recurring patterns (Goldenberg & Goldenberg, 2000; Minuchin, Lee, and Simon (1966). These patterns are often undetectable by outsiders and often occur so automatically among family members that their origins are poorly understood. Nevertheless, these unspoken rules play a significant role in determining how families organize their lives to maintain harmony and predictability within the family. In addition, the roles and responsibilities assigned to family members may be lasting. Looking back at your own family when you were a child, was a family member identified as the "helper", the "perfect" child, the "irresponsible child"?

Over the course of generations, the family unit transmits basic and lasting assumptions about the world to its members (Constantine, 1986). Moreover, the core of family membership is predicated on "the acceptance of and belief in a set of abiding suppositions or shared constructs about the family itself and its relationship with its social environment" (Goldenberg & Goldenberg, 2002). In this way, the family's way of being in the word is strongly influenced by family "narratives" or social constructions that have likely been passed down from previous generations. Thus families pass on values and perceptions about their interactions with society (e.g., "We never get a break; its always a struggle", "We are a strong family and have always been able to manage issues without help from others outside of the family"; "Problems within the family should stay in the family and not be discussed with others", "We always come out on top!", etc.). These assumptions may limit the family in decision-making (i.e., result in considering only a limited range of options and alternatives) or, alternatively to serve as an inspiration for creative problem-solving.

The family therapy literature has provided us with important information about the characteristics of families that function well and these characteristics have been influential in the conceptualization of our model. According to the literature, well-functioning families:

- Encourage the realization of each individual's potential.
- Specifically, the family provides the freedom for exploration and self-discovery and at the same time provides the individual family member with a sense of protection and security. This level of support enables individual family members to explore new opportunities.
- Adapt to changing needs, demands, and expectations.
- This flexibility enables families to cope with pressures that originate with individual family members, the extended family, community, and society (Rice, 1993).
- Promote positive relationships among family members.
- Attend to the personal needs of family members.
- Organize to manage daily tasks
- Prepare for change.
- Developmental, maturational, and environmental/social changes are a part of life and families must develop readiness to be able to handle unexpected crises and cope with stressors from the outside world and internal stressors.
- Demonstrate flexibility, collaboration, resilience, and the ability to adapt to changing external conditions.
- Goldenberg and Goldenberg (1998) have reported that well functioning families show greater recuperative ability, more flexibility and collaboration, and a greater degree of adaptation to changing external conditions compared to poorly functioning families.

Goldenberg and Goldenberg (1998) identified other characteristics of well-functioning families. These included the following:

- Demonstrate good communication skills.
- That is, family members exchange ideas easily and clearly.
- Clearly define expectations about roles and relationships.
- Show respect for individual differences and needs of all family members.
- Use effective problem-solving strategies.
- Preserve the identities of the family and individual family members.

- Specifically, well-functioning families permit individual family members to develop individual identities while maintaining the identity of the family. Despite this individuation, individual family members preserve their attachment to the family unit.

- Balance the needs of the family while addressing the interests and needs of all of its members.

- Accomplishment of this task often requires negotiation and creative problem solving especially when there are conflicting interests/needs among family members.

Two other important concepts from the family therapy literature have contributed to the development of our model. These include the following:

Families are dynamic, not static entities. This refers to the idea that both the family unit and individual members of the family experience developmental changes. Some authors have referred to specific developmental stages in family's that correspond to events that require some level of family reorganization with respect to roles, responsibilities, and the family's relationship with individuals and systems that extend beyond existing relationships. For example when the family's first child enrolls in school, the family necessarily has to develop a host of new relationships (e.g., school personnel, people associated with extracurricular activities, and peers and the families of peers). This is an important point since families may require very different types of support at different developmental stages. For example, DeMyer and Goldberg (1983) reported that parents of adolescent children with autism no longer felt a need for diagnostic information or more education on the nature and course of autism and that they tended to seek out counseling to help them manage feelings about autism less frequently than they did when their children were younger.

Families may be viewed as microcosms. Many authors refer to the family as a "training ground" because the social context of the family provides innumerable opportunities to learn about patterns of interaction (i.e., sharing, fighting, sacrificing, negotiating, cooperating, compromising, empathizing, etc.) that family members take into the outside world. Sibling interactions are considered especially important as siblings are thought to function as the children's first peer group.

▶ The Stressors are Real

Each family has its own unique style of coping with stress. In our work with families, we are continuously amazed at the strength and fortitude demonstrated by individual family members and the family unit as a whole as they face the challenge of ASD. While their response is remarkable, some of our families are reluctant to acknowledge the myriad of additional stressors associated with raising or living with a child with ASD or to acknowledge the impact of the associated, chronic stressors. At one extreme, we have encountered individual family members (often mothers) who view their emotional responses as abnormal because they believe that they should be able to manage the challenges better. While it is true that there are individual differences in family's (and individual's) ability to cope, the bottom line is that stress is real, not imagined. The professional literature provides strong support for the presence and the negative effects of stress.

Children with ASD have a unique constellation of symptoms. These include problems with attention, communication, socialization, learning (e.g., unusual learning styles, slow acquisition, poor maintenance, rote learning, difficulty generalizing skills learned to new situations), and behavioral/emotional control. These symptoms do not merely reflect developmental delay (i.e., slow progression through the normative course of development), but they are representative of atypical development (i.e., patterns of behavior not seen in typical development). While improvement in some of the symptoms may result as a function of intervention and maturation, some symptoms may become exacerbated with age and new challenging behaviors may emerge. Since ASD is considered to be a lifelong disorder, the challenges associated with ASD may persist across the lifespan.

We know from sound research that families of children with developmental disabilities experience significant levels of stress in coping with their child's special needs (Baker, Smithen, & Kashimal, 1991; Bromley & Blatcher, 1992; Van Hasselt, Sisson, & Aachi, 1989. Documented sources of stress encountered in the process of parenting a child with ASD include the unpredictable and uncertain course of autism (Bristol & Schopler, 1984; Koren, Chess, & Fernandez, 1978), prolonged dependency on parents and the continuous need for special care

(Howard, 1978), parental disappointment with delayed developmental milestones (Bentovim, 1972), decreased confidence in parenting skills relative to parents of typically developing children and children with other disabilities (Rodrigue, et al., 1990), worry regarding the child's ability to achieve self-sufficiency in the future (Wing, 1985; *Wolf & Goldberg)*, and the need for parents to either delay gratification regarding the child's attainment of specific goals or the need to forfeit goals (Kohut, 1966). The latter may apply to family goals as well.

As children progress through childhood to adolescence, the chronic and severe nature of existing behavior problems or the emergence of new, difficult to manage behaviors, may contribute to physical and psychological burnout in parents and in decreased community acceptance of atypical, aberrant, or socially unacceptable behavior (DeMyer & Goldberg, 1983). DeMyer and Goldberg have also identified concerns that are associated with increases in the size and strength of children with ASD as they approach adolescence. For example, if self-destructive or aggressive behaviors are present in the child's repertoire, there will likely be heightened concern about the safety of the child and the safety of others. In addition, increases in physical size and maturation may complicate completion of routine activities such as dressing, bathing, and toileting.

Parents also have to contend with the issue of juggling the dual role of parenting their typical children as well as their ASD child where issues of fairness related to adherence to family rules, allocation of time and attention, and differential expectations may come to the fore (Newson and Hipgrave, 1982; Howlin, 1988).

Research has also shown that ASD may increase marital stress and increase conflict between parents and their families of origin (DeMyer & Goldberg, 1983; Rodrigue, et al., 1990). Families have also reported limited opportunities for family recreation, which is an extremely important part of family life.

Parents may experience a strain on their family finances since care giving demands often prevent both parents from working. In addition, the costs of medial care, the "quest" for efficacious treatments, supplemental services, and quality respite care (i.e., particularly in communities where respite services are limited) can be exorbitant. We also know families who have spent considerable sums of money changing residences when they were forced to leave their homes because of complaints of neighbors (i.e., too much noise) or due to concerns about their child's safety (i.e., too much traffic on the street or the presence of swimming pool in the neighbor's yard).

Research has indicated that patterns of social withdrawal may occur soon after the birth of a child with special needs. Families may attend church less than they had previously attended and they may have less contact with extended family and fewer visits with neighbors (DeMyer, 1979).

▶ Why You Need to Care for Yourself and Your Family as a Whole

In addition to the aforementioned stressors, raising a child with ASD may negatively affect the physical and psychological health of the parents. Research suggests that parents of children with autism experience significantly more stress than parents of typical children and those with other disabilities (Wolf, Noh, Fisman, & Speechley, 1989). Unfortunately, becoming ill or otherwise incapacitated can become an additional source of worry. DeMyer and Goldberg (1983) found that parents experienced concerns about their own physical health, worry related to the possibility of illness, and thoughts about their own mortality. This same research revealed that 33% of the mothers in the study (i.e., mothers of preschool-aged children) had experienced mild, reactive depression and all parents reported heightened anxiety that stemmed from challenging behavior.

Parents are not the only ones stressed by having a family member with ASD. Sources of stress for siblings include social ostracism, sharing parental attention, and coping with having to sometimes assume a caregiver role. In addition, siblings struggle with personal needs that may conflict with those of the family (DeMyer & Goldberg, 1983).

Chronic stress increases the likelihood of family dysfunction and crises within the family (Kysela, McDonald, Reddon, & Gobeil-Dwyer, 1988). When comparing the aforementioned characteristics of well-functioning families with the specific stressors associated with raising a child with a handicapping condition (and specifically, ASD), it becomes readily apparent that there is a mismatch. For example, while "well-functioning" families tend to have good support networks, there is a tendency toward social isolation in a subset of families of children with ASD. Similarly, while "well-functioning families attempt to consider individual differences among family members and their separate needs and effective problem-solving strategies, the emotional, physical, and financial needs of raising a child with ASD may deplete the family's resources.

▶ Parent Training

Parent training involves teaching specific skills to parents to provide them with tools needed to successfully change behavior. There are two types of behavior that these strategies are used to change – skill deficits and behavioral excesses. The term "deficits" refers to the absence of skills that are age or developmentally appropriate (i.e., skills expected at a particular age or developmental level). Excesses are behaviors that occur with such high frequencies or intensities that they interfere with normative expectations (e.g., age-appropriate social interactions) or they are routinely observed at inopportune times. Regarding the latter, jumping and running may not be considered to be excessive behaviors on the playground, but they may be aptly labeled as behavioral excesses within the context of a classroom or church service. Thus, it is not the behavior itself that is "excessive"; rather, it is the interaction between the behavior and the environment that defines any given behavior as "excessive".

Teaching parents how to effectively change behavior has been found to reduce parenting stress (Breismeister & Schafer, 1998). This technology has been used with parents of children who manifest a variety of challenging behaviors (i.e., sleep problems, chronic feeding problems, oppositional and defiant behaviors, behavioral issues associated with attention deficit-hyperactivity disorder, habit disorders, and the skill deficits and excesses manifested in children diagnosed with ASD.

The majority of parent training strategies utilize principles derived from learning theory (applied behavior analysis, behavior therapy, and cognitive behavioral therapy) and the focus is on teaching children new responses to their environments. The methodology emphasizes analysis of antecedents and consequences that precipitate and maintain behavior (both wanted and unwanted, respectively). Within this framework, parents are taught to be consistent, change antecedents, environmental conditions, consequences for behaviors and to teach children socially acceptable alternative behaviors and coping strategies.

Systematic and controlled research has documented that teaching parents to effect behavior change is not only effective, but it is cost-effective. That is, the cost of providing effective interventions is less when parents participate as therapists. Moreover, the outcomes are more likely to persist over time. This makes sense for a number of reasons:

- Children spend the majority of their waking time with their parents within the family context.

- Problem behaviors often occur in the home setting or in the community.

- Treatment that occurs within the child's natural environment provide numerous opportunities to practice new skills within the criterion environment (i.e., home and community) and to maintain the behavior change.

- For children with ASD, teaching in the natural environment helps to generalize the learned behaviors to new settings.

- When parents become involved in behavior change at home, a clear message of family support is given to the child.

▶ Implementation of Family Interventions with ASD

During the evolution of family interventions, there has been an increased awareness that multifaceted interventions are often needed. Lutzker & Campbell (1994) present a point of view, similar to our own, that indicates that families are best served when they receive a variety of services that affect the social ecology of the family. It is important to note that models of service delivery can vary significantly. In more diffuse models, specific issues related to individual family members are identified and referrals are made to various agencies/professionals. Thus, a menu of services might be prescribed for a given family. That is, a sibling might be referred for counseling to address adjustment issues, parents might be referred to a different therapist to address issues associated with marital issues, and the parents might be referred to yet a different agency to address ASD-related, behavioral issues that are problematic within the home setting.

Our family-focused model is an example of a focused intervention model that differs from the diffuse model of service delivery in the following ways:

- It centralizes family issues related to ASD.

- It encourages individual family members to identify personal stressors within the family context and to utilize this information to select child-centered goals that serve the needs of all family members.

- The process of working together sets the stage for families to work together and to set mutual goals that address problems that interfere with harmonious family functioning which in turn has the potential for solidifying family unity and cohesiveness.

That is not to say that families will not require additional services. Examples include instances when some family members may need professional consultation to assist them in managing mood issues or when family members need help to re-establish productive communication between family members before they are able to participate in the process.

► Can Family-Focused Interventions be a Source of Stress?

Our position on this question is that if families devote an excessive amount of time to home interventions and the implementation of these interventions interfere with the family's ability to address the needs of other family members or the family as a whole, the answer to this question is clearly, yes. Our approach is to encourage families to think about home intervention within the context of the family unit and to make realistic decisions about time allocations for home intervention. In addition, we educate parents about the variety of empirically validated intervention strategies with a specific emphasis on program implementation that can be incorporated into the flow of everyday activities. For example, if parents want to work on increasing their child's independence with self-care, we talk with them about teaching strategies that they can implement when these activities occur naturally in the home. Just think about how many times you assist your child with brushing his/her teeth, eat a meal, or dress or undress. These are all teaching opportunities that should not be missed.

Also, we discourage parents from addressing too many goals simultaneously. Radically changing the way you run your household or the demands that you place on your child, may backfire. We view the introduction of home programming as a gradual process that evolves as a function of the readiness of the child and the family. By starting slowly and gradually increasing the amount of teaching time at home, you stack the cards in your favor. That is you create a scenario for success for both your child and your family. This is especially important because success tends to breed more success and failure may be so discouraging that families give up.

▶ Resiliency

It is no surprise that all families encounter chronic stressors, unexpected events that challenge the family, and crises. We all know some families that manage quite well when faced with adversity and others for whom stressful events seem to precipitate a negative chain of events. One characteristic of families who deal well with diversity is the family's resiliency. Resiliency refers to the quality that enables both the family and its individual members to utilize strengths and resources (i.e., competencies) to make self-corrective changes (Goldenberg & Goldenberg 2000). This resilience enables families to generate adaptive responses to stress. In fact, Hawley and DeHaan (1996) have noted that in some cases, families actually thrive and grow in their response to stressors. Goldenberg & Goldenberg (2000) have noted that the manner in which the family organizes itself, retains its cohesion, and communicates and problem-solves together in an effort to cope with stressors is a strong predictor of the family's ability to recover from these trying events. They also indicated that a strong support network and an affirming belief system may also contribute to the recovery of the family.

Walsh (1966) has suggested that a family's resiliency is shaped through adversity. That is, the way that families confront and manage disruptive experiences, buffer stress, and reorganize so that they are able to persevere with their lives, influences both the immediate and long term adaptation of the family and for individual family members. We believe in the importance of resiliency in families and believe that when families are encouraged, educated, and supported, that families can all make changes that impact their quality of life in a positive way.

▶ Collaboration with the School

Federal law requires parent involvement in the development of your child's educational plan. Prior to participating in the I.E.P. meeting, it might be a good idea to review your family oriented priorities and assess which goals the school might be able to help you achieve. For example, if you are selecting self-care skills as a priority, you could request that the skills you would like your child to perform at home are addressed within the school setting. Using your priorities as a guide, you should be able to duplicate the procedures at school, providing that it is appropriate to teach those skills in the school setting (i.e., self-feeding, but perhaps, not bathing). Similarly, if compliance with parent requests or increasing the ability to wait for parent attention are high priority goals, these goals could also be addressed within the school setting. At least in the initial stages of teaching, coordinating the specific skills to be taught in both settings is advantageous. By coordinating the goals taught at home and at school, you have the benefit of receiving extra instructional support.

3

Getting a G.R.I.P. on the Challenges

This chapter is about getting a "grip" on many of the issues that you and your family confront on a daily basis. In this chapter, you will be introduced to many important issues that need to be considered when starting a Family Individualized Enhancement Plan (FIEP). There are many challenges you may face in the process of the development of a FIEP that this chapter will address. The place to start is to help your family develop a realistic wish list that might help improve overall family functioning. This begins with GRIP. GRIP is our acronym (i.e., Growth, Relationships, Independence, Participation) that identifies family needs and translates directly into child-centered goals. GRIP is described in more detail later in this chapter. Consistent with our family focus model, your preparation for completing the GRIP will require you to think about your child within the family context. It is important that every family member is involved, either directly or indirectly at this stage. Below are some of the topics that will be discussed to help prepare you for completing the GRIP:

- Consideration of the needs of the family

- Consideration of the needs of the child with ASD

- Identifying stressors

- Brainstorming: Initial generation of GRIP wish list

- Assess family readiness for change

- Set priorities: Reach consensus on the priorities for wishes to address in your family's FIEP

- Evaluation of the resources available to assist in "wish" implementation

- Revision of GRIP Wish List

- Identification of warnings signs that you and your family are trying to do too much or that you and/or your family may need specific professional services

▶ Generate Your Wish List: Considering Family And Child Needs

As a way of helping you to think about the context within which to develop an appropriate wish list for your child and family, it is important to reflect upon the impact that raising a child with ASD has upon family functioning. In other words, identification of common needs to all families helps to put your own wishes into perspective.

Based both on research (see Chapter 2 for sources) and our experience with families, we have put together a list of the "Top 10 Family Needs" and the "Top 10 Child Needs" that we consider important for each family. We know that families will differ in what they consider to be the "Top Ten" for them, so, we have left extra space at the end for you and your family to list additional needs that are important to your family and for your child(ren).

▶ Top 10 Family Needs

1. **Financial:** Clearly, every family has monetary needs. Employment or a consistent source of income is needed to sustain basic needs such as food, clothing, and shelter, have insurance to cover medical expenses, and to provide some discretionary funds for school-related activities and family social activities. Additionally, many families value saving money for investment for the future. Even though the range of financial need may vary from family to family, basic financial resources are vital to providing a stable family life.

2. **Shelter:** It is important for all families to have a stable living environment with ample space for family members. This living space should be safe, comfortable, and provide privacy for family members when needed.

3. **Sense of Belonging:** In addition to having a place to call "home" (#2 Need), all family members need to feel connected with others. This need for affiliation extends beyond the family into the community at large. Thus, all family members should know and feel that they have an important role within the family. Additionally, family members should have

a sense of belonging in the community in which they live and be able to participate in activities they desire (e.g., participating in religious activities, playing sports, engaging in recreational activities, using community resources, etc.). Also, family members should feel an association and sense of comfort and support with their extended family.

4. **Acceptance**: Everyone in the family should have the same recognition and respect as participating members in the community, school, business, religious, and the extended family. Family members should feel welcomed by others who attempt to understand the family's circumstances and acknowledge their efforts.

5. **Autonomy**: As family members mature and develop personal interests, their independence to pursue such interests should be facilitated and supported to the best of the family's ability. Autonomy does not refer to separation from the family, but rather, signifies that a family member is defining his/herself more clearly as an individual within the family.

6. **Intimacy**: Family members should be able to be close to each other and share personal successes, secrets, disappointments, etc. with other family members. Family members should also be able to develop different kinds of intimate relationships with each other. For instance, siblings should be allowed to have special relationships that do not involve the parents, as appropriate. Parents need personal time to develop their own intimate relationship as a couple.

7. **Support**: (from the extended family/community): Support from others provides the family with understanding, compassion, and assistance. Families should have support in the form of assistance with personal and family endeavors or with solving dilemmas that a family might face. Support for a family can also come through the encouragement for the pursuit of personal expression, growth, and development. Families can also benefit from emotional support (e.g., having someone to listen to their concerns, fears, opinions, etc.).

8. **Leisure/recreation**: (personal/family): It is important that families schedule time to participate in enjoyable activities with family, spouse, friends or alone. For example, play is important in that it provides a relief and release from stress, for each family member, no matter their age. Recreational activities that involve the entire family create special bonds between family members and lasting memories of shared family activities.

9. **Flexibility**: A family needs to be flexible and accommodate changing circumstances, such as a parent getting a new job. Family's needs change throughout the course of the family's developmental continuum: thus each member needs to allow for some flexibility to adjust to these changing needs. An example of this might be having an extended family member, such as a grandmother, move into the family's home due to illness and the need for assisted living. Family members must be flexible in adapting to the changes that need to take place to accommodate the grandmother's needs as part of the family.

10. **Growth**: Each family goes through many changes and stages allowing the family to evolve in their relationships with each other and with the community. As a family experiences new exciting events, obstacles, and hardships together, they go through emotional and spiritual growth, both individually and as a family.

List Your Family's Important Needs:

_____

_____

_____

_____

_____

_____

_____

▶ Top 10 Child Needs

1. **Unconditional love:** Each child needs to feel loved, and secure in that love. Unconditional love refers to caring, respect and recognition that is a constant. It does not change as a function of achievement, failure, or stressful day to day interactions. Children should feel secure in their belief, even when their parents do not approve of their behavior, that they are still loved.

2. **Protection:** Every child should feel protected by their family from events, individuals, and settings that may endanger the welfare and safety of a child. Even though no one can be protected completely, every effort should be made to prevent and protect children from situations that may result in trauma, emotional and physical abuse, negligence, injury, or harm.

3. **Consistent Parenting:** While each child is entitled to unconditional love, each child is also entitled to having their parents teach them social norms and a sense of right and wrong. In other words, even though a parent should always love their child (Need # 1), a parent must provide their child(ren) feedback as to their actions in order to have the child develop to enjoy healthy social interactions. This is also how a child develops respect, empathy, responsibility, self-control, and achievement. Another important aspect of parenting is structure. Structure is like the scaffolding that is present when a building is being constructed. It is necessary to provide support and strength during the growth of the structure, and then, when construction is complete, it may be safely removed. Parents must provide structure to children to shape and enable growth in a positive direction, and protect from damaging influences. Structure is not always welcomed by a child, but it is always beneficial.

4. **Relationships with Family Members, Peers, and Others:** Similar to parents, children have needs to have special and different relationships with individuals within and outside the extended family. Children should be encouraged to play with and befriend other children. Additionally, children should understand the boundaries of their

relationships with familiar individuals and strangers. Children also need to be informed about harmful relationships they must avoid, and what to do if something bad happens.

5. **Developing Independence:** Children need to feel that they can depend on their families and are secure in that their basic needs will be taken care of, especially at a young age. If a child overhears that the family is having difficulties, then the child needs to be reassured that his/her needs will still be met, both emotionally and physically. As a child grows, his/her urge to explore the environment and the drive for new experiences increases. With appropriate boundaries, children should be allowed such independence to explore and manipulate, safely, his/her own environment.

6. **Play:** Play is an essential aspect of every child's life because it facilitates social/emotional development, concept development, creativity, and imagination. Typically, the nature of a child's play changes as he/she matures. Interactions with toys evolve from simple cause-effect relationships to complex use of multiple toys to enact familiar situations (e.g., playing house), create novel, imaginative situations (e.g., pretending to play movie or book characters). The social aspects of play is the most important, and develops from playing alone with simple toys (e.g., toy cars) to playing games and other activities with peers and family members. Having opportunities for frequent, uninterrupted, safe, and well-supervised play with other children and family members is critical for child development.

7. **Education**: Education allows children to develop their academic skills, learn to socialize outside of the home environment and increase their independence as they explore new interests, hobbies, and areas of knowledge. Formal education does not exclusively occur outside of the home. As children progress through the educational system, various levels of parent involvement and support is needed for child success. At home, children need a quiet place to study and the availability of their parents to assist with homework, to reinforce study skills, and to consolidate new ideas.

8. **Ability to communicate needs and wants:**   Children, of all ages, should feel comfortable to talk about different needs and desires they may have, including, but not limited to privacy issues, physical growth issues, emotional feelings and changes, and dissatisfaction with another family member, without feeling guilty or ashamed in doing so. As a child develops, their needs and wants change, and so must communication style and content, so that their wants and needs can be addressed to the best of the family's ability.

9. **Nurturance:** Children require not only sustenance to grow and develop, but also a nurturing environment that provides physical and emotional stimulation, as well as guidance, information, education, security, and acknowledgement as valued individuals.

10. **Consistent Role Models:**   Children learn new behaviors by watching their parents and siblings. They look towards adults for answers to the simple and complex problems they face. It is important that the adult role model(s) a child has are consistent (in that the adult adheres to their own statements of "what to do when…"). An adult role model should not be demonstrating to a child that "Do as I say, not as I do" is the lesson being taught.

List Your Child's Important Needs:

_____

_____

_____

_____

_____

_____

_____

_____

_____

_____

▶ Generating Your Wish List

We have provided the flow chart, below, to help guide you through the relevant issues when beginning to plan for your FIEP.

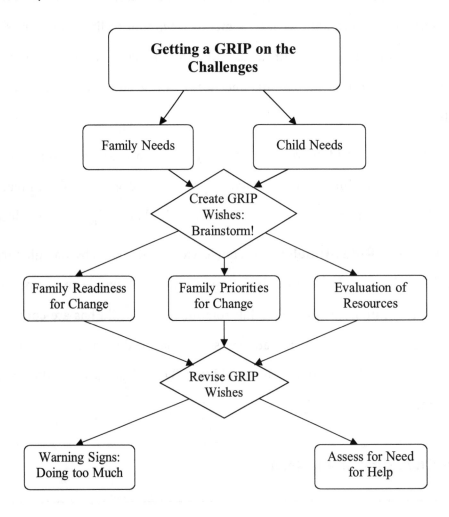

▶ Getting Started

   As we discussed in the beginning, this chapter will help you generate your wish list for your FIEP by using a process called GRIP. What is GRIP? GRIP is an acronym we use when starting the FIEP process. GRIP stands for *Growth, Relationships, Independence,* and *Participation.* Essentially, GRIP is part of a more general metaphor we use for this process. In this metaphor, your family is confronted with an obstacle in your life journey, such as the seemingly impassible river in our illustration (see page 47). At this point you need to ask questions about the direction and purpose of your journey. You'll then need to discuss a possible route with architects and engineers to create a 'blueprint' and then build a bridge to allow you to proceed past the river as an obstacle. This bridge has no purpose other than to assist you in pursuing your journey. You can think of the bridge as the path to achieving the wishes (skills or goals) you select (from your wish list) to assist in improving your family's functioning. The chapters that follow in this book provide you with information and skills to "GRIP" the challenges your family faces, both as a whole unit and as individuals. This chapter will assist you in tackling some of the preliminary challenges. By the end of the chapter you will be ready to begin the creation of your own FIEP.

G - **Growth**
R - **Relationships**
I - **Independence**
P - **Participation**

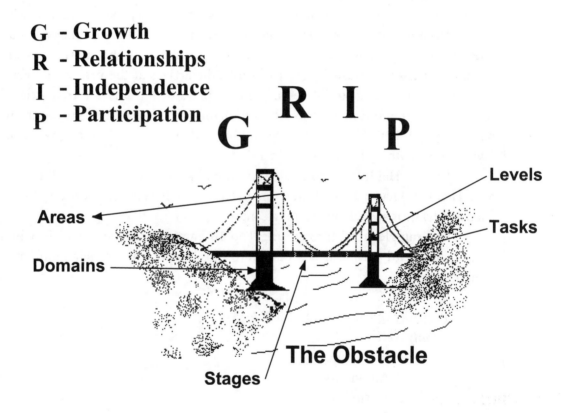

The Example Family

Throughout this chapter, you can follow the Example Family to see how to use the various worksheets. The Example family consists of Mr. and Mrs. Example, their daughter Heidi and their son Gary, who has autism. Heidi is 9 years old and Gary is 4 years old. Mr. Example has a full-time job and Mrs. Example works part-time, two days a week. Heidi is in the 4th grade. Gary attends a preschool for children with developmental disabilities. Gary is a very loving son and brother, as he likes to give his family member hugs and kisses. Gary needs his parents help in getting dressed, brushing his teeth, and combing his hair. He does not talk often, however, Gary understands most of what his parents ask of him and will occasionally speak. Gary has difficulty with transitions and breaks in his daily routines. For instance, if his mother takes an alternate route, due to construction, to the preschool in the morning, Gary becomes irritated and usually tantrums until he arrives at the preschool. Gary also has a limited range of interests. He only plays with trains and train-related toys. From time to time Gary is noncompliant with his parents. However, his parents report that he is usually noncompliant when they ask him to give up his favorite toy or when they turn off the TV.

At times, Heidi tends to treat Gary more like a toddler than a child of his age. Heidi also has a difficult time understanding why Gary does certain things, such as why he is scared of vacuum cleaners.

The Examples read through the Top 10 Family Needs and Top 10 Child Needs and identified the needs that were most important to their family and their situation.

Priorities of Family and Child Needs
Family Needs:
      1. Acceptance
      2. Autonomy
      3. Flexibility
      4. Growth
Child Needs:
      1. Unconditional Love
      2. Consistent Parenting
      3. Ability to Communication Needs & Wants
      4. Relationships with Family Members, Peers, and Others

One of the first questions to answer before deciding upon a wish list for your family goals for your FIEP, is to ask "What is stressing you out?" First, take a look at an example worksheet below.

Parents: What is stressing you out?
Rank order the items below that are causing your family stress. (Most stressful = 1)
_1_ Child Care
_3_ Financial Matters
_2_ Relationships in the Family
_5_ Family Schedules
_4_ Sibling Conflict
_7_ Marital Conflict
_8_ Behavior Problems
_6_ Limited Free Time
____ Everything is stressing me out!

Now, you fill one out!

Parents: What is stressing you out?
Rank order the items below that are causing your family stress. (Most stressful = 1)
____ Child Care
____ Financial Matters
____ Relationships in the Family
____ Family Schedules
____ Sibling Conflict
____ Marital Conflict

| _____ Behavior Problems |
| _____ Limited Free Time |
| _____ Everything is stressing me out! |

Let's take a look at your answers. If you ranked marital conflict, we recommend that you and your spouse seek professional consultation with a clinical psychologist, family-marital therapist, or social worker in your local area. We recommend this because it is known that marital conflict adversely affects children in the family. If you rank "Everything," this may be an indicator that you may be under significant, serious stress and we strongly recommend you seek similar professional consultation to assist you with stress-related issues before starting to develop your FIEP. As discussed in Chapter 2, it is typical that families with a child with autism experience heightened levels of stress. Thus, it is quite reasonable to seek therapeutic services for yourself or family members and you should not feel guilty or embarrassed for doing so. Remember that you are reading this book to help your child with ASD function better within your family and this is a commendable and difficult endeavor. Knowing that you or other family members may benefit from additional services is a step to help your family achieve the goals in your FIEP by addressing some of the family members' needs as well.

Let's not forget about the other family members. Siblings may also want to fill out the box on page 51. You may want to introduce the idea of being involved in the FIEP process as a family project. You could tell your children that you think it would be a good idea for the family to make some changes so that everyone in the family works together on things that bother them.

Depending on the children's ages, it may be important for parents to assist siblings in completing the box. You should not be surprised if your children don't want to participate in this process. Often children may think that the creation of a FIEP is unusual or may not understand the purpose of the worksheets or how to fill them out. We think that it is important to incorporate all of your family members' opinions, thoughts, and needs into the FIEP process. Here are two examples of ways to assist you in explaining the "What is Stressing You Out" box to your other children.

1) With regard to "Problems with Peer Relationships," think of the following things:

- Not fitting in

- Criticized by peers

- Not able to participate in activities with peers

2) With regard to "School Issues," think of the following things:

- Difficult time studying

- Not enough help from parents

- Not enough study time due to other responsibilities

- Too much noise

Siblings: What is Stressing You Out?

My Name:_____
Rank order the items below that are causing your family stress. (Most stressful = 1)
_____ Privacy
_____ Limited Parent Availability
_____ Relationships in the Family
_____ Problems with Peer Relationships
_____ School Issues
_____ Too Much Responsibility
_____ Feeling Unsafe
_____ Limited Participation in Extracurricular Activities
_____ Everything is Stressing Me Out!

My Name:_____

Rank order the items below that are causing your family stress.
(Most stressful = 1)

____ Privacy
____ Limited Parent Availability
____ Relationships in the Family
____ Problems with Peer Relationships
____ School Issues
____ Too Much Responsibility
____ Feeling Unsafe
____ Limited Participation in Extracurricular Activities
____ Everything is Stressing Me Out!

My Name:_____

Rank order the items below that are causing your family stress.
(Most stressful = 1)

____ Privacy
____ Limited Parent Availability
____ Relationships in the Family
____ Problems with Peer Relationships
____ School Issues
____ Too Much Responsibility
____ Feeling Unsafe
____ Limited Participation in Extracurricular Activities
____ Everything is Stressing Me Out!

The Example Family

Below, Mr. and Mrs. Example and Heidi completed the "What is stressing you out?" boxes one evening after dinner. Mr. and Mrs. Example were surprised that Heidi felt like she had problems with friends (peer relationships). All three decided that this would be a priority for change as they develop their FIEP.

Parents: What is stressing you out?

Rank order the items below that are causing your family stress. (Most stressful = 1)

2	Child Care
	Financial Matters
3	Relationships in the Family
5	Family Schedules
4	Sibling Conflict
	Marital Conflict
	Behavior Problems
1	Limited Free Time
	Everything is stressing me out!

My Name: Heidi

Rank order the items below that are causing your family stress. (Most stressful = 1)

	Privacy
1	Limited Parent Availability
2	Relationships in the Family
3	Problems with Peer Relationships
	School Issues
5	Too much Responsibility
	Feeling Unsafe
4	Limited participation in extracurricular activities
	Everything is stressing me out!

▶ Preparation: Complete Brainstorming & GRIP Worksheets

Now refer back to the flowchart. It is time to start creating your GRIP wish list. This process is best preceded by having one or more family brainstorming sessions. Below is a Partial Brainstorming worksheet to facilitate the generation of family wishes. You've already done some work in this regard! Refer back to the Parenting Myths table in chapter 2. You can use the erroneous beliefs identified in the parenting myths worksheet and stressors you've identified above to assist in completing the Partial Brainstorming worksheet. We have provided some examples of how this is done.

Partial Brainstorming Worksheet

Stressor	What would make it better?	Who benefits from the change?	To be used later	To be used later

The Example Family

At a family meeting, Heidi and her parents brainstormed 4 stressors using the "what is stressing you out?" boxes.

Stressor	What would make it better?	Who benefits from the change?	To be used later	To be used later
No time for parents to be alone (grocery shopping, going to dinner, etc)	Feeling less anxiety with a babysitter	Mom & Dad		
Difficulty explaining Gary to friends	Being able to explain to friends about Gary that doesn't make Gary seem weird	Heidi		
Feeling uncomfortable around Gary sometimes	Knowing what to say or do when Gary does something that I don't understand or don't like	Gary & Heidi		
Self-care needs make it difficult	Teaching Gary a morning and evening routine	Gary, Mom & Dad		

Each family member should complete the GRIP Wish List worksheet. Photocopy one for each family member and one for the entire family. Each family member should write in his/her personal wishes for the areas of GRIP. These wishes should be filled out with regard to each family member and the child with ASD. Try to write the wishes in a form that addresses problem areas, such as finding time alone with parents, learning to play with siblings, improving table manners, etc. Completing the GRIP Wish List worksheet may be difficult for your children if they are under 10 years old or have difficulty understanding the meanings of the words or the intent of the worksheet. It may be necessary for you to interview each sibling to gather his/her "wishes." Following the GRIP Wish List worksheet is an interview format that you may find helpful when interviewing your other children.

We then recommend everyone share their wishes and, together, create another GRIP that is specifically designated for the family. By doing this, you and your family will have a good starting point for identifying areas that need improvement, selecting family goals, and setting realistic expectations for your FIEP.

GRIP Wish List Worksheet

Family Member Name _____   Date _____

G: Growth: _____
                        _____

R: Relationships: _____
                        _____

I: Independence: _____
                        _____

P: Participation: _____
                        _____

GRIP is an acronym to convey the importance of four basic aspects of personal growth and happiness. These four aspects are growth, relationships, independence, and participation. To assist in completing this form, here are some possible examples.

Growth (development in areas such as):

- Physical

- Emotional

- Social

- Skills (e.g., riding a bike, learning to paint, play golf)

- Knowledge

Relationships:

- Expressing affection

- Communicating feelings (positive and negative)
- Building trust
- Expanding circle of friends

Independence:

- Self-care (toilet training, grooming, choosing wardrobe, etc)
- Earning money/allowance
- Personal responsibilities
- Self-direction (not needing to be told what to do)

Participation:

- Visiting friends and family members
- School-related activities
- Community activities (e.g., going to religious services, joining a volunteer organization, etc)
- Joining in and assisting with family activities (e.g., preparing meals, shopping, going to restaurants, completing group and individual chores, etc)

▶ Interview Format for the GRIP Wish List Worksheet

Below are questions for each GRIP area that you can ask your child to help them understand and communicate with you their wishes for his/herself and your child with ASD. These questions are just examples; we cannot guarantee that they will help every child understand this worksheet better, but we hope that they do make it easier!

Growth (development in areas such as):

- Is it hard to say that you feel angry sometimes? Embarrassed? Frustrated? Sad? Emotional
- Is there an activity or sport that you would like to learn (e.g., riding a bike, learning to paint, play an instrument)?
- Is there something you would like to know more about? For example, a foreign language, science, dinosaurs, etc.

Relationships:

- Do you wish that (family member) would give you more hugs or kisses?

- Is it easy or hard for you to talk to mommy or daddy about things that make you feel uncomfortable? If so, do want to share some of these with me now?

- Do you feel safe at home?

- Would you like to have more friends come over to the house?

- Do you think you have too few friends?

- Do you think it is hard to have friends because of anything?

Independence:

- Do you want to start picking out your own outfits for school?

- Would you like to earn your own spending money? Earning money/allowance

- Are there certain things that you would like to do on your own?

Participation:

- Do you feel like you have enough time to hang out with your friends and other family members?

- Are there any school clubs or sports that you would like to join?

- Community activities (e.g., going to religious services, joining a volunteer organization, etc)

- Are there things that you would like to do more as a family? (e.g., hiking, playing games, watching TV together, etc)

- Joining in and assisting with family activities (e.g., preparing meals, shopping, going to restaurants, completing group and individual chores, etc)

Congratulations, you have completed the first step in the process of "GRIP"ing the challenges! The next step is to address three important areas. These areas are crucial to selecting specific family wishes. The areas are: family readiness for change, family priorities for change, and evaluation of resources for change.

GRIP Wish List Worksheet (via Interview by Mr. Example)

Family Member Name <u>Heidi</u>   Date <u>11/03/03</u>

G: Growth: <u>I wish that I could learn more about the problems Gary has and why Mom & Dad need to spend so much time with him.</u>

R: Relationships: <u>I wish to be able to spend more time with my friends and be a member of the All-Star Girl's Club.</u>

I: Independence: <u>I wish that I would not have to bug Gary to help me pick things up.</u>

P: Participation: <u>I wish my family could go to more fun things together, like the movies and have Gary come with us, rather than have mom or dad stay at home with him.</u>

GRIP is an acronym to convey the importance of four basic aspects of personal growth and happiness. These four aspects are growth, relationships, independence, and participation. To assist in completing this form, here are some possible examples.

Growth (development in areas such as):

- Physical

- Emotional

- Social

- Skills (e.g., riding a bike, learning to paint, play golf)

- Knowledge

Relationships:

- Expressing affection

- Communicating feelings (positive and negative)

- Building trust

- Expanding circle of friends

Independence:

- Self-care (toilet training, grooming, choosing wardrobe, etc)

- Earning money/allowance

- Personal responsibilities

- Self-direction (not needing to be told what to do)

Participation:

- Visiting friends and family members

- School-related activities

- Community activities (e.g., going to religious services, joining a volunteer organization, etc)

Joining in and assisting with family activities (e.g., preparing meals, shopping, going to restaurants, completing group and individual chores, etc)

GRIP Wish List Worksheet

Family Member Name <u>Mrs. Example</u>   Date <u>11/03/03</u>

G: Growth: <u>I wish that Gary could increase his social and play activities so that he would do more age-appropriate things.</u>

R: Relationships: <u>I wish that Gary would have more friends and that his and Heidi's relationship would improve.</u>

I: Independence: <u>I wish that Gary would learn to pick out his clothes and dress himself independently.</u>

P: Participation: <u>I wish that Mr. Example and I could do more things together and feel safe with leaving a baby sitter at home or feel OK with leaving Gary at my sister's house to play with her children.</u>

GRIP is an acronym to convey the importance of four basic aspects of personal growth and happiness. These four aspects are growth, relationships, independence, and participation. To assist in completing this form, here are some possible examples.

Growth (development in areas such as):

- Physical

- Emotional

- Social

- Skills (e.g., riding a bike, learning to paint, play golf)

- Knowledge

Relationships:

- Expressing affection

- Communicating feelings (positive and negative)

- Building trust

- Expanding circle of friends

Independence:

- Self-care (toilet training, grooming, choosing wardrobe, etc)

- Earning money/allowance

- Personal responsibilities

- Self-direction (not needing to be told what to do)

Participation:

- Visiting friends and family members

- School-related activities

- Community activities (e.g., going to religious services, joining a volunteer organization, etc)

- Joining in and assisting with family activities (e.g., preparing meals, shopping, going to restaurants, completing group and individual chores, etc)

▶ Is Your Family Ready For Change?

Your family's motivation for change is an important part of being *ready* for change! Although individual family members may want specific things to change, they may have difficulty participating in the change process. Changes within the family require commitment on the part of all of the family members. For example, if a wish on your GRIP Wish List worksheet is to have siblings play together more appropriately, then each of the siblings will need to be ready to start changing, even just a little bit, for a FIEP to work. Completing a Family Readiness for Change Scale will help you to assess your family's ability to make changes and estimate how ready your family is to make a change in their lifestyle, daily activities, and overall functioning.

Following the Family Readiness for Change Scale on the next two pages, we present an example of a family contract. Once you have established that change is desired and possible, the contract helps structure family member's involvement and serves to minimize misunderstanding, confusion of responsibilities, and provides a concrete mechanism to commit to the process of change.

FAMILY READINESS FOR CHANGE SCALE

Below are several questions assessing your family's level of readiness for change. Read each question carefully and rate each question using a 5-point scale where 0 = "not much or not often," 2 = "fairly much or more often," and 4 = "very much or very often"

****

_____ How often has your family stated a desire or need for change?

_____ How often does your family discuss the current situation and its affect on family members?

_____ When change has been suggested, how much do family members cooperate with their part of the change plan?

_____ How much agreement is there among family members concerning starting a FIEP (as opposed to disagreement)?

_____ How optimistic (as opposed to pessimistic) does your family feel about achieving improved family functioning using this workbook?

_____ How much cooperation have family members shown in attempting to use this book to facilitate change?

_____ How often has a family member(s) discussed possible options for addressing a specific situation with your child with autism?

_____ If your family has scheduled family meeting times to discuss a problematic situation, how often has your family, as a whole, met together?

_____ **Total Score.** * A score between 21-30 indicates your family having high readiness for change. This is a level of readiness that will facilitate successful development of a FIEP. A score between 11-20 indicates a moderate level of readiness. Your family may need some extra encouragement along the way, but most likely will be able to make a commitment to change. A score between 0-10 indicates your family having a low readiness for change. Your family may want to reconsider whether implementing a FIEP is a realistic expectation.

*Please note: The distinctions between the levels of readiness for change scores are not research – based, rather they are based on clinical judgment and do represent rough estimates. The purpose of this scale is to assist with your evaluation of how "ready" your family is for change.

FAMILY READINESS FOR CHANGE SCALE

Below are several questions assessing your family's level of readiness for change. Read each question carefully and rate each question using a 5-point scale where 0 = "not much or not often," 2 = "fairly much or more often," and 4 = "very much or very often"

****

__3__ How often has your family stated a desire or need for change?

__3__ How often does your family discuss the current situation and its affect on family members?

__2__ When change has been suggested, how much do family members cooperate with their part of the change plan?

__4__ How much agreement is there among family members concerning starting a FIEP (as opposed to disagreement)?

__4__ How optimistic (as opposed to pessimistic) does your family feel about achieving improved family functioning using this workbook?

__4__ How much cooperation have family members shown in attempting to use this book to facilitate change?

__4__ How often has a family member(s) discussed possible options for addressing a specific situation with your child with autism?

__3__ If your family has scheduled family meeting times to discuss a problematic situation, how often has your family, as a whole, met together?

__27__ **Total Score.** * A score between 21-30 indicates your family having high readiness for change. This is a level of readiness that will facilitate successful development of a FIEP. A score between 11-20 indicates a moderate level of readiness. Your family may need some extra encouragement along the way, but most likely will be able to make a commitment to change. A score between 0-10 indicates your family having a low readiness for change. Your family may want to reconsider whether implementing a FIEP is a realistic expectation.

Please note: The distinctions between the levels of readiness for change scores are not research – based, rather they are based on clinical judgment and do represent rough estimates. The purpose of this scale is to assist with your evaluation of how "ready" your family is for change.

▶ A Family Pact: Contracting For Collaboration

It is helpful to formalize the willingness of family members to work together on common goals. Below, is an example of a contract that each family can sign to declare their commitment to the "cause."

<u>Our Family Pact</u>

- I understand that we are working together to improve our family life.

- I understand that we all have to do our part. This means that I might have to change the way that I have been doing some things at home. However, I know that other family members will also be making similar changes.

- I understand that there may be times when I have to be more flexible than in the past.

- I agree to participate in discussions about making changes at home.

- I agree to do my part to help with the change process.

- I agree to inform others when I am unable to fulfill my responsibilities.

- I agree to communicate openly about my feelings about changes at home.

- During family discussions…

- I agree to avoid critical feedback

- I agree to listen to what other family members have to say

- I agree to give everyone a chance to express their feelings and opinions.

- I agree to try to utilize coping strategies when frustrated and upset

- If I choose not to participate directly, I agree to support the efforts of others to the best of my ability.

_____   _____
Signature   Date

_____   _____
Signature   Date

_____   _____
Signature   Date

_____   _____
Signature   Date

_____   _____
Signature   Date

Family Priorities. The GRIP forms that family members completed should provide you with a starting point of your family priorities. At this point we will ask you to review and add or elaborate on your GRIP wishes. All GRIP wishes are important to your family, however, it is imperative to prioritize these wishes, otherwise, it will be too difficult to achieve all of the wishes at once.

There are five major child factors that influence family dynamics in families with children with ASD. Due to the impact of these factors on your family, we urge you to consider them in more detail with regard to priorities for your GRIP wishes. Each factor is presented to you in a way that specifically describes the influence of each factor on a family. Additionally, after reading each description, you and your family may decide that one or more factors are pertinent to your family's situation. If so, you can then add these factors as additional wishes to your GRIP form and prioritize these factors with your other wishes.

▶ Five Child Factors That Shape Family Dynamics

1. The need for continuous supervision

Depending on a child's functioning level, constant supervision is needed to prevent injury or accidents from occurring. If this is so, time available to do other tasks becomes limited as does the efficiency rate of completing other tasks, such as cooking, washing dishes, taking a shower, helping another sibling with homework, etc. Many families find themselves planning for each of these daily events so that someone can watch over the child with autism. For some families, a goal is needed to minimize constant supervision, such as teaching the child with autism independent activity skills, such as playing with toys, watching TV, or even staying within a specified distance from a parent.

Is this factor a priority for your family?   ☐ Yes   ☐ No   ☐ Not sure

Are there daily activities that should be doable tasks but rather are cumbersome obstacles?

List them here:

_____

_____

_____

2. Inability to communicate about needs and wants

Since many children with autism are nonverbal or have limited communication skills, it is difficult for parents and other family members to know what a child with autism needs. This can lead to a continuous guessing game as each family member attempts to figure out what the child with autism needs at any given moment. Sometimes, children will show increased behavioral problems, such as temper tantrums, crying, or self-injury, when communication difficulties arise. Family members experience increased levels of stress due to the pressure to understand the child's needs the first time around in order to prevent such consequences. Think for a moment of the numerous things that typical children will readily express to their parents. For instance, expressing that he/she feels ill. For some children with autism, it may be difficult to convey to their caregivers that he/she has a stomachache, fever, feels nauseous, or even has a pain in a specific body part. Other common examples that families encounter, are determining if their child has had enough to eat or is hungry, is bored with an activity versus he/she doesn't understand how to participate in a specific activity, or is experiencing pain (e.g., a stomach ache) versus being noncompliant (e.g., resisting to follow directions).

Is this factor a priority for your family?   ☐ Yes   ☐ No   ☐ Not sure

What needs or wants would you like to be more comprehensible (to family members and to your child with autism)?

List them here:

_____

_____

_____

3. Atypical relationships with family members

Most likely, your child with ASD takes up takes up most of one or two family members' time. Usually this is one of the parents. When this occurs, the relationships within the family change so that it is difficult to get "respite" from family members. This may lead to potential for increased conflict between family members.

Is this factor a priority for your family?   ☐ Yes   ☐ No   ☐ Not sure

What types of conflict are noticeable <u>now</u> between family members?
List them here:

_____

_____

_____

4. Atypical relationships with peers

Having a child with ASD in a family usually decreases opportunities for other family members to be active in activities outside of the home. For example, participation in sports or after school clubs becomes increasingly difficult and also limited for siblings. Also, parents may find less time available for visiting with friends or colleagues. Because many family members feel an obligation to help out more at home, care for the child with ASD, or feel guilty about leaving their family momentarily, isolation from peers increase, which may lead to an individual family member feeling the stress of family responsibilities or depressed due to the lack of peer social support and activities.

Is this factor a priority for your family?   ☐ Yes   ☐ No   ☐ Not sure

What types of peer relationships are limited for specific family members?
List them here:

_____

_____

_____

5. Atypical, difficult-to-manage behavior

Many children with ASD display behaviors that are not usually observed in other children. Or, some of the difficult to manage behavior one tends to think of may be exacerbated in a child with ASD or may not serve the same function for a typical individual as it does for an individual with ASD. Sometimes an individual's behavior may limit his/her participation in school programs or requires extraordinary resources. If you feel that your child with ASD may have difficult to manage behavior, then it is important to seek professional consultation. Recognizing the limits that this behavior may have on family goals is important. However, it is also realistic that positive behavior change may occur while working on family goals and child goals both at school and home.

Additionally, it may be difficult for some family members to understand such behavior and be confusing and frustrating at times. If this is the case, then it is important to have a professional provide your family with education regarding this topic and how to best cope with feelings of confusion or frustration.

Another way to help with prioritization of wishes is to take the number of total wishes your family has for its GRIP worksheet. Then, divide that number by three. Rank the wishes so that the top wishes that fall within the first third are assigned to "high" priority, the next third are "moderate" priority and the last third are "low" priority. It is important to keep in mind, however, that over time, given natural life circumstances, family and child growth and changing conditions, the assigned priorities or rankings may change and this is OK.

GRIP PRIORITY WORKSHEET

GRIP Wishes
(Write your and your family's wishes from your completed GRIP Wish List Worksheet and any new ones you have thought of. Then, assign each wish a priority)

The Example Family	
GRIP Wishes (Write your and your family's wishes from your completed GRIP Wish List Worksheet and any new ones you have thought of. Then, assign each wish a priority)	**Priority** (low, moderate, high)
Providing Heidi with education about autism	**High**
Parents spending more time with Heidi	**High**
Increasing the time Heidi spends with friends	**Moderate**
Heidi joining All-Star Girl's Club	**High**
Heidi & Gary communicating better with each other	**High**
Increase number of family activities	**Moderate**
Expand Gary's interests beyond trains	**Moderate**
Increase Gary's age-appropriate social skills	**High**
Teach Gary to dress himself without help	**Moderate**
Teach Gary to pick out his own clothes	**Low**
Increase the number of things Mr. and Mrs. Example do as a couple	**Moderate**
Increase tolerance for a babysitter	**Moderate**
Make transitions and changes in routine easier for Gary	**High**

A week following the assignment of levels of priorities given to each GRIP wish, meet again, as a family and determine if everyone still agrees upon the rankings made. If not, it is important to discuss which wishes are incorrectly ranked, and reassign the wish(es) to a different priority ranking/level. This can happen often, as one week an area of concern seems more immediate than at another time. If the priorities assigned to the wishes are still agreed upon, then you and your family are ready to move to the next step, which is to evaluate resources for the goals.

At this point you may be wondering how much time will this involve? The answer to that question is rather complex. The amount of time to develop a FIEP involves, the number of family members involved, the daily activities of each family member, ages of siblings, resources available, and many other variables. It is important to spend an adequate amount of time in order to implement the plan within the headset that certain aspects of your FIEP may change.

▶ What Are Your Resources?

First, it is important for all parents to be able to admit that needing help is not a sign of weakness. Seeking out help in the community and the various resources available, is key to successful planning and implementation of your FIEP. Prior to selecting goals for your family and child with autism, it is necessary to find out what resources are available to you. It is important to determine what services are offered by your state, county, and school district. Some community resources include respite, support groups, leisure and recreation programs for children, baby sitters with specialization in children with special needs, car pooling with other families, a clearing house for reliable information. The types of services available will depend on geographic location, funding sources, and available personnel. The local ASA chapter may have some of this information for you. You can also contact your school district and the state's department of education for more specific information about services offered in your area.

Another important resource to assess is whether there are family members who are willing to help and what capacity will they be able to help. Other family members, such as grandparents, aunts, uncles, cousins, etc may be willing to help pick up a sibling from an after school activity, babysitting, teaching one of the siblings (even the sibling with autism) a new skill, such as sewing or soccer. Determining the amount of time and type of activities that certain family members can assist with will help you choose goals with more flexibility and less of a burden on you to do everything. Since some of the family goals you may choose may not include spending time with the entire family, it is also important to find out what options you have for childcare. Is there someone to watch your child with autism (e.g., For how long?, During what hours?)? Do you have childcare for the other siblings? Are you willing and able to allow someone else to help your family? Answering yes to this question allows you to benefit maximally in the utilization of community and family resources. Think of the following issues when answering the above question:

- When assistance with childcare is available, do you accept it?

- Do you fear that something terrible will happen if you are away?

- Do you trust anyone to provide supervision for your child?

- If you do leave your child with someone else, can you enjoy your time away from home?

Let's take another look at your completed Brainstorming worksheet. You can now transfer the information to the Full Brainstorming worksheet to also evaluate resources. This is important for later in this chapter when you revise your GRIP wishes.

FULL BRAINSTORMING WORKSHEETS

Stressor	What would make it better?	Who benefits from the change?	What resources are needed?

The Example Family

At a family meeting, Heidi and her parents evaluated some of the resources that would be required to help ameliorate each stressor. This was more difficult than they thought!

Stressor	What would make it better?	Who benefits from the change?	What resources are needed?	What resources are available?
No time for parents to be alone (grocery shopping, going to dinner, etc)	Feeling less anxiety with a babysitter	Mom & Dad	Babysitter we can trust	Maybe an extended family member?
Difficulty explaining Gary to friends	Being able to explain to friends about Gary that doesn't make Gary seem weird	Heidi	Educational materials on autism that are age-appropriate	Ask a psychologist, school psychologist for references
Feeling uncomfortable around Gary sometimes	Knowing what to say or do when Gary does something that I don't understand or don't like	Gary & Heidi		
Self-care needs make it difficult	Teaching Gary a morning and evening routine	Gary, Mom & Dad		

Another critical aspect when searching for resources is to make sure that you are attempting to meet all of the family members needs. There should be some resources available for each family member. For example, is there a car pool available for after school activities? Time is an important resource that tends to be overlooked. In order to implement the family goals you select for both your child and family members, an adequate amount of time needs to be available. Are there times in the evening when all family members can get together for a family time activity?

▶ Conflicting Versus Complementary Needs

As you evaluate the immediate family members' needs, keep in mind that some needs are conflicting and others are complementary. As an example, for one sibling, the identified area of need may be increasing participation in social activities, such as swimming. This need may be complementary to other siblings needs, in that all siblings could take swimming lessons together. However, the needs may become conflicting when one sibling needs to be in one place and, at the same time, another sibling or family member needs to be elsewhere.

What are some complementary needs in your family?

_____

_____

_____

The Example Family

Some complementary needs in our family include:

- All family members would like to get more attention from each other

- Heidi's interest in after school activities may work out well with our (Mr. & Mrs.) wish to have Gary involved in more social activities.

What are some conflicting needs in your family?

_____

_____

_____

The Example Family

Some conflicting needs in our family include:

- If Heidi and Gary become more involved in after school activities, on the days that Mrs. Example works, no one will be able to provide transportation.

- Mr. and Mrs. Example want more time alone (to go out to dinner), yet do not have a babysitter available in the evenings.

If you have listed more than three conflicting needs, fill out the worksheet to help solve some of the conflicting needs and put them into perspective.

CONFLICTING NEEDS WORKSHEET

Conflicting Need	Family Member(s) Involved	Rating of Conflict (0-10, 0 very difficult, 5 neutral, 10 no conflict)	Alternative Solutions	Chosen Solutions

A key component for success having the involvement of all individual family members when you begin to evaluate the resources. With everyone's involvement in problem solving, assessing and evaluating resources, more negotiation and compromise can take place, as everyone is working together in the formulation of your family's FIEP.

▶ Revise GRIP Goals

Use the worksheet to assist your family in revising your family's GRIP wishes for your FIEP. You will use information you have gathered throughout this chapter to re-prioritize initial wishes and consider the most relevant wishes to meeting your family's and child(ren)'s needs.

The Revised GRIP Worksheet is designed to be used after the consideration of family and child needs, of readiness for change within the family, of family priorities, and the evaluation of resources has taken place. This worksheet assists in the re-priorization of goals for your family's FIEP. First, take the GRIP worksheets that each family member completed. Starting with one of the first GRIP wishes, write down the resources needed to assist in successful implementation of this wish. Then decide, as a family, if this particular GRIP wish is still a priority for your family. If so, is your family ready for this wish to be implemented?

Considering the necessary resources for this wish and your family's overall sense of readiness for such wish, is there consensus to keep the wish? If so, you can leave the wish as is until you begin the next phase of the FIEP model, in Chapter 4. If the wish needs modification, then your family can write the revised wish in the right hand column. After going through all of the GRIP wishes in this manner, you will have a complete list of GRIP wishes, prioritized, and ready for the application of the AIMM model to these wishes. It is very important that wishes are agreed upon as a family, since the focus of this book is to improve family functioning!

Revised GRIP Worksheet

Initial GRIP Wishes	Priority (low, med, hi)	Ready for Change?	Keep Wish?	Revised Wish (if needed)
Providing Heidi with education about autism	High	Yes	Yes	
Parents spending more time with Heidi	High	Yes	Yes	
Increasing the time Heidi spends with friends (e.g., joining All-Star Girl's Club)	Moderate	Yes	Yes	
Heidi & Gary communicating better with each other	High	No	Yes	
Increase number of family activities	Moderate	No	Yes	
Expand Gary's interests beyond trains	Moderate	Yes	Yes	
Increase Gary's age-appropriate social skills	High	Yes	Yes	Improve Gary's conversational skills with other children his age
Teach Gary to dress himself without help & pick out own clothes	Moderate	No	Yes	Teach Gary to dress and undress himself
Make transitions and changes in routine easier for Gary	High	Yes	Yes	

Revised GRIP Worksheet

Initial GRIP Wishes	Priority (low, med, hi)	Ready for Change?	Keep Wish?	Revised Wish (if needed)

▶ Don't Underestimate The Challenges

The end of this chapter is devoted to pointing out some of the areas that families of children with ASD face quite often and are relevant for the success of implementing your FIEP.

Knowing warning signs that signal difficulty in your FIEP is important, as it usually tells you that you or your family may be trying to do too much. Secondly, since having a family member with ASD does increase stress within and sometimes amongst family members, professional help from a psychologist, social worker, or therapist may be helpful.

Central to starting your family's FIEP, is your awareness of certain warning signs that your plan may be *unsuccessful*. If you notice any of the following signs, it is important to address a concern as soon as possible. Note: sometimes addressing a concern may mean that another professional is needed to assist with a problem or concern.

Warning Signs:

- Level of stress is increasing

- A family member is unhappy with the plan (stated or not)

- Your family meeting time to discuss progress in your FIEP is cancelled or postponed at least twice in a row

- After agreement, wishes seem "impossible" to implement

- Wishes in your FIEP are not being addressed in over 1 week

- Family members are finding excuses for not completing wishes

When to ask for help. Parents and families are under a considerable amount of stress given the typical challenges each family faces throughout their growth as a family, experience with certain environmental consequences, and other circumstances that are presented to a family at various, and usually unpredictable instances overtime. This stress increases exponentially when a family has a child with an ASD. Events taken for granted, such as trips to the grocery store, take on a tremendous amount of planning and flexibility for the family. Throughout our experience, we have known many families that begin to believe in certain ideas about family functioning. That is, that their family must be perfect or should be just like the family next door.

No two families are alike and no family is perfect. In fact, a sign of a healthy family is acknowledging that your family needs help and actively doing something about that. For instance, purchasing this book indicates the high value you place of your family life and your family's well-being and adjustment to having a child with autism.

It is key to be able to recognize signs or symptoms that may be suggestive that a problem you or a family member is experiencing cannot be addressed in this self-help book and needs professional attention. How do you recognize such signs? Below is a list of things that you or someone in your family may be experiencing.

- Not being able to sleep through the night

- Disruption in eating patterns

- Loss of interest in activities or social interactions

- Lack of enjoyment of normal life activities

- Feeling guilty about your situation

- Feeling overwhelmed

- Not feeling in control

- Loss of control

- Feeling that things will not get better

- Increase in headaches

- Increase in irritability

- Increased feelings of dizziness that occurs out of the blue

- Inability to relax – feeling tense or muscle tension

A first step is to talk to friend or relative to get perspective. Sometimes an outsider's point of view is beneficial and helps you see the situation from a different perspective. Additionally, friends and relatives who know you well can notice changes in your well-being, attitude, personality, and energy that may be indicative of a concern. We encourage you to listen carefully to advice you're getting from friends and relatives, especially if they have your best interest in mind. If you or a family member is experiencing the different characteristics for more than a month, then further consultation should be sought out. We stress that making decisions to seek out help, ask for advice, and even obtain additional services for yourself, spouse, or other family members shows your strengths and clear perceptions of the situation and are not a sign failure.

▶ Final Thoughts

This chapter introduced you to the many issues that one needs to consider before attempting to implement a family goal plan at home. After reading through this chapter, many parents will feel different emotions. It is important to monitor your feelings throughout this process as feelings are important indicators of when you may need professional help for a particular area addressed in this book. Professional help can be beneficial as it can help you manage your level of stress throughout this process, prevent depression, or help get through times when you may feel depressed or even overwhelmed in the process of having a child with autism. At the end of this chapter, did you feel an increased amount of stress, pressure, anxiety, depression or feel overwhelmed just from the discussion of the topics? If so, perhaps an independent, objective person can be of assistance to you.

As discussed in Chapter 1, it is important to be cognizant of the interventions that have scientific support. There are several resources that provide detailed information about such interventions. In this book, our model can be applied when using any one of the intervention strategies. The model is intended to provide families with a structure to select wishes for their child and family, implement these wishes, and with the ability to objectively determine success of chosen interventions.

৪০ ✠ ଓ

4

The Nuts and Bolts of Intervention: Take A.I.M.M.

Accepting the need for change is important for families to agree upon before starting any type of intervention, such as an FIEP. As an example, according to a large body of research, behavioral interventions are considered to be more acceptable than pharmacological interventions for children (Corkum, Rimer & Schachar, 1999; Power, Hess & Bennet, 1995). However, for most families, the degree of readiness for change and intervention is more positively related to pragmatics rather than attitude for making a change. Common problems that prevent a family from being ready to change include scheduling conflicts, child care restrictions, cost of necessary services, such as professional consultation, insurance coverage of services, etc. Even though your family may desire change, it may not be feasible given other constraints. Therefore, it is imperative that your family understands the limitations you have as a family with regard to the issues described above, as forces that are separate from general attitude towards change and commitment to change.

▶ What is A.I.M.M.?

A.I.M.M. is our acronym for Assess, Intervene, Measure, and Modify and it is the framework for behavioral intervention with children diagnosed with ASD. The model reflects the core components of the applied behavior analysis approach to intervention. Each of the components of the model is critical for developing teaching programs that work.

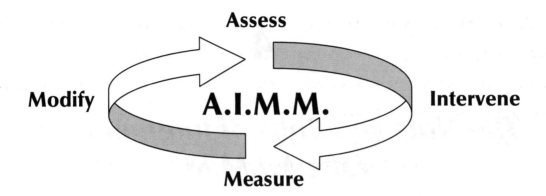

In the diagram, you will notice that each of the components of the model are interrelated; that is, each component is related to the others in important ways.

Let's start with Assess. This component is important because it gives us information about what to teach and can give us information about the teaching strategies that are likely to be the most effective.

There are various types of assessments that are specifically designed to measure different types of abilities/skills. These range from tests that are administered in a highly structured manner and measure abilities that are presumed to reflect intelligence, language ability, social competence, adaptive behavior (i.e., the ability to perform everyday tasks), motor skills, achievement (or ability on preacademic/academic skills). Other types of assessment measure child ability on a series of skills outlined in a specific teaching curriculum (i.e., self-help skills, language skills, or social behaviors) that outline skills expected at a particular age or developmental level or within a specific classroom. Still other assessment formats evaluate the interaction of child characteristics and the environment (i.e., how environmental factors such as group size, teaching ratios, etc. affect the child's ability to function in specific environments). Individualized assessment is essential in the treatment of ASD as no two children are alike. While a more comprehensive discussion of the issues related to assessment is presented in the next chapter (Chapter 5), several points are important here.

The first point is best phrased in the form of a question: How does assessment relate to treatment planning? In other words, how will assessment help you teach your child important behaviors?

The next point refers to a question that you might be asking yourself right now: I have no formal training in assessment. Can I do this? The answer is "yes" and we will provide you with instructions and materials to help you collect information for treatment planning (Chapter 5). The text box below highlights the importance of assessment.

Ways that Assessment Directly Influences Teaching

- Identify skills that you want to teach or behaviors that you want to change.

- Identify prerequisite skills that need to be in your child's repertoire for teaching to be successful (i.e. following directions, attending skills).

- Conduct specific assessments to collect information about your child's level of ability on skills of interest or on the current rates of behaviors that you want to change.

- Determine what level of support (i.e., prompts and cues your child will need in order to perform a specific skill)

- Continue to assess child progress on teaching tasks. *Assessment is strongly related to ongoing measurement of child progress on teaching programs.*

Once you have identified the behaviors that you want to teach or change and have measures that reflect the status of these behaviors, you are ready for the next step in the A.I.M.M. model, **Intervene**. The text box below outlines important components of this phase of the model.

Steps to Intervene

1. Identify teaching strategies that are likely to be effective.

2. Have a plan of how to keep your child's motivation high (i.e., your child's level of interest in the task and your child's desire to perform well) during teaching activities.

3. Consider where and when the teaching will take place (i.e., optimal teaching environments and times of day).

4. Develop individualized treatment programs. These should consist of a step-by-step outline of the teaching process that takes into account the supports that may be necessary at the beginning of the teaching process and a plan to reduce the number and types of supports so that your child can perform the skill independently.

5. Devise a plan to measure progress. Measurement involves monitoring your child's responses. Are the responses correct, incorrect, or partially correct? Are prompts needed to cue appropriate responses or is your child able to make correct responses independently?

6. Implement programs.

Measure is the next component of the model. The accompanying text box outlines the importance of measurement in the teaching process.

Why Do We Need to Measure?

- Ongoing measurement is critical because we need to know whether or not the teaching program is effective. Our philosophy is that lack of progress reflects an inadequate program. If progress is not being made, the program must be modified.

- Recording child progress on both individual goals and progress on mastering sequences of goals is important because we do not want to teach isolated goals, but meaningful and functional sequences of goals.

- Evaluating progress on a frequent basis prevents wasting precious instructional time on ineffective teaching programs.

The last component of the model is **Modify.** Modification of teaching programs is essential to insure that your child continues to make progress on the goals that you have selected.

When to Modify

- If progress is faster than anticipated, add new goals or modify existing goals to maximize skill development.
- If progress is poor, assess impediments to learning. Modify instructional methodology and assess the effect on learning.

▶ What Else Do I Need to Know to Develop Successful Teaching Programs?

Identifying skills to teach or behaviors to change. Since we view learning as behavior change, a definition of behavior is also in order. Behavior, for our purposes, will be defined in the following way:

Behavior is an action or series of actions that is/are observable.

Because behavior is observable, it is thus measurable.

Using this definition, it is easy to categorize the acts of walking, sitting, running, eating, talking, and smiling as behaviors. Many other words are commonly used in our descriptions of actions and interactions. For example, we describe people as being happy, sad, angry, frustrated, etc. While these terms may be useful in communicating ideas to other individuals in our culture, they are not necessarily useful to us in the process of behavior change. For example, we can say that Johnny gets angry when his teacher is working with another child (when he does not have her complete attention). We cannot measure anger, per se, because we cannot see anger. We can, however, measure the specific behaviors that Johnny engages in when this situation occurs. More specifically, when we observe Johnny in the classroom setting, we see that when the teacher turns to work with another child, that Johnny begins to cry, he gets out of his seat, and attempts to leave the teaching area, lowers his head, his face flushes, he stomps his feet, etc. It is this precision of observation that allows us to formulate effective intervention.

As a second example, Amy's teacher has reported that she gets frustrated when trying to assemble an 8-piece puzzle. Frustration is just a vague term used to casually describe a situation where a task seems to produce a negative emotional reaction. Since we cannot directly measure frustration, it would be difficult to develop a program to increase frustration tolerance. In addition if we were able to devise such a program, it would be difficult to assess changes in her behavior that result from program implementation because of the difficulty we would have in identifying frustration. Observation of Amy's behavior indicates that the following behaviors typically occur when Amy is "frustrated".

- After finding the pieces that fit along the outer edge of the puzzle, Amy usually tries to fit a puzzle piece into the center of the puzzle.

- Following one or two unsuccessful attempts, Amy turns the puzzle upside down and finds another toy to play with.

It is important to understand that we do not intend to deny the presence of emotions or to negate their importance. Quite the contrary, too often emotional difficulties and anxiety in individuals with ASD are not fully acknowledged or effectively addressed. In contrast, our current discussion is focused on promoting growth and behavior change, not just labeling problems or giving them 'lip service'. In order to accomplish our goals in a responsible manner, we must be precise in our evaluations. Just as a physician looks beyond a patient reporting that she is "not feeling well" (i.e., measuring the patient's temperature, ordering blood work or other laboratory tests, etc.), we need to obtain more detailed information beyond identifying an emotional reaction. Defining behavior in a way that is measurable provides us with several advantages as follows:

- We can communicate about behavior more effectively and precisely to prevent misunderstanding

- We can target specific behaviors for teaching

- We can develop teaching programs to build deficient skills

- We can assess the effectiveness of our teaching programs

- We can plan more precisely for future needs and placements

Defining Behavior in Measurable Terms. As indicated above, the need to define behavior in a way that is measurable is rooted in our need to be both precise and objective with respect to the assessment of, and in the development of, interventions for behavior change. In our daily interactions with our children, it is sometimes difficult to maintain objectivity. There are many factors that may influence our ability to be objective about child behavior. One factor that plays a significant role is our desire to see the children make progress. This factor can affect our objectivity in two ways. First we may have a tendency to be somewhat more lenient in our criteria for child performance. Conversely, we may become more strict in our criteria and create a situation in which it is difficult for the child to be successful.

Another factor that influences our objectivity is our own emotional state. We have all experienced days that have been so trying that an ordinary incident seems like a catastrophe. Defining behavior in a way that is measurable helps us to maintain objectivity and consistency with respect to assessing child behavior.

A good definition of behavior should specify the behavior in a manner similar to that of a dictionary definition. The definitions should include all possible instances of the behavior as well as exclude those aspects of behavior that are not relevant. Three pairs of definitions (i.e., inadequate and adequate) are provided below as an illustration:

Behavior	Inadequate Definition	Adequate Definition
Aggression	Whenever Sam is mean to others	Any time Sam engages in a forceful, physical action directed towards another (e.g., hitting, scratching, bites, pinching, kicking). "Forceful" means physical contact that results in an audible noise, causes the recipient pain or discomfort, leaves bruising or other marks, or is rated as more intense than the social norm for age appropriate and developmentally appropriate physical contact.
Tantrums	Whenever Tanya has "fits"	Any time Tanya exhibits an emotional outburst consisting of any 2 of the following behaviors

		that persist for a duration of 30 seconds or longer: cries excessively, screams, stomps feet, or flails arms and legs when the antecedent to the behavior is not physical injury or illness
Cooperative play	Whenever George plays nicely with others	Any time George shares a particular toy with another child in such a way that he permits a peer to use his toy(s) for at least 30 seconds while he is playing, alternates turn-taking with toys, or manipulates toys to enact activities of joint interest.

In addition to defining specific behaviors, it is necessary to define instructional goals in a way that is measurable. Below are some examples of how to define behavior in a way that is measurable. A closer look at the task objectives above indicates that a good objective specifies the conditions under which the behavior will occur, what the child is required to do, and the criterion for successful completion of the task.

▶ Teaching Made Easy

In this section we will discuss four types of teaching strategies namely, teaching your child a new behavior, teaching your child to perform an already acquired behavior with more proficiency, teaching your child to spend more time engaging in "wanted" behaviors (i.e., increasing the amount of time the behavior is performed), and teaching the time and place for engaging in specific behaviors.

Teaching a new skill (e.g., a skill that is not currently in the child's repertoire) is a time consuming process and one that requires a good deal of effort on the part of both the parent and the child. New skills are learned best when they are taught in small, sequential steps. Once we have identified the specific skill that we want to teach, the first step is to break the skill down into a series of smaller steps, the sum total of which, comprise the skill we wish to teach. The logic here is that it is assumed that if a child can perform all of the component parts in sequence, he/she is able to perform the skill. We call the process of identifying the component steps of a skill a **task analysis**.

For the purpose of demonstration, the following outline lists the specific steps involved in teaching a child to write his name. Please note that each step of the task analysis specifies a child-centered behavior (i.e., it identifies the behavior that the child is expected to perform).

Skill: Writing Name

1. Picks up pencil
2. Holds pencil correctly
3. Makes mark on paper
4. Traces horizontal lines
5. Traces vertical lines
6. Traces diagonal lines
7. Traces curved lines
8. Traces letters of name
9. Fills in missing parts of letters
10. Writes first letter of name independently and traces remaining letters
11. Writes first two letters of name independently and traces remaining letters
12. Writes first three letters of name independently and traces remaining letter
13. Writes name independently
14. Writes name within specified guidelines
15. Writes name on assignment sheets

A second example of a task analysis is presented below for teaching a child to cross the street.

Skill: Crossing the Street (no streetlight)

1. Stops at the curb.
2. Indicates presence of a moving vehicle.
3. Remains at curb until vehicle passes.
4. Looks to the right and indicates the presence or absence of vehicle while remaining at curb when an adult points in that direction and asks the question, "Is a car coming?"
5. Looks to the left and indicates the presence or absence of vehicle while remaining at curb when an adult points in that direction and asks the question, "Is a car coming?"

6. Looks both ways independently and responds yes or no when asked the question, "Is it safe to cross?"

7. Looks both ways independently and makes decision to cross or to stay at curb without prompts.

A third example of a task analysis is presented below for independently completing household chores.

Skill: Completing Household Chores

1. Associates buzzer as a cue to access chore list.
2. Looks at chore list and identifies the first task to be completed.
3. Gets materials needed to complete the first chore.
4. Begins the first task specified on chore list.
5. Completes the chore on list to parent satisfaction.
6. Puts materials away.
7. Looks at the chore list to identify second task.
8. Gets materials needed to complete a second task.
9. Begins the second task specified on chore list.
10. Completes second task to parent satisfaction.
11. Puts materials away.
12. Takes a break.

It should be noted that there are many ways to break a skill into component parts and there is really no correct or incorrect task analysis for any given skill. The critical element is to be sure that the skill increment from one step to the next is small enough so that you are certain that with a minimal amount of practice, the component can be mastered. It is important that the requirements for task performance be reasonable and within the range of your child's capabilities. This will ensure that both you and your child will meet with success in the teaching interaction. It is also important to know that when using a task analysis as a guide, it may not be necessary to teach all steps in the sequence. You may skip steps that your child is able to complete (i.e., (s)he already had the skill in his/her repertoire prior to the start of the teaching program or (s)he learned the skill during the teaching interactions. Also, if you find that your child has difficulty learning a specific skill component, that step may broken down into additional skill components to make learning easier.

▶ Suggestions and Cautions Regarding the Teaching of New Skills

Mastery of certain prerequisite skills often facilitates acquisition of new behavior. For example, in order to participate in most functional skills, your child will need to be reasonably skilled in a cluster of skills that we have referred to as "learning to learn" skills. These skills included basic attentional skills such as eye contact, non-verbal imitation, and following simple directions. Once these skills have been acquired, they provide a foundation upon which to build new skills. Below are two examples of how these basic skills facilitate learning new behaviors.

1. **Speech acquisition:** By looking at the teacher's or parent's face/mouth (e.g., attention to relevant cues), children receive information regarding the formation of the mouth for the production of specific sounds/words. Using his/her ability to imitate motor movements (in this case, facial movements) children are able to imitate the facial configuration that accompanies the sound emitted by the teacher. Observation and imitation then, are skills that are prerequisite to verbal imitation - the skill we are attempting to teach.

2. **Face washing:** Suppose we want to teach a child who exhibits limited verbal skills how to wash his/her face. If the child readily attends to the adult upon request and has acquired good imitative skills, the adult may incorporate these skills into the teaching program. Utilizing the task analysis presented below, the adult may assist the child in completing all of the steps in the face washing sequence except the last step, hanging the towel up after use (see below). At this point, the adult models (demonstrates) the appropriate action for the child, i.e., hanging up the towel after the child's face has been dried. It is good practice to pair nonverbal cues (i.e., modeling) with verbal labels in order to teach your child the verbal equivalent of the targeted skills. Next the adult hands the child a towel and says, "Hang up the towel" ; "You do it!". When the child has mastered this stage of the program, the adult proceeds to model and label larger chains of behavior. In this example, the next stage would be to have the child dry his/her face and then hang up the towel. Note that the teaching proceeds from the last step in the

sequence to the first. This procedure is called backward chaining and will be discussed in more detail later in our discussion.

Skill: Face Washing

1. Turns on water
2. Picks up soap
3. Wets soap
4. Soaps hands
5. Puts soap on face
6. Scrubs face
7. Rinses face
8. Turns off water
9. Picks up towel
10. Dries face
11. Hangs towel on rack after face has been dried

Once your child has demonstrated that (s)he is able to imitate specific chains of behavior, you should stop modeling the behavior so that the child can perform the skill independently. However, since each demonstration was repeatedly paired with verbal cues, the verbal cues should now be sufficient as cues for performing specific behaviors. As performance becomes more consistent, the verbal cues should be eliminated so that your child is able to perform the skill independently.

► Other Prerequisite Skills

In addition to basic attention skills, mastery of certain skills or concepts may be necessary prior to teaching your child a particular skill. For example, let's suppose that your want to teach your child to count 10 objects. Counting to 10 by rote can be considered a prerequisite skill since being able to recite numbers in sequence is necessary for accurate counting. In like manner, several prerequisite skills are needed for telling time using a standard clock. These include the ability to identify numerals 1-12, to count by 5's to 60, to count by 1's to 60, and to discriminate between the big and the small hand on the clock. The prerequisite skills for telling time on a digital clock are different from those listed above. In order to read a digital clock, the only prerequisite skill is the ability to recognize numerals to 59. One final example addresses the prerequisites necessary for teaching shoe tying. Your child must have fairly well developed fine motor dexterity in order to learn to tie his/her shoes.

The key point (which cannot be overstated) is that it may be very difficult, if not impossible, to teach a new skill if your child does not have an adequate foundation upon which to build the new skill. Therefore it is critical to examine the components of the novel skill as well as the skills currently in your child's behavioral repertoire to determine the presence or absence of the basic skills.

Skills already in your child's repertoire: Utilizing strengths in your child's repertoire. Children often engage in specific behaviors even though these behaviors have not yet acquired functional value or are not yet performed at mastery levels. In other words, your child may spontaneously engage in a behavior, but may not be able to use the behavior to effectively interact with or to modify the environment or use the behavior skillfully or purposefully. Take for example a pre-verbal child who has a limited number of sounds in his/her babbling repertoire. When planning to implement a language acquisition program, it is advisable to begin training with those sounds/words that the child has already demonstrated that he/she is capable of producing than to select targets that are not currently in his/her repertoire. Joanne's parents noticed that their daughter spontaneously produced the sounds "ma", "ca", and "da". They developed a labeling program to teach Joanne to use these sounds to name things/people in her environment. She was taught to say "ma" when presented with a picture of her mother or when someone pointed to her mother and asked, "Who's this?". Similarly, "da" was used to label "dad", and "ca" became the label for car.

Teaching your child to perform a skill better. Another form of behavior change is to teach children to perform certain behaviors better, i.e., with more skill. Using an example from the area of self-feeding, suppose we are working with Donald, who is able to feed himself using a spoon. While the basic skill is in Donald's repertoire, observation during feeding indicates that a substantial portion of his food winds up on the table, on the floor, or in Donald's lap. We might want to improve the proficiency of his skills, e.g., scooping more effectively, holding the spoon straight as it is brought to his mouth, etc. The first step in developing a program would be to develop a task analysis of the skill, "eating with a spoon". The steps might include the following:

1. Uses open palm of non-dominant hand to hold bowl in place.
2. Grasps handle of spoon with dominant hand.
3. Guides spoon into dish with the bowl portion of the spoon facing upward.
4. Scoops a spoonful of food onto spoon.
5. Brings spoon to mouth holding the spoon parallel to the table.
6. Removes food from the spoon.
7. Returns spoon to the dish or to table.

If Donald is able to successfully complete steps 1-4 and steps 6 and 7, but has difficulty with step number 5, the program might begin by having Donald complete steps 1-4. At this point, Donald's mother would physically assist Donald by bringing the spoon 3/4 of the way to his mouth. Donald's job would be to bring the spoon to his mouth. Donald's mother would continue with this prompting procedure until Donald successfully completed this stage of the program. Then, she might begin to reduce or fade out her prompt by providing assistance only to the halfway point from the dish to Donald's mouth. As Donald's progress continues, she again fades the prompt by providing assistance only 1/4 of the way. Finally, Donald will be expected to bring the spoon from his dish to his mouth without spilling.

Increasing the length of time the behavior is performed. Another way we are able to change behavior is to increase the amount of time the behavior occurs. For example, your child may remain seated for only short periods of time. In school or at the dinner table, it may be desirable to increase the amount of time that your child remains in his/her seat. Similarly, we may want to increase the amount of time your child is able to play appropriately with toys or pay attention to his/her teacher.

Using sitting at the dinner table as an example, you would begin by assessing the amount of time that your child sits at the table after being called to dinner. Several measures of sitting duration should be taken at different times so that you can compute an average for the number of minutes that your child remains seated (i.e., sum of the total number of seconds/minutes their child is seated divided by the number of measures collected; 27/5).

Number of minutes at table	
	5.0
	4.0
	2.0
	7.0
	9.0
Total minutes:	27.0
Average:	5.4

Having this assessment information serves two purposes. First it provides a measure of your child's ability before you begin a teaching program which, in turn, enables you to measure progress towards your goal. Second, it gives you very important information about where to begin your teaching program. Specifically, if your child is only able to sit for 5.4 minutes on average, you would be expecting too much if the first step in your teaching program was to have your child sit for 10 minutes.

Teaching the time and place for specific behaviors. The last type of behavior change we will address in this section, is changing behavior in such a way that it only occurs at certain times, places, or in the presence of very specific cues. In other words we want to teach the child to attend to specific cues present in a given situation and to engage in behavior that is compatible with the environmental cues. Take for example, a young child who has just learned to say the word, "mommy". The child learns very quickly that every time she says the word, "mommy", she receives a tremendous amount of hugs, kisses, and praise. Initially, the child calls all women "mommy". However, not all women react as positively towards her as her mother does when she calls them "mommy". As a result, she learns over time to use the word "mommy" only when referring to her mother.

Another example of discriminating the appropriate circumstances for specific behaviors follows. Children can be taught that it is O.K. to run and shout outside during recess, but that these behaviors are not allowed in the school building or in the classroom.

Applying the concepts in your assessment of your child. The example, below, is an example of how to complete the Decision Making Worksheet: Goal Selection. A blank worksheet for you and your family to complete follows the example.

Decision-Making Worksheet: Goal Selection - Strength of Skill in Your Child's Repertoire					
Potential Target Behavior	**Is the skill absent?**	**Does your child have the prerequisite behaviors needed for skill? If "No", what's missing?**	**Does your child engage in the behavior, but below expected levels for his age? (i.e., mastery)**	**Is the behavior in your child's repertoire, but does not occur at age-appropriate rates? (i.e., it needs to be done more often)**	**Does your child engage in the behavior, but at the "wrong" time or place or only infrequently exhibits the behavior in the "right" place? Explain.**
Sitting at the dinner table	☐ Yes ☑ No <u>Comments</u> Janie is capable of sitting for long periods of time when she is engaged in tasks that she enjoys.	☐ Yes ☑ No <u>Comments</u> Janie does not follow verbal directions. Maybe we need to work on teaching her to come to the table when called for dinner. Also dinner is frustrating for her because we insist that she use utensils for eating. I guess dinner time is not pleasant for her.	☑ Yes ☐ No <u>Comments</u> Janie is four years old. She should be able to join the family for dinner without major disruption or conflict.	☑ Yes ☐ No <u>Comments</u> No additional comments.	☑ Yes ☐ No <u>Comments</u> No additional comments.
Coming when called	☑ Yes ☐ No <u>Comments</u> None	☐ Yes ☑ No <u>Comments</u> Janie does not orient to others when they talk to her unless they are right in front of her and effort is made to establish eye contact.	☐ Yes ☑ No <u>Comments</u> None	☐ Yes ☑ No <u>Comments</u> None	☐ Yes ☑ No <u>Comments</u> None

Decision-Making Worksheet: Goal Selection - Strength of Skill in Your Child's Repertoire					
Potential Target Behavior	Is the skill absent?	Does your child have the prerequisite behaviors needed for skill?	Does the child engage in the behavior, but below expected levels for his age? (I.e., mastery)	Is the behavior in the child's repertoire, but does not occur at age-appropriate rates? (I.e., it needs to be done more often)	Does your child engage in the behavior, but at the wrong time or place?
	☐ Yes ☐ No	☐ Yes ☐ No	☐ Yes ☐ No	☐ Yes ☐ No	☐ Yes ☐ No
	☐ Yes ☐ No	☐ Yes ☐ No	☐ Yes ☐ No	☐ Yes ☐ No	☐ Yes ☐ No
	☐ Yes ☐ No	☐ Yes ☐ No	☐ Yes ☐ No	☐ Yes ☐ No	☐ Yes ☐ No
	☐ Yes ☐ No	☐ Yes ☐ No	☐ Yes ☐ No	☐ Yes ☐ No	☐ Yes ☐ No
	☐ Yes ☐ No	☐ Yes ☐ No	☐ Yes ☐ No	☐ Yes ☐ No	☐ Yes ☐ No
	☐ Yes ☐ No	☐ Yes ☐ No	☐ Yes ☐ No	☐ Yes ☐ No	☐ Yes ☐ No
	☐ Yes ☐ No	☐ Yes ☐ No	☐ Yes ☐ No	☐ Yes ☐ No	☐ Yes ☐ No
	☐ Yes ☐ No	☐ Yes ☐ No	☐ Yes ☐ No	☐ Yes ☐ No	☐ Yes ☐ No
	☐ Yes ☐ No	☐ Yes ☐ No	☐ Yes ☐ No	☐ Yes ☐ No	☐ Yes ☐ No
	☐ Yes ☐ No	☐ Yes ☐ No	☐ Yes ☐ No	☐ Yes ☐ No	☐ Yes ☐ No
	☐ Yes ☐ No	☐ Yes ☐ No	☐ Yes ☐ No	☐ Yes ☐ No	☐ Yes ☐ No

▶ Tools of the Trade

While the above discussion focused on specific characteristics of the skills that you might want to teach, it did not provide you with sufficient information about "how" to teach. The list below identifies important components of teaching programs and specific techniques that you will need to successfully teach new skills. The information presented here is not meant to be a comprehensive course in all aspects of applied behavior analysis (ABA), but rather is intended to be an introduction to basic ABA concepts and principles that you will need to get started. You will need to consider the following:

- How behavior is learned.

- How to use techniques to effect behavior change (learning). How to motivate your child to act differently.

- How to identify the time and place for teaching

- How to make sure that the skills learned are maintained (maintenance).

- How to make sure that the skills learned are used in new settings or when similar situations occur (generalization).

These topics will be discussed in more detail in the sections below.

How behavior is learned. Cues in the environment play a major role in eliciting behavior. We will use the stimulus-response-consequence model (S-R-C) to describe the sequence of events that occur. Definitions of these terms follow:

> **Stimulus:**   an object or event that sets the occasion for a particular behavior to occur
>
> **Response:**   the behavior that the child performs following the presentation of the stimulus
>
> **Consequence:**   what follows the response

Because these components are critical to the teaching sequence, we will describe each of them in more detail and provide examples to explain how they are helpful in understanding the learning process.

Stimulus. The term, stimulus, encompasses a wide variety of objects and events. In our daily lives, specific stimuli serve to provide cues that enable us to determine the behavior that is appropriate given the specific set of circumstances. For example, when driving your car down the street and the traffic light turns from green to yellow you immediately begin to slow down. The yellow light has become a stimulus that sets the occasion for us to "slow down". Of course, a red light is a stimulus to bring the car to a complete halt.

We have learned to respond consistently to many other signals in our environment. We answer the telephone when it rings, we get out of bed when the alarm clock rings, we say "hello" to people when they greet us or smile, and we tend not to approach people who look cross or angry. When we teach new behaviors, we teach children to respond in a particular way to a specific stimulus or set of stimuli. Several examples follow.

Susan is a 5 year-old child who exhibits speech and language delays. Her primary method of communication is to point to things that she wants. If the desired object is out of her view, she will take her mom or dad by the hand, lead them to where the item is located, and will then point to indicate her desire or need. Susan has been learning to imitate a large number of words. However, currently she does not use these words communicatively, i.e., to label objects or events. A teaching program was recently implemented in an effort to teach Susan to use her speech for communication. The program requires that when Susan points to a desired object, her parents/teacher ask Susan, "What do you want?". If Susan does not respond verbally, the significant adults in Susan's environment engage in the following teaching sequence:

Parent/teacher:	"What do you want?"
Susan:	Points to the desired object.
Parent/teacher:	"Cookie". Immediately after Susan imitates the modeled response, the adult asks: "What do you want?"
Susan:	"Cookie".

Susan's response is followed by receipt of the cookie and lots of praise for her verbal behavior. After many repetitions of this teaching interaction, Susan will learn that the question, "What do you want?" requires a verbal response. The goal here is to change Susan's response to the stimulus from a non-verbal to a verbal one.

In an effort to teach independent classroom skills, David's teacher devised a program to teach David to get his lunch box in preparation for lunch. The need for the program was determined by the observation that David did not respond to the request to get his lunch box, but rather remained in his seat as if he had not heard the teacher's request. The specific stages of the program follow.

1. Lunch trays are placed on the table to provide additional cues that it is lunchtime.

2. The teacher gives the request to David as follows: "David, get your lunch box, please". Immediately after giving the instruction, the teacher walks David over to his cubby and assists him in getting his lunch box and bringing it back to the lunch table.

3. After several repetitions of step 2, the teacher presents the request as above, walks David to his cubby and waits for him to take his lunchbox and bring it to the table. If David requires assistance, the teacher provides it. Once David completes this stage on 3 consecutive days, the teacher proceeds with step 4.

4. The teacher presents the request and walks David halfway to his cubby. When David is able to go to his cubby, get his lunch box, and return to the table with his lunch box in hand on three consecutive days, the teacher continues with step 5.

5. The teacher presents the request, "Get your lunch box, please".

6. If David does not respond, the teacher assists David in getting out of his chair and turns him so that he is facing in the direction of his cubby. No further assistance is provided if David proceeds to complete the appropriate sequence of behavior.

7. The last stage of the program, of course, is for David to complete the entire sequence independently.

How stimuli are used in the teaching interaction. There are several guidelines that should be followed when using instructions in the teaching interaction. Prior to presenting the instruction the parent or teacher should maximize the probability that the child is paying attention. Frequently directions such as, "Look at me", "Look at the picture", "Sit quietly", or "Fold your hands" are used to interrupt any ongoing behavior which might be distracting and to focus the child's attention for presentation of the instruction.

Task instructions or questions should be simple and to the point. If, for example, we want to teach a child to identify body parts (e.g., head, nose, foot) it might be difficult for a child to understand what he was required to do if the instruction was given in the following manner:

"O.K. Johnny! You're going to work on learning to touch your head today. When I say, 'Touch your head,' I want you to do this (the parent then models for Johnny how he should touch his head). Are you ready? Touch your head! If you are right, I'll give you a tickle!"

The following is an example of providing clear concise instructions (boldface type indicates that this word is exaggerated by the teacher).

Teacher: "Johnny, look at me."

Johnny: Makes eye contact with the teacher.

Teacher: "Touch your **head**."

Johnny: Makes no response.

Teacher: Takes Johnny's hand and gently guides it so that it touches his head while at the same time saying, "Touch your head".

Teacher: "Touch your **head**."

Johnny: Touches his head.

Teacher: "Good job! You touched your **head**!

Please note that not only were the task instructions clear, but that the feedback presented to Johnny was equally clear. We will discuss feedback in greater detail later in this chapter.

A second consideration when teaching a new task is to ensure that the instructions are easy for the child to discriminate. A program written to teach recognition of printed words may consist of several word lists each of which contains five words. Two word lists are presented below.

List A	List B
boy	boy
bed	girl
box	house
book	car
baby	school

At least in the initial stages of teaching reading, List B would probably result in more child success than List A because the words in List B:

- Look very different and therefore are easy to discriminate from one another

- Have very different spelling patterns and configurations which also make them easy to discriminate from one another

- Sound very different and therefore, facilitate auditory discrimination of the words

- The points made in this section are as follows:

- Instructions and questions must be discrete

- Instructions should be simply and clearly stated

- Instructions should contain vocabulary which is within the child's current level of comprehension

- Instructions must be easily discriminated from other stimuli presented within a similar context

▶ Types of Child Responses

A response consists of the behavior that your child engages in following the presentation of the stimulus. Five types of behavior may occur in response to a request or direction given by a teacher or parent. These include the following:

- a correct response

- an approximation of a correct response

- an incorrect response

- no response

- an inappropriate response (e.g., tantrums, disruptive behavior, verbal refusals, etc.).

If your child consistently engages in a correct response, it is probably safe to assume that (s)he understands the direction/question and has the skill in his/her repertoire. A high frequency of approximations could be interpreted to mean that your child understands what is expected, but that (s)he needs to improve the quality of the skill being required.

High rates of inconsistent responding (i.e., when your child only sometimes or rarely responds correctly in the presence of a specific direction or question), nonresponding, and inappropriate responding are harder to interpret. That is, it is difficult to say with any degree of certainty whether or not the behavior has been learned. If your child frequently engages in incorrect responses, nonresponding or inappropriate responding, the following questions become important:

1. Was your child paying attention to the question/direction?

2. Did your child understand the direction?

3. Does your child have skill to perform behavior being required?

4. Is your child adequately motivated to perform the task or skill that (s)he is being asked to perform?

Answers to these questions can be obtained through systematic assessment. Several guidelines are outlined below:

- If poor attention is suspected to be the culprit, assess your child's response to the question when his/her attention is directed towards the speaker or to the task materials prior to presenting the question or direction (e.g., "Look at me" or "Look here" while pointing to the materials).

- If poor comprehension is hypothesized to be the cause of poor performance, you can set up situations designed to determine which parts of the instruction your child does not understand. For example, if the task involves following directions that involve placing common objects in specific locations, you can ask your child to "give you" or to "point to" specific objects to see if (s)he recognizes them by name before including them in a more lengthy and complex direction.

- If specific skills are weak or absent from your child's repertoire, your child may have difficulty completing more complex tasks. For example, if the teaching program has targeted "dresses self completely" and your child has difficulty with the fine motor coordination needed to fasten buttons or tie shoes, it is likely that your child will have difficulty completing this program. You may want to try the dressing program using pull over shirts and Velcro fastened shoes.

- If poor motivation to perform the task is suspected, you can assess the impact of motivation on your child's performance. That is, you can assess performance under different levels of motivation (e.g., social praise, giving your child his favorite toy after (s)he has finished dressing, or making your child's favorite breakfast food available following dressing to see whether specific consequences effect performance.

▶ Supports for Learning: Prompts and How to Use Them in the Teaching Process

A prompt is a cue that functions to assist your child in making a correct response. Prompts are used when your child responds incorrectly or does not respond to directions (verbal or nonverbal). Prompts can also be utilized in the beginning stages when we have every reason to believe that the child will not engage in the behavior spontaneously. Referring back to one of the previous examples that depicted an instructional sequence for teaching Johnny to touch his head, the teacher employed both a physical prompt (i.e., gently guiding Johnny's hand to touch his head) and a verbal prompt ("Touch your head") to help Johnny understand the specific behavior he was expected to perform. Commonly used prompts and examples of their use are described in the table below.

Type of Prompt	Definition
Physical prompts	providing physical guidance to enable the child to perform the desired behavior.
Verbal prompts	providing the child with verbal instruction. A verbal prompt may consist of simply restating the original request or may include a series of verbal cues that help your child successfully complete the task
Gestural prompts	providing a motion cue (performing the action, pointing, or nodding to indicate) that encourages correct responding
Visual prompts	using written cues, picture cues, signs, or size or color cues to increase the likelihood that your child will make the desired response

▶ Application of Prompts

Physical prompts. Mr. Grayson is teaching Gloria how to follow the direction, "Come here". Implementation of the program involves recruitment of a second person, Mrs. Grayson. In the early steps of the teaching program, Gloria is escorted to within 3 feet of her father. As soon as he presents the verbal instruction, "Come here", Mrs. Grayson gently nudges (the physical prompt) Gloria from behind in the direction of her father. This prompt ensures that Gloria responds correctly to her father's instruction for which she is rewarded.

Physical prompts are sometimes referred to as physical guidance. The degree of physical guidance that you give your child should be directly related to your child's ability on a specific task. "Hand-over-hand" prompting to complete an entire task sequence is a legitimate strategy in the early stages of teaching. However, as your child masters the skill or components of the skill, the amount of physical prompting given should be reduced.

Verbal prompts. Mrs. Smith is working at home on teaching Artie how to brush his teeth. Artie has successfully completed all of the stages in the program and is able to complete each component of the task sequence. However, he is having a little bit of difficulty completing the task independently particularly with respect to brushing thoroughly. Mrs. Smith has decided to use verbal prompts to help Artie successfully complete the task. Therefore, as Artie begins to brush his teeth, she reminds him to brush in specific locations as follows: "Brush the top; brush one side; brush the other side; brush the bottom, etc."

Another example of using verbal prompts follows in the context of teaching addition with carrying. Given the problem: $14 + 8 =$ the teacher would wait for the child to add 4+8 and then remind the student to "Write the 2 in the ones column and then carry the 1".

Gestural prompts. One method of gesture prompting is the use of a "model". When a model is used as a prompt, the parent demonstrates the behavior that their child is supposed to perform. Returning again to Johnny's task, the teacher could prompt for the correct response by touching her head, thus providing feedback regarding the desired behavior.

Signs can also be used as gestural prompts especially when the sign clearly depicts the action that you want your child to perform. By way of example, the sign for "stand up" involves making a "V" with the index and middle finger of your right hand and placing your fingertips on the palm of your left hand while holding your hand vertically. Especially when used with children who have significant language comprehension problems and relatively good visual skills, these gestural prompts may be more meaningful than verbal directions. If gestural prompts are initially paired with verbal directions and gradually eliminated, you can teach your child to respond to the verbal directions alone.

Another use of gestural prompts is to direct your child's attention (i.e., to a task, an event of interest, or to a speaker in an social interaction). Suppose you are working on teaching your child to put on his/her shoes and that during the teaching interaction your child begins to look away from the task. Pointing to indicate where your child should be looking may be preferable to verbalizing instructions, as "too many words" may be confusing.

Visual prompts. There are multiple ways that visual prompts can be used in teaching interactions. For example, capitalization or size could be used as a prompt to help your child identify his/her name as illustrated below:

Instructional Steps	Capitalization Child's name is Malik	Size Child's name is Sally
Step 1	**MALIK** Jan	**Sally** Jane
Step 2	**MALIk** Jan	**Sally** Jane
Step 3	**MALik** Jan	**Sally** Jane
Step 4	**Malik** Jan	**Sally** Jane
Step 5	**Malik** Jan	**Sally** Jane

The chart illustrates the use of "within stimulus prompts" or prompts that are embedded in the stimulus itself. In both examples, the level of prompting is systematically decreased so that discriminations can be made without the prompts.

Another example of a visual cue is the use of pictures or words to help children initiate or continue social interactions. The table below shows how prompts can be gradually decreased in a cue card that scripts a social interaction designed to be used to invite a peer to play.

Teaching Step	Script as Presented to Your Child
1	Joey, do you want to play with trucks?
2	Joey, do you want to play with_____?
3	Joey, do you want _____?
4	Joey, _____?
5	?
6	No visual prompt.

▶ General Guidelines for Effective Use of Prompts

Prompts are important tools in the teaching process and, when used effectively, they can expedite new learning and provide your child with important information about parental and teacher expectations (what response is being asked for, when certain behaviors should be performed, etc.). The rationale for using prompts is to help your child make the desired response without errors to increase the likelihood that (s)he makes the necessary connections between what is being asked (the stimulus) and the desired response. However, there are also risks or pitfalls associated with the use of prompts that you need to be aware of when you anticipate incorporating these techniques into your teaching programs. Important points to keep in mind when using prompts include the following:

- While prompts are helpful in assisting your child in making new responses, they should only be used in the initial stages of teaching and eliminated (or faded) as soon as possible (see discussion, below). This is because, many children become dependent upon prompts and rely on parental or teacher prompts for performance. If prompts are not systematically reduced, your child's ability to function independently may be impeded.

- There are two general strategies for using prompts, "most to least" and "least to most". In the first, more assistance is given in the early stages of teaching. As the teaching program progresses, the degree of prompting is systematically reduced so that your child is doing more of the work. In the second strategy, you allow your child the opportunity to make the response independently. If the response is incorrect or otherwise inadequate, prompts are added (a verbal prompt, then perhaps a verbal prompt with a model, etc.) to help your child make the desired response. One of the problems with the "least to most" method of prompting is that the child is permitted to make incorrect responses.

- Prompts and cues that do not involve the presence of the instructor (i.e., parent or teacher) are considered easier to fade out so that your child can perform skills independently. These include visual prompts that are embedded in the stimuli (as in the color and size prompts described above) and picture or written cues.

Shaping. Shaping is a technique that focuses on gradually and systematically altering behaviors already in your child's repertoire so that they become functional skills. Shaping is a process that occurs when we reinforce slight changes in the desired response (i.e., child behavior) so that it gradually comes to resemble the criterion behavior (i.e., the target behavior that we are hoping to achieve). The focus is on gradual change in the your child's response (i.e., the quality of the response, the duration of the response, etc.) while the stimulus stays basically the same. When using a shaping procedure, we reinforce successive changes in behavior.

Fading. Fading is the process used to eliminate prompts. This technique focuses on gradual changes in the stimulus while the response remains stable. When implementing a fading procedure, the goal is to systematically reinforce a child's response as you change the stimulus so that the stimulus gradually resembles the stimulus that your child will encounter in the natural environment. In the example included in the section on visual prompts, selecting his/her name in an array of two, the color and size cues were gradually faded so that the child would be able to make a correct response (the same response throughout the fading procedure) under naturally occurring task conditions. Some important characteristics of fading are listed below:

- Fading involves changing stimulus control (i.e., environmental events that set the stage for responding)

- Fading occurs along dimensions (characteristics that can be measured) of stimuli, volume, intensity of visual cues, number of prompts, pressure of teacher's hand while guiding a child's response, complexity of an environment, etc.

- Fading may also occur across changes in a general situation or setting; i.e., fading to more traditional classroom settings. Again, the stimulus conditions change (i.e., the physical dimensions of the classroom and the teacher:student ratio), while the child's response(s) remains the same.

Differentiating between shaping and fading. The differences between shaping and fading can be difficult to understand. The table below, summarizes the essential differences in bold face type. Similarities are listed in regular typeface.

Shaping	Fading
Reinforces gradual changes in child responses	Responses stay basically the same, throughout
Controlling stimuli remain the same throughout the shaping process	Controlling stimuli change over time and gradually match those that will be present in the natural environment.
Method of gradually changing behavior that emphasizes child success	Method of gradually changing behavior that emphasizes child success
Minimizes child errors	Minimizes child errors

Instructional methodologies. Both shaping and fading are powerful instructional methods for teaching children with ASD new skills. There are many ways of using these effective instructional methodologies such as in discrete trial teaching. Discrete trial teaching refers to presenting highly discriminable stimuli in a very precise sequence under very low distraction and high motivation conditions. It is often used to teach initial and/or very difficult skills. It may be used in conjunction with naturalistic or incidental teaching methods as well. Relatedly, massed practice relies on frequent repetition (which is what many of us do when we practice a skill over and over to become very good at it, like practicing a tennis serve, a dance move, or basketball shots). Then there is distributed practice, which is the opposite of massed practice and relies on maintaining the skill over extended periods of time and in a sense being "ready" to perform the skill. It takes great skill and extensive training to effectively use all of the myriad of effective behavioral intervention methodologies and to apply them correctly based upon the unique characteristics of each individual child. It is not critical that these methodologies be used in a "cookie cutter" or "one size fits all" manner (Anderson & Romanczyk, 2000). Chapter 10 provides you with some resources to learn more about these instructional methodologies.

▶ Consequences: How to Motivate Your Child

A consequence is defined as an event that follows a response. Although there are innumerable possible consequences that may follow any given behavior, only one class or type of these will be addressed at this point in our discussion - positive reinforcement. Positive reinforcement is defined as a consequence which strengthens the behavior it follows. For example, if a child receives cheers and high fives from teammates for finishing a race, the child is more likely to participate in another race in the future. In other words, if the social praise (e.g. cheers and high fives) is functioning as a reinforcer then we will observe a strengthening of the behavior (i.e., participating in a race).

In their book, How to Select Reinforcers, R. Vance Hall and Marilyn Hall (1980), list 5 basic rules for reinforcement. These rules are discussed below.

Rule 1: An object/event can only be considered a reinforcer if it increases the strength of a behavior. In the above example, if receiving candy for correct responding does not increase the frequency of eye contact, it is not a reinforcer for that child on that particular task.

Rule 2: An event that may function as a reinforcer for one child may not be a reinforcer for another person. For example, one child may enjoy being hugged and tickled. When these events follow correct responding, the child is motivated to perform well. However, for a child who resists physical contact with others, hugs and tickles may not be reinforcing. In fact, this second child may respond incorrectly in an effort to avoid being hugged or tickled.

Rule 3: In order for a reinforcer to be effective (at least in the initial stages of teaching a new behavior) it must immediately follow the target behavior. As the time delay between the occurrence of the behavior and the delivery of reinforcement increases the likelihood that the behavior will increase, decreases.

Rule 4: Reinforcement must be contingent upon the presence of the desired behavior. This means that the child must perform the desired behavior in order to receive reinforcement.

Rule 5: When teaching a new behavior, reinforcement should occur each time the behavior occurs. After the behavior has been acquired, the behavior can usually be maintained with less reinforcement.

Types of Reinforcers. A wide variety of items and events may serve as effective reinforcers. A reinforcer is always defined by its effect, not just by its characteristics. Several classes of reinforcers and examples of specific reinforcers are presented on the next page.

Type of Reinforcer	Examples
Primary	• Edibles (candy, crackers) and liquids (fruit juices, soda)
Tangible	• Material items such as toys, books, games
Privileges and activity	• In the school setting, privileges and activity reinforcers might include helping the teacher in the classroom, delivering messages, erasing the blackboards, correcting papers, helping with lunch preparation, or earning free time to play a game or read a book. • In the home setting, examples of privileges and activity reinforcers include staying up 1/2 hour late to watch a favorite T.V. show, receiving a favorite dessert, spending an overnight with a friend or with a special relative, spending exclusive time with one or both parents, or special activities such as fishing, shopping, or eating out at a favorite restaurant.
Social	• For some children, adult attention is highly reinforcing. Verbal praise ("Good work!"; "Nice job!"; "Terrific!") and age-appropriate physical contact (e.g., hugs and tickles for young children; pats on the back for older children) may be extremely effective reinforcers.
Conditioned	• Conditioned reinforcers (points, tokens, money) are symbolic. They are not terribly reinforcing in their own right, but their value lies in the ability to exchange these symbolic reinforcers for primary or tangible reinforcers or privileges and activity reinforcers. Money is perhaps the most familiar and highly valued symbolic reinforcer. However, children will often work very hard to earn points or tokens which, like money, may be exchanged at a later date for primary, tangible, privilege, or activity rewards.

▶ When Behavioral Treatments Are Not Enough. Can Medication Help?

Despite the fact that modern pharmaceutics are tremendously useful as frontline interventions to manage many psychiatric disorders (e.g., depression, anxiety, obsessive compulsive disorder), there is no single medication or group of medications that can "cure" the core symptoms of ASD, namely, marked impairment in social interaction, communication, and restricted repetitive behavior. However, there sometimes is a role for the use of medication in the management of some of the behaviors that may be part of the clinical picture.

Decision-Making. Making the choice to try medication is often a difficult one for families. Many factors contribute to the decision-making process. These include the following:

- Family attitudes towards medication:

  — Many people equate medication with "chemicals" and they tend to prefer more "natural" interventions (i.e., diet, dietary supplements, natural remedies, or behavioral interventions).

- Past personal experience with medication or stories about medication use:

  — In their quest to minimize the behavioral excesses associated with ASD, many parents have attempted medication trials. If there was little or no change in the troublesome behaviors, if "the behavior got worse", if there were unwanted side effects or unsatisfied expectations (i.e., "problematic behaviors decreased, but Johnny seemed so "out of it" or "Susie's activity levels decreased markedly but her language did not improve") or the positive effects of the medication were short-lived (i.e., the medication seemed to work at first, but the results did not last), parents may be reluctant to pursue another medication trial.

As with all important decisions, you need to do your homework and access accurate information to help you weigh the pro's and con's of medication use. It is important to be aware of what you can realistically expect and the current limits of available medications. The following list provides a summary of information that we frequently share with our families regarding the reality of the use of medication.

- Medications may be useful in the management of behavior problems associated with autism (i.e., aggressive behavior, tantrums and irritability, distractibility, self-stimulatory and self-injurious behavior, etc.), but do not "cure" autism.

- The majority of research studies investigating the effectiveness of medication and side effects have focused on adults. There are relatively few well-controlled studies that focus on the effects of medications on children and adolescents.

- Response to medication is highly individualized. Some children will be responders and others will be non-responders. Some children will experience no or mild side effects while others will experience numerous untoward (negative) effects.

- At the present time, there are no good predictors that identify children who will respond positively to medication and those who will not. Finding an effective medication can be a trial and error process.

- In most cases, parents will not see the effects of the medication immediately. It is common practice to start with low doses of medication and to gradually increase the dose until a therapeutic level is reached. Behavior change is usually seen when the dose approximates the therapeutic range for a specific medication. Thus, it is important to be patient and allow a sufficient amount of time to evaluate the medication's effectiveness.

- Varying the dose of medication can have a differential effect on behavior. In other words, changes in some behaviors are seen at a specific dose, while other behaviors are unaffected. As the medication is increased, the beneficial effect seen in the initially changed behavior may disappear, but positive effects are seen in other behaviors. This is referred to as a dose-response curve.

- Long-term use of medication may be needed since autism is a life-long disorder.

- It can be dangerous to stop some medications "cold turkey". Parents should always consult with the prescribing physician before discontinuing medication.

- Using more than one medication to achieve a goal is not an uncommon practice. Medications interact with one another and there may be some medications that boost the effect of another medication. Also, given the complexity of some of the behavior problems our children exhibit, more than one medication may be indicated to treat different types of problems (e.g., seizures and hyperactivity).

Guidelines for Appropriate Medication Use. There are many sources of useful information concerning the complexities of medication use with children. One important reference, that concerns both children and adults, is the <u>Psychotropic Medication and Developmental Disabilities: The International Consensus Handbook</u> (Reiss and Aman (Eds.), 1998). These authors provide specific recommendations concerning psychotropic medication(s):

- Should not be used as punishment, for the convenience of staff, or as a substitute for efficacious psychosocial interventions. The Handbook also stipulates that medications should not be used in quantities that negatively impact upon quality of life.

- Must be used within the context of a coordinated, multidisciplinary care plan with a primary focus on improving an individual's quality of life.

- Administration must be based a psychiatric diagnosis of a "specific behavioral-pharmacological hypothesis" that results from a full diagnostic and functional assessment.

▶ Decision-Making: Behavioral Treatment or Medication?

When considering the preferred treatment for a specific behavior or set of behaviors, it is important to become familiar with the characteristics of the proposed treatment, characteristics of the target behavior, and characteristics of the individual. The table below provides more detail about some important factors.

Characteristics of the Proposed Treatment	
Degree of risk	What are the risks associated with the treatment? Do the potential side effects outweigh the potential benefits?
Effectiveness	Is there well-controlled research evidence indicating that the treatment is effective?
Efficiency	Assuming that there is evidence that the treatment is effective, can the treatment impact upon the behavior in a timely manner so as to minimize risk? In other words, how long will it take to see positive effects from the treatment?
Acceptability	Is the treatment acceptable to caregivers? Does the treatment meet with social norms. In other words, is the treatment acceptable to the greater community?

An understanding of the characteristics of the target behavior is also important in the decision-making process. Each behavior has a unique history in the life of the child. A more detailed definition of terms is presented in the table below.

Characteristics of the Target Behavior	
Severity	Degree of danger that the behavior presents to the individual or others.
Frequency	How often the behavior occurs? Does the behavior occur too infrequently or too often?
Cyclical nature of the behavior	Do instances of the behavior cluster around certain time periods? That is are there periods of time during which the behavior does not occur and other times during which the behavior occurs with some regularity?
Degree to which the behavior results in exclusion	Does the presence of the behavior result in exclusion of the child from normative, age-appropriate activities (i.e., exclusion from educational and social opportunities) including participation in routine family activities?
Occurs fairly reliably in presence of specific antecedents and maintained by specific consequences	Is the occurrence of the behavior predictable? That is, are there specific events that set the occasion for the behavior (antecedents) or specific events that follow the occurrence of the behavior that maintain the behavior (i.e., consequences).

Child characteristics also contribute to the decision-making process. No two children are alike: they differ in their learning histories, the strategies they have developed to compensate for their deficits, the relative strengths in their repertoires, their response to reinforcement and motivating events, the number and intensity of unwanted behaviors, and their intervention histories. Therefore, it is important to evaluate the child-treatment fit for each child. Interventions that may be effective with one child may be highly disruptive and ineffective for another.

Child characteristics	
Awareness	How aware is your child about the effect of his/her behavior on others? Does (s)he show remorse or regret after engaging in behaviors that are harmful or that disturb others? Does your child understand cause and effect relationships (i.e., the relationship between his/her behavior and environmental consequences)?
Motivation	Is your child motivated to change his/her behavior? Is your child responsive to activities/events that could be used to motivate behavior change?
Physical Development	Your child's physical development can be a factor in the decision-making process. Larger and stronger children can be more difficult to manage (e.g., remove from potentially volatile situations so as to protect them and others) and block potentially dangerous behaviors.
Age	The age of your child relates to learning history (i.e., what your child has learned, interactions with his/her environment and how well established these behaviors have become in your child's behavioral repertoire). Age also relates to size and strength (i.e. factors related to the potential danger to self and others and the difficulty that others will have protecting the safety of the child and others).
History of response to treatments	This relates not only to prior history with interventions to reduce unwanted behaviors, but also your child's history with learning new behavior-contingency relationships. Prior history of your child's response to various treatments may also effect your attitudes towards specific treatments.
Supports	What is the breadth of support for behavior change? Implementing behavioral interventions may require a support network to assist in the implementation of programs to effect behavior change. In other words, there must be a good match between the demands of intervention and available resources.

To provide you with a perspective on just a few of the variety of medications available, the following table presents a sample of medications used for specific behavior concerns. This table is not intended to recommend specific medications and is not an exhaustive list. We present it as a starting point for pursuing the complex issue of medication use.

Medications Sometimes Used for Aggression, Self-Injury, and Stereotyped Behavior		
Medication	Reported effects	Possible side effects
Haloperidol (Haldol) Antipsychotic	Sedative; Reduction of stereotypies; few effects on self-injurious behavior aggression	Excessive sedation, involuntary muscle contortions, Parkinson-like movements, restlessness, seizures
Lithium carbonate Mood stabilizer	Decreased aggression in MRDD	Neurological, hematologic effects (agranulocytosis), rash, nystagmus, oculgyrus crisis, jaundice, low blood sodium, water intoxication.
Carbamazepine (Tegretol) Tricyclic anticonvulsant	Temporal lobe and limbic seizures, control assaultive behavior or episodic dyscontrol	Neurological, hematologic effects (agranulocytosis), rash, nystagmus, oculgyrus crisis, jaundice, low blood sodium, water intoxication
Naltrexone (Revia) Opiate blocker	Decreased activity, irritability, restlessness	
Risperidone (Risperdal) Atypical neuroleptic	Reduction in aggressive and self-injurious behavior. Improvements reported on Aberrant Behavior Checklist, Conners, CARS, and YBOC.	Weight gain, insomnia, agitation, anxiety and headache, orthostatic hypotension, dizziness, tachycardia, cardiac arrhythmias, seizures, mild, dose-related Parkinsonian symptoms, and Neuroleptic Malignant Syndrome. Excesssive sedation, involuntary muscle contortions, Parkinson-like movements, restlessness, seizures
Quetiapine (Seroquel) Antipsychotic	Behavior and social improvement.	Somnolence, headache, agitation, insomnia, orthostatic hypertension and dizziness, weight gain. Minimal cardiac arrhythmias, rare seizures. Side effects more favorable than other atypical neuroleptics
Olanzapine (Zyprexa) Atypical neurolelptic	Behavior and social improvement.	Risk of Parkinsonian symptoms(> than Risperdal), akathisia, weight gain, fatigue, stiffness, agitation, increased aggression, exacerbation of OCD symptoms in some. Not associated with seizure or agranulocytosis.
Clozapine (Clozaril) Atypical neurolelptic	Decrease in aggressive, compulsive and repetitive behaviors, self-injurious behavior, and improved social behavior	Mild restlessness, sedation, and orthostatic hypotension, nausea and vomitting, weight gain, seizures, and low incidence of agranulocytosis

Medications Sometimes Used for Aggression, Self-Injury, and Stereotyped Behavior		
Medication	**Reported effects**	**Possible side effects**
Clomipramine (Anafranil Nonselective cyclic antidepressant	Reliable decreases in obsessive compulsive behavior, repetitive stereotypies, and some reductions in aggression and self-injurious behavior	Anticholinergic, CNS (tardive dyskinesia, akesthesia), cardiovascular, gastrointestinal, endocrine. Dry mouth, drowsiness, tremors, dizziness, blurred vision, urinary retensive, insomnia, nightmares, constipation, & may induce seizures …
Fluoxetine (Prozac) SSRI	Decrease compulsive behaviors, self-injurious behavior, aggression	Nausea, weight loss, anxiety, nervousness, insomnia, restlessness
Sertraline (Zoloft) SSRI	Improvement in behavior problems	Nervousness, nausea, headaches, insomnia, dry mouth, constipation, urinary retention, rashes

▶ Evaluating the Effectiveness of Treatments

Treatments for ASD needs to be monitored carefully to make sure that desired changes are occurring and that there are few, if any, adverse effects associated with the treatment(s) implemented. The mechanism for monitoring treatment effects is assessment. The issues and "how to's" of assessment for this purpose is discussed in Chapter 5 (Assessment).

Beware of anecdotal claims for the claimed "miraculous effects" of some specific treatments. We use the term anecdotal here to indicate the absence of well-controlled research to document the effectiveness of treatments.

In the recent past there was a lot of interest generated in the media regarding a medication, Fenflouramine. Justification for its use in the treatment of autism was based on the findings that some children with autism exhibit dysregualtion of 5HT. Fenflouramine is an indirect agonist that realeases 5HT presynaptically and blocks its uptake from 5HT. Ongoing use may result in reduction of brain 5HT.

While the initial studies reported a decrease in whole-blood levels of serotonin associated with improvement in scales measuring social and sensory functioning and decreases in abnormal motor movements (Ritvo, Freemen, Geller, and Yiwiler, 1983). Initial clinical reports and field trials reported remarkable successes. However, subsequent controlled research has not supported the efficacy of Fenfluramine in reducing stereotyped behaviors or the efficacy of Fenfluramine in reducing the core symptoms of autism. In addition, research has also identified many negative side effects: weight loss, excessive sedation, loose stools, and irritability. There was also concern that long term use of Fenflouramine may result in irreversible changes in 5HT neurons. Other reports indicated that pulmonary hypertension and cardiac valvulopathy were associated with Fenfluramine use. Due to the numerous and severe risk factors, Fenfloruamine has been removed from the market.

Considerations. There are important considerations that must be taken into account when evaluating the risks and benefits of various treatments for children diagnosed with ASD. Behavioral and pharmacological treatments may be used together and all forms of intervention should be rigorously evaluated. There are, however certain specific cautions regarding pharmacological treatment.

- Individuals with autism and developmental disabilities are susceptible to the same range of adverse medication effects as the general population.

- Early identification of adverse medication reactions in individuals with developmental disabilities may be complicated. The challenge (for professionals and parents) is differentiating between the signs of adverse medication effects and functional deficits (e.g., slurred speech, confusion, clumsiness, stereotypies, (e.g., dyskinesia), psychiatric symptoms, and coexisting medical problems.

- Expressive language deficits may limit children's ability to communicate about symptoms. While some individuals may have the language to communicate about medication or treatment side effects, they may have limited understanding that the symptoms they are experiencing may be medication-related (e.g., dizziness).

- It is important to be aware of and to have your physician monitor drug interactions. These are changes that occur in the effect of a medication or in the way the medication passes through the body when two or more medications are administered simultaneously.

- The above issue is extremely important because many children with ASD are on multiple medications (polypharmacy) for management of medical problems that may coexist with ASD (e.g., seizure disorders).

- Children with ASD often present with complex behavioral issues. There are no standard solutions for managing the myriad of educational, emotional, and medical needs. Treatment must be individualized and monitored.

- Because individual responses to treatment vary, the effects and side effects must be continuously assessed and managed.

ജ ✠ ☙

5

Assessment

The first component of the AIMM model is assessment. It is the lynchpin that holds together all our efforts to help the child and family members. It should not be viewed as simply a professional requirement, or bureaucratic procedure or legal requirement. While such things are factors that can influence assessment and create problems, for our purpose, focusing on the child and family's specific needs is our starting point as well as our continuing anchor point.

▶ Family Involvement in the Assessment Process

Many aspects of assessment are highly technical and require great expertise. In many instances you will be the consumer of information. However, you will also have a critical role as a provider of information and as a keen observer of your child's behavior. Family participation in the assessment process should begin immediately with your service providers and should be an on-going process. Family members should expect to be asked, repeatedly, questions about many issues, such as:

- Health history
- Developmental history
- Functional skills: communication, self-help, play, social interaction
- Problem behavior
- Participation in home activities
- Participation in community activities
- Description of family relationships and structure
- Family psychological, financial, and support resources

- Family stress

- Time management issues

- Current priorities for child

- Child rearing philosophy

Perhaps nothing is more frustrating for parents than the process of assessment of their child. Assessment is a misunderstood process that is extremely complex and varied in its application. It has a format and structure that is unfamiliar to most people, and typically proceeds more slowly than a parent would desire. There are many seeming contradictions, such as references to "standardized assessment" even though often professionals will use different tests and combinations of tests for the same child, setting the stage for wondering which professional is 'correct' in their assessment. As a parent it appears inconsistent and doesn't seem to capture what you know about your child. In this chapter we will help you through this process and help you become an active participant in the assessment process.

First, objective measurement of child development, performance, abilities, and behavior is a critical component in the treatment of children with ASD. It is not a luxury and is not just an academic exercise. Assessment is part of the complex process of diagnosis, goal selection, educational placement decisions, and evaluation of progress and treatment outcomes. Each of these processes requires a different assessment strategy. One of the most important aspects of assessment is its use in treatment planning (i.e., what goals to teach and in what sequence to teach) and in treatment evaluation (i.e., measuring the success of treatment/teaching strategies).

▶ Diagnostic Assessment

A diagnosis provides a perspective on the development of the child. A diagnosis results from a formal process that uses a commonly agreed upon set of criteria. In the United States, this criteria comes from the fourth edition of the Diagnostic and Statistical Manual of the American Psychiatric Association (DSM-IV, TR, 2000). This manual presents a series of factors, symptoms and behaviors that are used to define each diagnosis. Interestingly, however, this system does not specify the method of determining the diagnosis. Thus different diagnosticians may use different tests, or in some cases none at all, in determining a diagnosis. However, there are important aspects of the child's development that must be considered if ASD is suspected, such as:

- Review of medical history: including illnesses, neurological examinations, medication history (past and current medications), eating and sleep disorders, and family history of psychiatric and developmental problems.

- Assessment of language

- Assessment of cognitive functioning

- Assessment of social functioning

- Assessment of adaptive skills

- Prior diagnostic history and other current diagnosis/diagnoses (the technical term is comorbidity, meaning the simultaneous occurrence of more than one diagnosis)

- Review of educational history (i.e., learning rate and style, resources needed for classroom management)

- Behavior problems: frequency, intensity, and duration

Currently, the diagnosis of ASD is a qualitative process, not a quantitative process. That is, there are no specific medical, psychological, neurological, educational, or behavioral tests that can conclusively make the diagnosis. We must rely on the qualitative evaluation of the above sources, in conjunction with the DSM, to make a diagnosis. Because of this, it is possible for clinicians to disagree on the specific diagnosis. This speaks to the complexity of the disorder, the wide range of expression and severity of symptoms. This can be frustrating, but it is the nature of the disorder.

It is also important to understand that a diagnosis may change. A diagnosis simply describes the child's current development. While the diagnosis of autism is typically stable over time, it is not unusual for very young children to receive changing diagnoses over time. As the child gets older certain characteristics are easier to assess, such as speech and language development. While this may seem distressing in the sense of 'why can't they get it right', it is more the case that a diagnosis does not have the meaning most people think. It does not specify a cause or imply permanency. It is a statement of current development. This is why the assessment for diagnostic purposes can be rather circumscribed and performed fairly quickly compared to assessment for treatment/educational intervention.

▶ Standardized Tests

It is important to understand the purpose of standardized testing if you are to make sense out of the process your child will experience in being given a diagnosis, applying for services, and selecting treatment and having periodic evaluations performed. Standardized assessment is one important component of the overall assessment process. Standardized tests are designed to measure a child's ability by obtaining samples of their performance on various tasks under specific testing conditions. That is, each child is given the same instructions, in similar settings, for specific time periods and there are objective criteria for determining whether a response is correct or incorrect. The tasks included in standardized tests have been found to be good measures of the skills being tested (e.g., attention, visual perception and discrimination, spoken language, language comprehension, school readiness, reading, spelling, arithmetic, acquired knowledge, reasoning, memory, novel problem solving, etc.). That is, the child's performance on the test should relate to performance on similar tasks, be similar to his performance on other tests that measure the same abilities (i.e., a child's performance should be similar on two memory tests that are designed to measure the same skills), and may predict the child's future performance.

Another hallmark of standardized tests is that the child's responses are tallied to obtain a 'raw score' (e.g. the number of items correct) which is then converted to more useful but technical statistical scores: standard scores, T-scores, percentile ranks, age and school grade equivalents. These scores provide information about the child's ability relative to other children of similar age. In the process of standardizing tests, the test items are administered to large numbers of children of various ages to determine average scores for each age group. Mathematical analyses are conducted to determine performance levels that are indicative of average, above or below average performance levels, and performance levels that are indicative of significant problems or impairment. (If you really want to go into specific detail about standardized tests, there is a parent-friendly book that would serve as a good reference: Braaten, E. & Felopulos, G., 2003).

The results of standardized tests are helpful in identifying global areas of deficit and patterns of deficits. We use the term 'anchor point' to describe their function. That is, standardized testing provides a method of identifying where the child's development falls in comparison to children with typical development. In this way it is like locating your position on a map. Knowing where you are is critical to reaching your destination.

We have found that for many parents a point of confusion and frustration is the mistaken belief that standardized testing should measure the child's skills at his best and describe his potential. Quite the opposite. Standardized testing, as the name implies, is <u>not</u> adjusted to the characteristics of the specific child. In fact all standardized tests warn of 'breaking' standardization – that is, trying to elicit better performance from the child by changing the way information is presented, giving more time, repeating questions, providing external motivation, etc. When one breaks standardization, the results are not interpretable. As a parent you want to insure the professional performing assessments is 'going by the book' and not being innovative in a misguided attempt to paint a brighter picture. Inaccurate information is dangerous, just as if a medical professional told you your cholesterol was lower than it actually was because you were 'trying hard' to keep to your diet.

In contrast, there is a form of assessment that specifically <u>is</u> adjusted to the child in order to elicit optimum performance and understand the contribution of various factors to how the child behaves and performs. This is referred to as behavioral or functional assessment (described later in this chapter). This form of assessment is unfortunately often underutilized but crucial to effective intervention.

Sole reliance on standardized tests for evaluating the progress of children is not recommended, as these tests tend to be insensitive to the small increments in learning often observed. Thus, a child may make progress on all his educational goals within a given school year and not show gains on standardized test scores. Progress is best measured via multiple methods of assessment.

When interpreting standardized test scores, it is important to recognize that a variety of situational factors that will effect how your child responds. Remember such tests are intended to measure performance under a 'standard' situation, not to obtain optimal ability. Factors such as familiarity of the examiner, change in routine, current health, fatigue, past history with test situations, ability to comprehend instructions and attend to relevant stimuli, noise and heat levels in the testing room, distractions in the testing room, may significantly effect test performance. In the testing situation, these situational, organismic, and environmental characteristics often interact in ways that make it difficult for the child to participate. However, understanding these influences provides important information about atypical and unusual reactions your child has to such situations. In turn this information can be used to select important goals that serve to teach a child to be able to participate more effectively. Such skills are commonly referred to as 'test-taking skills'. As an aside, we often gauge progress by carefully examining the changes in child behavior in areas such as attention, following directions, waiting, not disrupting test materials, etc, that reflect achievement of goals specifically targeted to these important skills that allow a child to interact in assessment and teaching situations.

Thus, interpretation of information obtained during standardized assessment should not only involve attention to summary scores which provide information about overall levels of performance in the skill areas evaluated by the test, but should also consider the patterns of performance and behavior observed during testing. This improves accuracy of interpretation, which then influences goal selection, which in turn produces meaningful change in the child's performance. The table below provides an example of the types of changes that might be observed across testing sessions.

Initial Testing of Language Comprehension	Retest Using Same Language Test
Child had difficulty remaining in seat	Child remained in seat throughout session
Child was unable to attend to test materials	Child carefully looked at test materials before making a response
Responding was random; the child did not consider response choices. In other words, the child pointed with little or no regard to the examiner's instructions	Child pointed to several pictures on request; performance declined when items became unfamiliar

When measuring the progress of children who exhibit severe learning problems, another problem may arise with the use of standardized tests. Many of the tests used in educational settings are not sensitive enough to detect what may be significant changes in a child's acquisition of skills. Therefore using test scores as the only measure of child progress may be misleading and should always be accompanied by objective information regarding child progress on specific, educational goals and observations within everyday activities. Despite the limitation of standardized testing, it is our opinion that standardized test scores continue to be useful as global indicators of progress and provide a context for our expectations for habilitative outcomes.

▶ Developmental and Behavioral Checklists, Inventories, and Rating Scales

An assessment method that does not rely on the child's performance within a traditional assessment setting, is the use of checklists, inventories, and rating scales. These measures frequently rely on an informant (parent, guardian, teacher, or other individual having first-hand knowledge of the child's behavior in a variety of circumstances). The informant provides information about whether or not the child is able to perform the behaviors in question (i.e., motor skills, social skills, concept development, expressive and receptive language) or indicates the presence or absence of specific behaviors (i.e., age-appropriate social behaviors or maladaptive behaviors).   Many of these instruments have been standardized and, as a result, the child's level of functioning in a given area can be compared to that of same aged peers.

These measures, then, provide the examiner with information about the child's performance in certain environmental settings much in the same way that standardized tests provide information about performance on specific tasks; i.e., they indicate the degree to which the child is functioning relative to his peers.   However, unlike the standardized tests described above, they do not require the child to perform skills under highly structured testing conditions. As a parent or concerned adult, it is sometimes difficult be fully objective, which can limit the use of these measures. However, this is the rationale for multi-method assessment: not to place reliance on any one measure, but rather to use of pattern of convergence of information to make decisions.

▶ Systematic Behavior Analysis and Functional Analysis

Systematic behavior analysis is the process through which critical variables that effect performance, learning and behavior can be identified. Conducting a behavior analysis requires a systematic plan for observing behavior. It requires the examiner to generate a series of questions about the child's behavior/performance and how different environmental and personal variables affect behavior/performance.   Systematic, quantitative observations are made of the child's behavior/performance in different situations and this leads to a set of hypotheses based upon the data analysis.

Next starts the process of functional analysis. By manipulating one variable at a time, it is possible to begin to identify the variables that significantly influence (increase, decrease, maintain, elicit) behavior patterns.   The process can be likened to carrying on "mini" experiments. If, for example, you were interested in assessing how different events affect a child's response accuracy, you would likely present the task in the same way, but change the consequences for correct performance (e.g., no specific consequence, verbal praise, or the opportunity to play Nintendo for 5 minutes following a correct response). By analyzing the number of correct responses the child made over the course of multiple sessions in which each of the aforementioned consequences was used, it would be possible to begin to identify environmental events that increase performance. This process is the counterpart to standardized testing. In functional analysis we seek to find the optimum performance and understand behavior problems.

Because behavior changes as a function of a variety of influences, it is not sufficient to say that a child is "unmotivated", "distractible", "overactive", "aggressive", or "stubborn" when describing a child's behavior. Such labels simply tell us there is a problem, but not how to deal with it. Rather, it is necessary to specify the conditions under which these behaviors occur, i.e., "Johnny is distractible when the teacher is instructing a group of three or more children", but "is very attentive when working individually with his teacher". Identifying the conditions that affect a child's behavior/performance is crucial in the development of effective interventions.

Systematic behavior analysis and functional analysis are complex processes and should be conducted and supervised by trained individuals. It is not something that a parent, or teacher, or service provider can perform without specific training. In the same way that you want the professional conducting a diagnosis to be professionally qualified, the same is true for behavioral 'diagnosis'. There are many excellent texts on the subject, such as Maurice, Green, & Luce (1996); Maurice, Green, & Foxx (2001); and Scheuerman & Webber (2002). Just as with standardized tests, analysis and interpretation of behavior analyses and functional analyses are complex, but a very powerful tool in effective intervention.

▶ Using a Curriculum to Assess Child Abilities

An important assessment process, particularly for choosing educational goals, is the use of curriculum based assessment (Scheuerman and Webber, 2002). In the same way that typical education follows a curriculum, which in essence is a sequenced series of skills that are to be taught, use of a specialized curriculum for assessment purposes is an essential component in developing an educational and habilitative goal plan for a child with ASD. We strongly urge parents and professionals to use a curriculum. It provides context for decision making and can help you find your mistakes quickly. Each child is different and will have different goals, sequences, learning rate, and outcome. A curriculum allows you to share collective experience rather than try to 'reinvent the wheel' for every child.

In the 1970's we began work on a goal selection curriculum. The ongoing development of the Individualized Goal Selection Curriculum (Romanczyk, Lockshin & Matey, 2000) is specifically designed for young children with autism and related developmental, learning, and emotional disabilities. It has continuously evolved over the last 20 years. It does not provide a lock step or rigid sequence of goals and tasks, but rather provides a comprehensive guide or "road map" in 19 areas of development felt to be important for child progress. While it is organized in a developmental sequence, once again it is not expected that a child would simply progress through each particular item in sequence. Rather, it serves as an assessment tool, a guide, and provides a format for setting priorities.

The Individualized Goal Selection Curriculum (IGS)

Habilitative Domains
I. Communication
II. Behavioral/Emotional
III. Social
IV. Preacademic/Academic
V. Life Skills

Instructional Level
I. Basic Skills Training
II. Integrated Skills
III. Functional Skills
IV. Independent

Goals
I. Explicit - Written
II. Individualized
III. Precise Data Collection
IV. Rigorous Evaluation

Instructional Formats
I. Focused Instruction
II. Experiential Learning
III. Enrichment/Stimulation
IV. Skill Integration Activities

Child

Behavioral Expectations
I. Learning Readiness
II. Social Awareness
III. Social Norms
IV. Self-Regulation
V. Respect for Others
VI. Sensory Awareness
VII. Independent Learning

Required Resources
I. Large group
II. Group
III. Small group
IV. Individual
V. Multiple

I.G.S. Curriculum Areas

1. Maladaptive Behavior
2. Attentive Skills
3. Speech
4. Receptive Language
5. Expressive Language
6. Concept Formation
7. Gross Motor Skills
8. Self-Help and Daily Living Skills
9. Social Skills
10. Reading
11. Fine Motor Skills
12. Written Communication
13. Arithmetic
14. Cultural Skills
15. General Information
16. School Related Skills
17. Life Relevant Skills
18. Leisure Skills
19. Emotional & Self-Control Development

Structurally it is composed of 19 areas of development and within each area are levels of development. Further, within each level, there are stages of development, and in turn within each stage, there are specific behaviorally referenced tasks. The tasks then serve as the focus for activities and intervention. Because these tasks are logically grouped under stages and levels of development, this organizational structure represents a filter approach in which one can use the area delineation to specify broad goals, the levels serve to set priorities within areas, the stages in turn represent specific deficit components within the levels of priority, and finally, the tasks serve as the day-to-day activities to be conducted by staff in addressing the child's needs.

During the course of both formal (i.e., assessment) and informal interactions (i.e., everyday activities within the home or school setting), parents and staff can begin to compile a list of the child's strengths and weaknesses. While use of information obtained via formal assessment and observation may suggest broad areas for intervention, using a curriculum serves as a much more specific guide that provides sequences of skills in the areas of interest that can be helpful in the process of specifying the goals that will comprise a child's individualized goal plan. An example from the I.G.S. Curriculum format is presented below:

Area 5

Expressive Language/Communication

Level 1. Basic communication

    Stage 1. Self-initiated vocalizations

        Task 1. Emits any sound to communicate intent

        Task 2. Emits multi syllabic vocalizations in social contexts

    Stage 2. Use of gestures

        Task 1. Produces nonspecific gestures/signs to communicate

        Task 2. Uses gestures to indicate desire for object in proximity

        Task 3. Uses gestures to indicate desire for object that is not visible

    Stage 3. Use of mands

        Task 1. Uses vocalization to indicate basic wants

        Task 2. Uses single word to indicate want

Task 3. Uses multiple words to indicate want

Level 2. Labeling

Stage 1.

Task 1. Produces consonant-vowel combination in response to an object

Task 2. Labels familiar objects with a single word/sign/symbol

Task 3. Labels body parts

Use of this curriculum as an assessment tool is illustrated for a child with impaired language skills. Assume that the child has multiple sounds in his repertoire and that he uses the sounds in a social context. This suggests that he is able to produce sounds and is attempting to communicate, but he has not yet demonstrated the ability to use words to label objects or events. Review of the first page of the Expressive Language Communication Area (see above) from the Individualized Goal Selection Curriculum, provides a list of skills that should be assessed as necessary to achieve the goal of increasing functional communication (i.e., uses vocalization to indicate basic wants, and uses single words to indicate want). Assessment of the child's abilities would likely occur in a variety of settings (e.g., observation in different environments and within the context of ongoing interactions with adults and children). As an example, a teacher or speech therapist might hold up an object and ask, "What is this?" or to display an array of preferred toys and ask, "What do you want?" to determine the extent of a child's labeling vocabulary. Data collected during these observations are not only useful for identifying appropriate starting points for teaching, but they also serve as pretreatment measures of the child's ability. The examiner would also likely be concerned with measuring the frequency and interpretability of the child's vocalizations and identifying the conditions under which the child performs best (e.g., when asked to identify toy preferences versus objects that are less interesting to the child). Information collected from this type of assessment is critical in the selection of short and long-term goals.

To re-emphasize, we strongly urge the use of a curriculum. It is not the case we can say one curriculum is better than another, but that misses the point. A curriculum helps you structure your decisions, assists in keeping perspective on goal priorities, and guides you to proceed in a systematic fashion.

▶ Evaluating Child Progress

A neglected type of assessment involves monitoring child progress. In typical educational settings or follow-up evaluations, routine assessment of child progress tends to occur on interval schedules (i.e., weekly spelling tests, report cards at the end of marking periods, a yearly re-evaluation) or on ratio schedules (i.e., assessing knowledge gained at the end of a unit of instruction). Programs that utilize applied behavior analysis strategies tend to record data on child behavior and performance on a much more frequent response basis so that the data may be analyzed to evaluate progress in the global sense, but more importantly, to signal the need to investigate impediments to learning on a continuous basis. That is, rather than waiting a significant amount of time to assess if progress is being made, this evaluation is on-going so that frequent adjustments to teaching and intervention programs are made in order to optimize success. In this context, assessment is continuous.

So, what should you expect to take place with a behavior analysis? First, it is important to remember that behavior analysts use the term behavior quite generically. In contrast, often when people use the term behavior in the context of ASD they mean some form of problem behavior. We will give examples in later chapters, but in general a useful distinction is that behavior analysts attempt to measure objectively actions of the individual. As mentioned above, rather than infer characteristics such as he's bored or she's unfriendly, we wish to measure observable behavior so that we can directly work on improving skills.

As a general strategy, we also want to measure multiple behaviors simultaneously so that we can understand the <u>system</u> of behavior, not just the behavior that grabs our attention. Thus we would measure and assess multiple effects of our 'mini-experiments' and interventions, such as:

- Positive effects - Behaviors expected to change as a function of intervention

- Positive changes in related behaviors

- Negative changes in the behavior of interest

- Negative, unplanned changes in related behaviors
- Potential side effects: parent/teacher observation is particularly critical

In order to interpret our observations we must have in place a basis for comparison. That is, how do we measure and interpret change? Is it a significant or meaningful change? Some of the procedures we use are:

- Baseline measures (monitor the behavior before doing anything)
- Repeated measures (don't rely on a single observation)
- Use multiple observers
- Trained observers
- Observe in multiple settings
- Systematic schedule for measurement (not 'when you can')

► Summary

Assessment will confuse and frustrate you. This is especially true when you want your service provider to 'do something' and they speak to you about more assessment. In fact that is the mark of a good service provider – one who tries to figure out causes before intervening. But there can also be misuse of assessment. That is, performing assessments and evaluations that simply tell you where you child's development is at the moment, but not providing guidance for intervention. You will have to be assertive to make sure that assessment is directly relevant to your child's needs. It is always best to understand a situation before trying to intervene. We sadly see many families who have 'tried everything' except obtaining sound assessment that then directs treatment decisions.

6

Intervention

This chapter will address several topic areas related to intervention. The first section will focus on preliminary issues that need to be addressed prior to beginning in-home teaching. The remainder of the chapter will be devoted to demonstrating how to use the assessment data (i.e., assessment of child and family needs, prioritization of goals and assessment of child ability) to develop home teaching programs. We will provide you with examples of home programs that have been successfully implemented by parents in our school. The examples chosen are derived from the "Top 10" child and family needs outlined in Chapter 3. Our goal is to provide you with the "basics" that you will need to create an environment that supports in-home teaching and to develop individualized, instructional programs for your child that address skills that many of our parents have identified as important. We recognize that every family's needs are different and expect that the examples may not be directly relevant for everyone reading this book. Be assured that after reading this chapter you will still have the tools needed to develop teaching programs that are important to you.

▶ Benefits of Using a Curriculum Guide

When developing an educational program, it is important to have a plan of action. Use of a curriculum guide (or more than one guide) can be helpful when you are planning a home teaching program. Because these guides were designed as compilations of instructional goals, you can browse through them to get ideas about skill sequences. This will likely save you time and energy because creating your own skill progressions can be time intensive. In our program, we also use the Individualized Goal Selection Curriculum (Romanczyk, Lockshin, & Matey, 2000) when conducting assessments to determine starting points for intervention. Once we have identified an area of need, we systematically assess the child's level of performance on skills contained in that area of need and identify reasonable starting points.

Children learn best when complex skills are broken down into small components and are taught sequentially. Therefore, it is often useful to select behaviors from a curriculum guide that provides teaching sequences for a variety of developmental areas. Outlining or sequencing the skills to be taught has several advantages as follows:

- It facilitates child learning.

- When teaching new behavior, a skill sequence enables the teacher/parent to develop a program that encourages the child to utilize skills that have already been mastered.
- It provides continuity for both the teacher/parent and the child.

If you plan to use a curriculum guide, we advise you to thoroughly review a variety of guides before purchasing one or more since they can be somewhat expensive. As indicated above, curricula vary considerably on the dimension of organization. Some curricula are developmentally based and suggest that a child must progress through each step of a particular developmental sequence in order to achieve mastery of developmentally later skills (e.g., crawling before walking). Other curricula focus on a restricted range of possible teaching goals (e.g., expressive language), and may even provide teaching strategies, but do not contain the broad range of skills that you might want to address at home.

Two excerpts taken from the Individualized Goal Selection Curriculum (Romanczyk, Lockshin, & Matey, 2000) are presented below to provide you with examples of logical skill sequences within specific areas. While developmental sequences were consulted in the development of the guide, the curriculum is not designed to be used in a lock-step manner. Instead, the sequences were designed explicitly to serve as guides for teachers and parents in the process of educational planning. The content within each curriculum area (19 in all) are subdivided into Levels, Stages, and Tasks. The topic headings represent an increasing level of specificity. According to the description of the authors, the behaviors at the "Task" level can be thought of as representing immediate or short term goals, while the targets at the "Stage" level and beyond, represent longer term goals.

Excerpts from the Social Skills and Fine Motor areas are presented here to illustrate the organizational structure used in the I.G.S. Curriculum.

Skills Sequence for Social Skills

Level 1. Non-Verbal Interaction
    Stage 1. Passive tolerance of close proximity of a person
        Task 1. Looks at people
        Task 2. Smiles at people
        Task 3. Plays, sits, or lies on floor within ten feet of another person
    Stage 2. Passive tolerance of physical contact
        Task 1. Tolerates being picked up
        Task 2. Tolerates hugs
        Task 3. Tolerates tickles
    Stage 3. Initiation of physical contact
        Task 1. Reaches for people
        Task 2. Sits on lap of adult
        Task 3. Leads adult by hand to show something or to seek help
        Task 4. Hugs spontaneously
Level 2. Verbal Interaction
    Stage 1. Verbal etiquette
        Task 1. Greets people appropriately
        Task 2. Says, "please"
        Task 3. Says, "thank you"
        Task 4. Says, "excuse me" when interrupting
        Task 5. Answers the telephone appropriately
        Task 6. Takes telephone messages appropriately
        Task 7. Makes introductions
        Task 8. Refuses politely
        Task 9. Accepts invitations and gifts appropriately
    Stage 2. Conversational skills
        Task 1. Answers simple interpersonal questions
        Task 2. Gives full attention to the speaker
        Task 3. Answers questions asking for common information
        Task 4. Holds a conversation for a five-minute period
Level 3. Play Skills
    Stage 1. Isolate play
        Task 1. Shows interest in play things; rings bells, shakes rattles
        Task 2. Independently manipulates objects for 5 minutes
        Task 3. Uses simple toys independently; string toy, ball, stacking ring
        Task 4. Initiates own play activities

Task 5. Plays with more than one toy at a time

Task 6. Enjoys solitary play, does not put toys in mouth

Task 7. Acts out simple stories or songs

Stage 2. Parallel play

Task 1. Plays near other children with same type of toy

Task 2. Plays in a group of other children

Task 3. Alters activity when toy is removed

Task 4. Plays appropriately with two toys

Task 5. Shares occasionally upon request

Stage 3. Co-operative play

Task 1. Enjoys roughhousing, physical play

Task 2. Cooperates in simple games with adult or child, e.g., peek-a-boo

Task 3. Offers toy to adult or child

Task 4. Imitates adult/child behavior with toys (squeaks doll, bounces ball)

Task 5. Shares upon request

Task 6. Takes turns

Task 7. Follows teacher directions

Task 8. Recalls simple game rules and plays games independently

Task 9. Participates in play upon request

Task 10. Invites another child to engage in play activity

Task 11. Initiates sharing

Skill Sequence for Writing Skills

Level 1. Prewriting

Stage 1. Readiness

Task 1. Holds pencil or crayon

Task 2. Makes scribbles with pencil or crayon

Task 3. Draws within varying guidelines

Stage 2. Tracing

Task 1. Traces vertical lines

Task 2. Traces horizontal lines

Task 3. Traces circles

Task 4. Traces letters

Task 5. Traces numbers

Level 2. Copies From a Visual Cue

Stage 1. Simple copying

Task 1. Copies lines

Task 2. Copies shapes

Stage 2. Complex copying

Task 1. Copies letters

          Task 2. Copies numbers
          Task 3. Follows left-right
          Task 4. Copies words
Level 3. Independent Writing
      Stage 1. Basic linear configurations
          Task 1. Draws shapes
          Task 2. Prints name
          Task 3. Prints numbers
      Stage 2. Advanced writing
          Task 1. Prints words
          Task 2. Prints sentences
          Task 3. Writes in cursive

► Age and Developmental Issues

Although age and development may appear to be synonymous, they are not. For our discussion, "age" will refer to chronological age. "Developmental age" reflects functional status and is determined by comparing the skills in a child's repertoire to those of other children and determining at what age along the continuum the child's ability falls. Thus, it is possible for a child who is chronologically five years old and has impaired language and social skills, but average motor skills, to be functioning "developmentally" at a two-year old level in overall language development, at a two and one half year old level on a measure of global social skills, and at a five year old level on measures of motor skills. This distinction is important as they have implications for goal selection.

Age appropriateness of skills. "Age-appropriate" typically refers to those activities that we would expect non-handicapped children of the same age to perform. Clearly the term does not imply that children with learning and behavior problems should be expected necessarily to perform at the same skill level that non-handicapped children of the same age are performing. Rather, it suggests that we select tasks for our children that minimize the discrepancies between children with handicapping conditions and their peer group.

Let's suppose we are working with a twelve-year-old child who is severely delayed in all areas of development. Our long-term goals for this student include preparation for work in a vocational setting and independence (to the extent that is possible) in daily living skills. One of the target areas selected for instruction is visual discrimination. Having assessed this area, it was determined that instruction should begin with a sorting task. There are a variety of tasks that we could develop to teach the student to sort. These include sorting colored blocks, simple pictures, or miniature toys. However, if we consider the "age-appropriateness" of these tasks (i.e., are these tasks that the child's same-aged peers would engage in?) we would have to reconsider the nature of the task. Given our long range goals for this student and his age, several more appropriate and functional tasks come to mind. Several illustrations of age-appropriate skills take into account the child's current level of functioning, the long-term goals, and the functional nature of the task are presented below.

Age-Appropriate Skills				
Child's age	Long term goals	Target skills	Age-appropriate tasks	Functional utility
7	1) Mainstreaming into a third grade classroom	1) Independent seatwork 2) Follows complex directions 3) Works quietly without interfering with others 4) Takes turns	1) Completes basic skills worksheets 2) Follows teacher directions to complete classroom assignments 3) Follows simple game rules 4) Waits appropriately for a turn	Age -appropriate classroom behavior and ability to delay gratification and maintain social interactions with minimal adult supervision
12	1) Prepare for vocational setting 2) Prepare for independent living	1) Sorting 2) Completes tasks independently 3) Prepares lunch 4) Follows a daily schedule	1) Sorts nuts and bolts 2) Sorts socks 3) Sorts silverware 4) Uses schedule to organize daily tasks 5) Makes and packs a complete lunch	Vocational training and independent living

Referring back to our twelve-year-old child, it would be highly inappropriate to utilize preschool materials (e.g., the colored blocks or miniature toys mentioned earlier) to teach the sorting task. Although this child's skill levels may be similar to those of a preschool child, age appropriate materials must be used for the following reasons:

- To preserve the dignity of the child
- To approximate normalization

Developmental appropriateness of skills. This term refers to the presence of a skill repertoire that is often considered to be necessary before certain other skills can be learned. Some examples of developmental sequences follow:

- Children crawl before they walk
- Children must have number concepts (counting and an awareness of quantity) before they can learn to add quantities with understanding
- Children must imitate sounds before they can imitate words

It is important to note that these skill sequences are based on normative development. In other words, non-handicapped children typically follow these stages of development. However, when applying these sequences to children who exhibit developmental delays, we realize that they do not always hold true. Many of our children begin to walk before they learn to crawl and some of our students learn to imitate words even though they have never imitated sounds.

While there are always exceptions to rules, developmental sequences are useful in that they give us some guidelines as to what expectations we can have for children at various ages. This is important so we do not ask children to perform skills that their same-aged peers cannot do. On the other hand, strict adherence to developmental sequences can have detrimental effects. The discussion below highlights some problems with this line of thinking.

Some people feel that if a child does not perform certain skills in a developmental sequence that it is critical to reverse direction and go back to teach the skills that are missing from the repertoire. This strategy often results in implementing tasks that are age inappropriate and non-functional. Moreover, if the child is performing functional skills at a higher level, why spend precious instructional time on skills that may not enhance the child's skill repertoire.

Developmentally Appropriate Skills with Age-Appropriate Activities				
Child's age	Long term goals	Target skills	Age-appropriate tasks	Functional utility
7	Mainstreaming into a third grade classroom	Independent seatwork, follows complex directions, works quietly without interfering with others, takes turns	1) Completes basic skills worksheets 2) Improving listening comprehension 3) Playing board games 4) Waiting appropriately for a turn	Age-appropriate classroom behavior and ability to delay gratification and maintain social interactions with minimal adult supervision
12	1) Prepare for vocational setting 2) Prepare for independent living	Sorting	1) Sorts nuts and bolts 2) Sorts socks 3) Sorts silverware	Vocational training and independent living

▶ Preliminary Tasks for Intervention: First Things First!

Estimating Time Commitment and Evaluating Resources. Before you design teaching programs to be implemented at home, we strongly urge that you consider the following issues:

1. How much time can you realistically devote to teaching?

2. Who else is available to help with implementation of teaching programs?

3. What type of instruction is needed to affect "functional" behavior change? What we mean by "functional" is behavior change that impacts significantly on your child's ability to participate in activities at home and in the community.

4. How can you get the most gain with the least amount of effort?

Instructional time: how much time can you realistically devote to teaching? If you are like the majority of the parents that we work with, this question, while seemingly simple, is a very difficult one for parents to answer. What makes the response so difficult is the conflict between parental desire and reality. More specifically, if implementing home programs was your only responsibility, the amount of time you could allot to teaching might be infinite. However, given the challenge of managing the multitude of tasks that you need to accomplish in any given day (i.e., maintaining gainful employment, keeping current with household management tasks, attending to the needs of your other children, maintaining relationships with extended family members, peers, maintaining community ties, etc.) available time can be limited.

Your response to the question about time allocation is important because it will help you to set boundaries/limits that will result in more realistic goal selection and implementation. Remember, that teaching your child new skills is a process. The benefits are typically not immediate, but they accrue over time. The crucial measure of success is not how many programs you are implementing at any one time, but instead is your child's progress on the teaching in place. From a cost-benefit perspective, we feel that achievement of a few goals that make a difference in either your child's ability to function better at home or in community settings or that make a difference in family stress levels is far more beneficial than making limited progress on many goals with no noticeable changes in your child's level of functioning or benefit to the family unit.

Therefore, the first item on the agenda for planning in-home instruction is to identify a realistic time allocation for teaching. We urge you to be conservative in this regard for a very specific reason. If you initially overestimate the amount of time that you allot for teaching and cannot fulfill your expectations, you may be disappointed or worse, feel as if you have failed in your endeavor. If, on the other hand, you allot too little time, you can always readjust your time allotment. The benefit of the second strategy is that you gain information about time management in your household and can then systematically test the limits of what is manageable (i.e., gradually increase the amount of teaching and assess the impact on overall family functioning). Moreover, you will have demonstrated that you can, in fact, incorporate teaching into your everyday activities and that means that you have already been successful.

Who else is available to help with implementation of teaching programs? Obviously, the more people available to implement teaching programs, the more time can be allotted to teaching at home. Involving siblings or other family members is an option. However, it is important to consider the participant's age (i.e., home teaching may be too taxing for grandparents and inappropriate for young siblings) and ability to learn to implement programs acceptably.   Special issues apply when considering the inclusion of siblings in home teaching programs. These include, but are not restricted to, sensitivity to the siblings' need to engage in normative peer interactions and extracurricular activities and to manage their own responsibilities (i.e., homework and household chores). Some of the families that we work with are fortunate enough to have access to some respite care. Depending upon the limits of their job descriptions and training, respite workers are able to implement some simple teaching programs in their scheduled time. However, parents must be prepared to teach their respite workers how to implement home programs and to supervise program implementation at least initially. Other families have found that they have been able to involve older, more experienced baby sitters in the same types of teaching activities.

Another, often overlooked resource is your child's school program. If you identify specific goals that you would like to address at home, it may be possible for your child's teacher to address that goal at school. By coordinating teaching programs, it may be possible to increase instructional time on skills that will make a difference a home. In addition, some school districts provide "extended day" services. Again, requesting that providers focus on goals that will be beneficial to family life may provide another resource for instructional time.

You may find it helpful to review the items below to assess whether or not these are issues you wish to pursue.

- Do you use existing resources?
- When assistance with child care is available, do you accept it?
- Do you fear that something terrible will happen if you are away?
- Do you trust anyone to provide supervision for your child?
- If you do leave your child with someone else, can you enjoy your time away from home?

Specification of family responsibilities. As referenced in the section on "Who can help?", above, it will be important to clarify each family members' role in the home teaching process. This issue goes hand in hand with the issue raised in the next section on scheduling family activities.

Issues that should be clarified with members of your family include the following:

1. Identifying family members who are able to implement teaching programs (i.e., parents, older siblings).

2. Recruiting family support from those family members who are not actively teaching. Their explicit support is needed so that they do not undermine your teaching efforts. Examples of support that younger siblings can provide include not instigating or reinforcing unwanted ASD behaviors. Examples of support that can be provided by other adults, older children in the home include respecting the primary home programmers' method of responding to both wanted and unwanted behaviors. Another type of non-instructional support that family members can provide is assistance with household tasks, which directly impacts the amount of time that you can devote to teaching.

3. Getting agreement from family members to abide by limits set by the primary caregiver(s) and home programmer(s). This issue applies to both immediate and extended family members (i.e., grandparents) and is important because these family members are often involved in at least some aspects of child care. Although they are generally well-meaning (i.e., they are genuinely trying to intervene "to make situations better"), their responses may inadvertently interfere with or sabotage progress on home programs.

4. Being sensitive to the developmental issues of siblings. It is important remember that while siblings may want to assist with home teaching and while they may be very capable, they have their own developmental tasks to accomplish. Clear definition of their roles can safeguard against having siblings take on the role of mini-teachers and can limit their feelings of responsibility and ownership.

▶ What Type of Instruction is Needed to Affect "Functional" Behavior Change? & How Can You Get the Most Gain with the Least Amount of Effort/Time?

These two questions interface the questions presented in Chapter 4 when you completed the Decision Making Worksheet: Goal Selection form that we provided. At this point, you should refer to your completed Decision Making Worksheet: Goal Selection so that you can use the information that you generated to help you answer the question of time allocation. The chart below provides some guidelines (i.e. "general rules of thumb") to help you with decision-making in this regard.

Guidelines to Assist with Time Allocation for In-Home Teaching

Skill is absent in repertoire

- Generally speaking, a considerable amount of time and effort is need to teach skills that are not in a child's repertoire, especially if the prerequisite skills are absent

- When skills are virtually absent decisions need to be made about the best setting for instruction: Should instruction begin with intensive teaching in a distraction-free environment, or could your child benefit from instruction in the natural environment?

- If problems with attention, concentration, language comprehension, or motor skills interfere with your child's ability to perform the target skill, these prerequisite behaviors may need to be taught first.

Prerequisite behaviors needed for performance of the new skill are already present in your child's repertoire

- If the prerequisite skills needed for learning the new skill are present in your child's repertoire, acquisition of the new skill should move more quickly.

- Sometimes, it is possible to use the prerequisite skills as a bridge to teach more complex behavior. For example, a common strategy for teaching the arithmetic concept of addition, is to give children practice with joining sets via counting (e.g., 3 objects + 2 objects = 5 objects).

- Intensive instruction in a quiet, distraction free environment is often beneficial for teaching important prerequisite skills. This strategy can expedite learning of basic skills that may be impeding progress on other goals.

Skill is present, but quality of response is poor

- Improving the quality of a response is often easier than teaching the response from "scratch". One teaching tool that is often employed for this purpose is shaping. When implementing this strategy, parents would systematically reinforce "successive approximations" to the desired response.

- However, if your child has been performing the skill at an inferior level for a long period of time and has a long history of being reinforced for this level of performance, it may be wise to reteach the skill using prompts and prompt fading techniques.

- Instruction can take place in a quiet setting with limited distractions or in the natural environment.

Skill is in your child's repertoire, but does not occur with sufficient frequency (i.e., the behavior does not occur often enough)

- Increasing the frequency with which a response occurs also tends to be easier than teaching the skill from "scratch". Often, altering the antecedents (i.e., events that signal the occasion for the response) in combination with reinforcement can be effective in increasing the frequency of this response.

- Teaching in the natural environment (i.e., the settings in which you want the behavior to occur) is often indicated.

Skill is present, but your child has difficulty determining where or when the behavior should be performed.

- Depending on the level of the behavior (i.e., it's disruptive, destructive, or harmful effects), instruction in differentiating appropriate settings may need to be either intensive or intermittent. If your child is adept at using visual cues (i.e., pictures or words), it may be beneficial to use picture cues to help your child associate expected behaviors with specific settings (i.e., church = sitting quietly).

- Differential reinforcement strategies that focus on systematically fading the frequency of reinforcement, should most often be part of the teaching method. That is, you should reinforce your child for behaving appropriately for the specific setting at regular intervals and systematically increase the length of the interval so that it approximates age or developmentally-appropriate expectations.

- Given the focus on teaching your child to differentiate settings for specific behaviors, teaching should occur in the natural environment.

After you have applied the guidelines to the skills that you want to teach, complete the following worksheet.

Anticipated Teaching Time Worksheet		
List the skills that will require intensive instruction	How often will you teach each skill? Number of teaching sessions each day.	How long will each session be scheduled for? How many minutes will each session last?
List the skills that you will teach in the natural environment	How often will you teach each skill? Number of teaching opportunities you expect to have each day.	How much extra time will you have to allot to for these naturalistic teaching trials?
Totals		

Now that you know how many teaching sessions that you want to complete each day and who is going to assist you with the teaching, it is important to schedule these activities so that you increase the likelihood that they will occur on a regular basis.

▶ Scheduling

We live in an age where there never seems to be enough time to do all of the things that we need and want to do. In the average household, parents are continuously juggling work, household maintenance, attending their children's sporting events, preparing and serving dinner, fulfilling various family and social obligations, attending school conferences and other meetings related to parent involvement in their children's school programs, preparing and overseeing celebrations (birthdays, anniversaries, etc.), maintaining religious affiliations, scheduling family outings, chauffeuring, etc. The thought of adding just one more thing to the schedule could be that "straw that breaks the camel's back"

Of course, there are individual differences regarding people's ability to manage time. We're sure you all know people who have their daily activities scheduled to the minute. There are others, however, who "fly by the seat of their pants'. We often find that when we talk to parents about what a typical day in their home looks like, that they have considerable difficulty generating a typical schedule.

There are three very important reasons that we spend time discussing household schedules with parents. The first is that the majority of children diagnosed with ASD do best in structured environments. The second reason that we are interested in household schedules is because we are continuously looking for or trying to create opportunities for teaching. If you perceive that there is no time, no systematic teaching will take place in your home. However, with a little reorganization and some creativity (i.e., thinking outside of the box), we can sometimes find time where there once was none. The third reason that we focus on household schedules is related to providing enough teaching opportunities so that learning can occur. If instruction or intervention on emerging skills is delivered in a sporadic, haphazard manner, the learning process is likely to be "bumpy".

Family issues aside, children diagnosed with ASD tend to benefit significantly from the use of schedules. This is because, schedules decrease ambiguity and provide children with a specific structure and clear expectations for tasks and activities that will take place. This type of structure has been demonstrated to have a positive effect on the behavior of children diagnosed with ASD (references). In our own clinical experience, we have used schedules to teach our children the following skills:

- Delay of gratification

- Acceptance of minor variations in normal routines

- Decrease disruptive behavior and complete after school routines without incident

Detailed examples of how to teach your child to use picture schedules are located in Chapter 9: Family Successes.

In addition to using child-centered picture schedules, we have found that the explicit use of publicly posted family schedules can increase the consistency with which children are supervised by family members. As a result, risk of danger to our children is decreased.

Which type(s) of schedules will be most helpful to you and your family? In this section, you will read about various types of schedules that may help you organize your child's or your family's activities. The table, below, provides additional detail about most of the schedule types including who should be included in the schedule, the information necessary to make expectations clear, and the frequency with which the schedules need to be updated. As you read through the information contained in the table, we urge you to think about which schedules might be useful to organize your child's or your family's activities.

Type of schedule	Person(s) involved	Information contained	Frequency of updates
Household schedules	All family members	Time of day and necessities, appointments, teaching interactions, child supervision, sporting events, family activities, etc.	Daily or weekly depending upon how far in advance family members generally learn about these types of events
Safety supervision schedules	Participating family members	Time and who is "on call" for child supervision	Daily or weekly depending upon the regularity of the schedules of participating family members
Home therapy schedules	Service providers	When sessions will be scheduled	As needed.
Activity schedules for your child(ren)	Your child and potentially other family members	Specific activities/chores that your child is expected to engage in represented by pictures or words (depending upon your child's ability level). Numerals emphasizing the order of events and/or the start time and end time of the activity/chore if your child is able to tell time. Finally, the schedule could include the specific person or people who will be available for your child during these times.	As needed.
Task completion schedules for you child	Your child	Pictures of specific task components (i.e., sequences of pictures that illustrate how to get dressed, brush teeth, make a sandwich, etc.	As needed.

The example below illustrates the use of a family schedule to organize weekday morning activities. The X's indicate that no specific activity is assigned to the specific family member.

Family Schedule: Morning Activities				
Time of Day	**Mom**	**Dad**	**Joey**	**Samantha**
6:00 AM	Wake up Prepare lunches	X	X	X
6:30 AM	Wake up Joey	X	Wake up Bathroom Wash up	X
6:45 AM	Implements "Dresses self independently" program	Wake up & wake Samantha	Self-dressing	Wake up, wash & get dressed
7-00 AM	Breakfast Implements "Feeds self with a spoon program"	Breakfast	Breakfast Feeds self with a spoon	Breakfast
7:15 AM	Same as above.	Shower	Same	Packs backpack
7:30AM	Showers	Supervises children	Reads book on couch or plays on computer if he earned sufficient points during dressing and breakfast program	Waits for bus Boards bus
8:00AM	Goes to work	Gets Joey ready for bus. Implements "Puts on coat program".	Puts on coat, hat, and gloves	X

This schedule is a good example of how you can explicitly identify the responsibility of each family member. Moreover, it demonstrates how you can schedule time to teach new skills within the context of ongoing, everyday activities. It is important to remember that we are not suggesting that you schedule every waking minute in this manner. Instead, the schedule is intended to provide you with a method for managing your family's time to maximize the efficiency of completing important individual tasks. How and when you chose to use such a schedule depends entirely upon your family's needs.

Before leaving the topic of scheduling, we want to point out that there are a number of opportunities within any given day to capitalize on naturally occurring household activities to decrease the burden of child supervision or/or to create teaching opportunities. The method that we suggest for finding these "often overlooked" opportunities is outlined in the table below:

Identify household tasks that anyone can do if they have mastered specific basic concepts	Skill(s) needed to perform task.	Review the list of your child's strengths and weaknesses. Is there a match between the basic skills required and your child's strengths? Place a check mark in the box for Yes and an X for No
Setting the table	Matching placement of silverware to a visual pattern of silverware placement	
Sorting laundry – pre wash	Sorting by color	
Sorting laundry – post wash	Sorting by garment	
Putting clothing away after laundering	If pictures of clothing items are placed on your child's dresser, this task becomes a "match to picture task	
Making the bed	Following simple directions	
Putting silverware away: Emptying the silverware holder from the dishwasher (knives excluded)	Sorting by shape	
Use your imagination to identify two other tasks of this kind		

Congratulations! You have completed a task that will help tremendously with planning your home teaching program. Reward yourself by taking a break!

▶ Coping Strategies

During this challenging process of family and child development, it is important to be mindful of strategies that you can use to maintain a positive and optimistic outlook and to manage expected fluctuations in mood. The list below outlines some of these strategies.

- Generate positive self statements to support your own adherence to the plan. Consult with trained professionals to assist you with developing an overall plan, evaluating progress, and to provide support during the process of behavior change.

- Use or learn relaxation and/or anger management strategies.

- Set realistic goals.

- Have both long and short range goals.

- Collect data to monitor progress on personal, family, and child oriented goals.

Enhancing communication. Throughout the process of family change, maintaining good communication with family members can help to ease tensions, provide relief from stress, share needs, and rejoice in successes. Areas you can focus on include:

- Improving communication related to affect.

- Improving the ability to ask questions to clarify information or misconceptions.

- Improving the ability to ask for help.

- Creating a home environment wherein family members can express feelings and voice opinions.

Applying the techniques from Applied Behavior Analysis to modify your behavior/affect. Remember the following techniques that were introduced in Chapter 4?

- Successive approximations

- Fading procedures

- Manipulating antecedents

- Reinforcement

In this section we will show you can apply these very same techniques to help you make important changes in your behavior that in turn, can have a very positive impact on your family functioning.

Successive approximations. Recall that this technique involves systematic reinforcement of approximations to the desired behavior. The application of this technique to personal behavior change is straightforward.

If, for example, leaving your child under someone else's supervision is anxiety/stress provoking, you could use the following shaping program to help you achieve the goal of being able to let others care for your child.

Step 1. Have a responsible caregiver supervise your child at home while you occupy yourself with activities that are out of the line of sight of your child.

Step 2. Gradually increase time away from your child. Leave our child with a caregiver that you trust for 5 minutes (i.e., to take a walk around the block. Reinforce yourself for being brave. Upon your return, get a behavior report from the caregiver. Reinforce your child for good behavior if the report is good. Make a list of "issues" that may have arisen in your absence and begin to brainstorm solutions. Once your child demonstrates the ability to tolerate your absence for very short periods of time, go to Step 3.

Step 3. Same as Step 2 except that you should increase the time that you are away from home to 10 minutes (i.e., take a drive to the grocery to pick up several items). Reinforce you child as above and don't forget to reinforce yourself for being brave.

Step 4. Continuing with the procedure above, increase your absence from home in small intervals until you are able to engage in a necessary or preferred activity for normative durations (i.e., grocery shopping, parent teacher meeting, a workout at the gym).

Manipulating antecedents. Manipulating antecedent events can also be a useful strategy to reorganize activities and to clarify expectations within your household. One way that you can routinely incorporate use of this technique into your daily activities is to review the family schedule and each family member's responsibilities at the start of each day.

A second application that goes hand in hand with the example demonstrating the use of successive approximations in achieving the goal of expanding the range of caregivers for your child involves planning for opportunities during which your child can experience positive contact with potential caregivers.

Other changes in antecedent events that can increase the likelihood of positive outcomes follow:

- Complete tasks that may cause your child stress (i.e., complete meals if eating is problematic, bathing if bath time is problematic). Do not expect the caregiver to complete tasks that are difficult for **you** to do with your child.

- Restrict access to some favorite activities (e.g., specific movies, books, toys) and make them available only when caregivers are with your child.

- Leave plenty of preferred snacks (ideally the healthy ones) and preferred activities for the caregiver and let your child know in advance that these will be dispensed by the caregiver. Using a picture schedule that associates the activities/snacks with the caregiver might also be helpful.

- If your child is accustomed to using picture schedules, organize a schedule of activities and place a picture of mom and dad at the bottom of the schedule, indicating that you will return after the activities are completed. Review the schedule before the caregiver arrives.

Reinforcement. There will be many opportunities for you to reinforce yourself and your family members during the change process. Reinforcement is a crucial component for success. As you may recall, reinforcement increases the likelihood that the behavior will recur. Although you may think that we are being trite by mentioning this point, you would be surprised at how often we would forget to reinforce appropriate behavior if we did not remind ourselves to do so.

Opportunities for reinforcement include, but are not limited to:

- Reinforcing yourself for developing a plan and for adhering to the plan.

- Reinforcing your child for behavior change.

- Reinforcing family members for supporting the plan and for their participation in the play.

▶ Putting it All Together: Developing Teaching Programs

In this section, we will be providing you with a step-by-step procedure for developing home teaching programs. We will accomplish this by using specific case examples so that you are able to see how the information collected from the assessment data (i.e., your child's strengths and weaknesses), information about clearly defining the goal, and information about the selection of instructional methods and teaching environments are used to create teaching programs. The examples that we selected for this purpose relate directly to the Top 10 Child Needs that were outlined in Chapter 3. Those that will be highlighted include the following:

- Protection
- Play
- Communicates Needs and Wants
- Independence

Before we begin, there are several things that you should know. The first is that it is not our intent that you should implement the programs as they are written here. The case examples are only meant to provide you with information about the process of developing home teaching programs. If we recommended that you use these programs exactly as they are written, we would be violating one of our most sacred principles, namely, that *no two children are alike and that programs need to be individualized to address their unique needs.*

Therefore, we strongly urge you to use these programs as guides. If the goals address needs that are relevant to your family or child, please modify the program to reflect the unique characteristics of your child and family. If you do not find the goals relevant, don't despair. You will have the opportunity to create your own programs at the end of the chapter.

It is also important for you to know that there is not a "right" or "wrong" way to teach a skill. For any particular skill, there are a variety of strategies that could result in skill acquisition. If you are anxious about making the wrong choice(s), do not fret. The method we are teaching you is self-correcting if you keep records of your child's performance on the teaching programs. We refer to this process as data collection and if you recall, in the section describing the A.I.M.M. model, interpreting your data will tell you whether your strategies are effective or ineffective.

A word of encouragement and support. Although this process may feel over-whelming, we urge you to use the coping strategies outlined above to help you persevere. Specific applications are outlined below:

1. Start with a single program. The idea is to shoot for success.

2. Use shaping. Begin with a program that you expect will be relatively easy to develop and implement. Starting with a skill that is emerging in your child's repertoire is the best place to start. Your focus would then be on increasing the quality of your child's response, the frequency of your child's response, or teaching your child to use the skill in specific settings. You can always tackle more complex or challenging skills in the future.

3. Be patient. Remind yourself that behavior change takes time. Use positive, self-affirming statements during the waiting period (e.g., "Things will get better in time," "It takes a while before I'll see change," "It's a lot of work now, but it will pay off in the end.")

4. Reinforce. Reward yourself for your efforts.

5. Be realistic. Recognize when you need assistance. Remember, you do not have to be a superhero.

▶ Examples for Program Development

The format. We will introduce each example by providing you with a context for the program selected. The overview will include the following information:

*   A brief description of child including review of strengths and weaknesses that are relevant to the teaching goal

*   A summary of family needs

*   Discussion about the selection of the teaching goal (i.e., rationale) and how goal fits with long term planning.

Once the context for the teaching program is established, we will address the process of writing the teaching program. Topics reviewed here will include the following:

*   Clearly defining the behavior

*   Deciding when and where to teach

*   Outlining the teaching method. Teaching tools and choice points.

*   Preparing for each teaching session (listing what you will need for each program)

*   Implementing the teaching program

The four following examples we present will involve Ricky, Lilia, Jose, and Beth.

Ricky - The Child Need addressed in the following teaching program is: Protection.

General Description. Ricky is a 4 year old boy. He has poor expressive and receptive language skills, is extremely active, and likes to run. Moreover, Ricky has no sense of danger. This means he frequently runs into the road, climbs on structures that are unsafe, opens cabinets and frequently "gets into things". On several occasions, he has opened containers whose contents are toxic if ingested. Obviously, this was a source of great concern for his parents.

Strengths	Weaknesses
Ricky has successfully completed an eye contact program and reliably responds by looking at the speaker when his name is called	Ricky tends to wander away from parents or adult in most settings.
Ricky is eager to please his parents and works well when correct responses are reinforced with preferred items/activities	Poor adherence to behavioral limits for safety
Ricky has completed a sitting at table program, so he understands the direction, "Sit down."	Difficulty transitioning from one activity (e.g., running) to other activities (e.g., walking).

Family Issues. Given the potential harm that could result from Ricky's behavior, his parents feel compelled to have him "in sight" 24 hours a day. This places tremendous strain on the household as the time allotted to watching Ricky, prevents completion of other important family tasks including spending leisure time with their other children. Ricky's parents are reluctant to leave Ricky with a babysitter because they are concerned that the sitter will not be vigilant enough and Ricky will get hurt.

Program Essentials

Target Skill: Follows functional directions upon request

Teaching Tool: Massed practice and Verbal prompting

Comments: Due to the immediate importance of teaching Ricky this skill, his parents chose massed practice over spaced practice in the natural environment, and verbal prompting. Massed practice will let Ricky and his parents practice this skill many times in different situations. Because Ricky is a slow learner, and response well to his parents assistance, his parents decided to incorporate verbal prompting to help Ricky learn the skill.

Clear Definition:
When presented with the verbal direction, ("Ricky, sit down"), Ricky will look at his mom or dad (the speaker) by turning his head to look in the direction his parent. Ricky will follow the direction and sit down for the designated period of time. Ricky should never be more than 8 feet away from his parents.

Reinforcers: Social Praise (e.g., Great job listening to me! I like how you sat down so quickly, Ricky!") and Hugs

Schedule of Reinforcement: A continuous schedule of reinforcement will be used so that every time Ricky responds correctly, he receives both hugs and social praise.

Data Recording: What I will record: Correct responses, Prompted correct responses (this is scored when Ricky first responds incorrectly, but after a second try, he responds correctly.) and Incorrect responses (this means that Ricky does not sit down after a second direction.). Schedule for data collection: Data will be collected on a continuous schedule so that we can closely monitor Ricky's progress

Ricky's parents decided to practice this teaching program as often as possible, considering its importance to teaching Ricky safety skills at home.

Plan for Maintenance of Skills after Acquisition: To maintain Ricky's ability to follow the direction, "sit down," parents will continue to have sessions, but less often (4-5 times each week). When Ricky has 90% correct responses for two weeks in a row, Ricky's parents will begin to transfer this skill to new settings (see below).

Plan for Transferring Skills to New Settings: Follow the same teaching procedure as above, the skill will be taught in known places and with familiar people. For example, the teaching session may be at Ricky's grandmother's house, his Uncle's backyard, etc. After Ricky's has 90% appropriate responses for two weeks in these different settings in response to his parent(s) directions, have Ricky's babysitter, Grandmother, and Uncle also give the directions.

Other situations Ricky's parents choose to generalize this skill to:
1. Grandmother's house   2. Front yard   3. Restaurants   4. Movie Theater

Preparation:

Set up the situation as outlined in the current step. Ricky should also be in close proximity to his parents (no farther than 8 feet away).

Skill: Follows Functional Directions   Start Date: Schedule:

Step	Teaching Step	How do I know if s/he's right?	What do I do if s/he's wrong?	When do I move to the next step?
1	A parent will be sitting in a chair with Ricky standing in front of him/her. Parent says, "Ricky, sit down." When presenting the directions, Ricky should be no further than 1 foot away from his parent.	Ricky will respond within 3 seconds of the direction by stopping his activity and sitting down on the floor/chair for 5 seconds. Give Ricky praise and a hug to allow Ricky to get out of his seat/up from the floor. Score this as a correct response on your data sheet.	If Ricky does not sit down within 3 seconds, repeat the direction, "Ricky, sit down." If he still does not sit down in 3 seconds, then say the direction again and gently physically prompt Ricky to comply. Score this as incorrect.	Ricky must have 90% correct responses for 5 teaching sessions in a row before moving to step 2.
2	A parent will be sitting in a chair with Ricky standing in front of him/her. Parent says, "Ricky, sit down." When presenting the directions, Ricky should be no further than 3 feet away from his parent.	Same as in step 1.	If Ricky does not sit down within 3 seconds, repeat the direction, "Ricky, sit down." If he still does not sit down in 3 seconds, then say the direction again and gently physically prompt Ricky to comply. Score this as incorrect.	Ricky must have 90% correct responses for 5 teaching sessions in a row before moving to step 3.
3	A parent will be sitting in a chair with Ricky standing in front of him/her. Parent says, "Ricky, sit down." When presenting the directions, Ricky should be no further than 3 feet away from his parent.	Ricky will respond within 3 seconds of the direction by stopping his activity and sitting down on the floor/chair for 10 seconds. Give Ricky praise and a hug to allow Ricky to get out of his seat/up from the floor. Score this as a correct response on your data sheet.	If Ricky does not sit down within 3 seconds, repeat the direction, "Ricky, sit down." If he still does not sit down in 3 seconds, then say the direction again and gently physically prompt Ricky to comply. Score this as incorrect.	Ricky must have 90% correct responses for 5 teaching sessions in a row before moving to step 4.
4	A parent will be sitting in a chair with Ricky standing in front of him/her. Parent says, "Ricky, sit down." When presenting the directions, Ricky should be no further than 5 feet away from his parent.	Same as in step 3.	If Ricky does not sit down within 3 seconds, repeat the direction, "Ricky, sit down." If he still does not sit down in 3 seconds, then say the direction again and gently physically prompt Ricky to comply. Score this as incorrect.	Ricky must have 90% correct responses for 5 teaching sessions in a row before moving to step 5.
5	A parent will be sitting in a chair with Ricky standing in front of him/her. Parent says, "Ricky, sit down." When presenting the directions, Ricky should be no further than 8 feet away from his parent.	Same as in step 3.	If Ricky does not sit down within 3 seconds, repeat the direction, "Ricky, sit down." If he still does not sit down in 3 seconds, then say the direction again and gently physically prompt Ricky to comply. Score this as incorrect.	Ricky must have 90% correct responses for 5 teaching sessions in a row before moving to generalization.

Note   Parent must conduct at least 10 trials during each teaching session.

Lilia - The Child Need addressed in this teaching program is Independence.

General Description. Lilia is an 11 year old girl with excellent receptive vocabulary, but poor expressive language skills. Lilia's parents have noticed that she is increasingly interested in the telephone, especially when her older siblings are talking on the phone. Lilia has tried to answer the phone a few times, without supervision, which has resulted in Lilia becoming upset because she is unable to answer appropriately and the person on the other line hangs up. Lilia's parents felt that learning how to answer the phone was an age appropriate skill and a way to increase Lilia's ability to help out at home and be more independent.

Strengths	Weaknesses
Lilia is able to greet others appropriately, in a pleasant tone of voice and using appropriate, yet limited speech	Lilia has difficulty knowing what to say to others if a parent is not near
Lilia enjoys helping out at home	Lilia is sensitive to the reactions of others to her behavior
Lilia has excellent receptive language skills	

Family Issues. Lilia is able to take on a different role in the family, with more responsibility. This will increase verbal and social interactions between Lilia and her siblings. Additionally, when this teaching program is complete, Lilia will be able to have more independence, requiring less parental supervision.

Program Essentials

Target Skill: Answers the telephone appropriately

Teaching Tool: Role Playing & Verbal Prompting

Comments: The ability to choreograph teaching sessions is very important for teaching this skill to Lilia. Therefore, role playing was chosen over incidental teaching to ensure for a higher level of success in the natural environment for Lilia. Given Lilia's poor reading ability, verbal prompting was chosen to teach Lilia what to say rather than the use of cue cards.

Clear Definition:

After hearing a phone ring, Lilia will appropriately answer the phone by saying hello and asking who is on the other end and to whom they would like to speak. Lilia will then relay the information to the intended party or inform the caller that the individual is not available.

Reinforcers: Social Praise

Schedule of Reinforcement: A continuous schedule of reinforcement will be implemented.

Data Recording: What I will record: Correct response; Prompted Correct response ((this is scored when Lilia first responds incorrectly, but after a second try, she responds correctly); Incorrect response (this means that Lilia does not answer the phone according to the specific teaching step after given a verbal prompt).

Plan for Maintenance of Skills After Acquisition: When Lilia finishes all steps of this teaching program, Lilia's parents will continue to teach her the skill, twice a week, until Lilia achieves.

Plan for Transferring Skills to New Settings: When Lilia has maintained her skill, as outlined in the "Plan for Maintenance of Skills After Acquisition" section, her parents will begin to allow Lilia to answer the telephone, when it rings from a different caller. Depending upon Lilia's performance, Lilia may still need verbal prompting and close supervision at first. Both supervision and verbal prompting can be faded, as Lilia becomes more proficient at answering the phone with fewer prompts and assistance.

Preparation:
Make sure Lilia is in close proximity to the house telephone. Another parent will need to have a cell phone or other way to call Lilia at specified times.

Schedule:
This program will be practiced three times a week; Monday, Tuesday, and Thursday at 7:00pm.

Skill: Answers the telephone appropriately	Start Date:		Schedule:		
Step #	Teaching Step	How do I know if s(he)'s right?	What do I do if s(he)'s wrong?	When do I move to the next step?	
1	Have another parent call the house phone using a cell phone. When the phone rings, inform Lilia that the phone is ringing and ask her, "Will you please get the phone?"	Lilia should answer the phone and say "Hello." The other parent should ask to speak to her Mom/Dad and Lilia should say, "Who is calling" and after a response from the parent, she should say, "Wait one minute." Reinforce Lilia with enthusiastic praise such as "Great job answering the phone!" Score this as correct.	If Lilia does not answer the phone correctly, model the correct response by telling Lilia to watch (as you show her what she should say). Score this as incorrect.	When Lilia has answered the phone correctly for 10 times in a row.	
2	Have another parent call the house phone using a cell phone. When the phone rings, inform Lilia that the phone is ringing and ask her, "Will you please get the phone?"	Lilia should answer the phone, say hello, ask who is calling, ask who he/she would like to speak to and say "wait one minute." Reinforce Lilia with enthusiastic praise such as "You did a nice job answering the phone!"	If Lilia does not answer the phone correctly, model the correct response by telling Lilia to watch (as you show her what she should say). Score this as incorrect.	When Lilia has answered the phone correctly for 10 times in a row.	
3	Have another parent call the house phone using a cell phone. When the phone rings, inform Lilia that the phone is ringing and ask her, "Will you please get the phone?"	Lilia should answer the phone, say hello, ask who is calling, ask who he/she would like to speak to and say "wait one minute." Then Lilia should tell this information to the intnded person (e.g., "Mom, Dad's on the phone." Reinforce Lilia with enthusiastic praise such as "You did a nice job answering the phone!"	If Lilia does not answer the phone correctly, model the correct response by telling Lilia to watch (as you show her what she should say). Score this as incorrect.	When Lilia has answered the phone correctly for 10 times in a row.	
4	Have another parent call the house phone using a cell phone. When the phone rings, inform Lilia that the phone is ringing and ask her, "Will you please get the phone?"	Lilia should answer the phone, say hello, ask who is calling, ask who caller would like to speak to, relay the information to the intended person or inform the caller that the intended person is not available.	If Lilia does not answer the phone correctly, model the correct response by telling Lilia to watch (as you show her what she should say). Score this as incorrect.	When Lilia has answered the phone correctly for 10 times in a row.	

Notes:

Jose - The Child Need addressed in the following teaching program is: Play.

General Description. Jose is a 6 year old boy who is highly dependent upon his mother or father to be present at all times. Jose usually plays inappropriately with toys, (e.g., he uses them in a self-stimulatory manner). Additionally, Jose rarely chooses to play with toys. Instead, he takes things, such as pieces of newspaper or tissues to wave in the air.

Strengths	Weaknesses
Jose has completed an imitation of simple actions (clap, wave,) program	Jose uses objects out of context or for an unintended use
Jose responds well to social praise from his parents	Jose usually needs another adult to be present when he manipulates objects
Jose has excellent fine and gross motor skills	Jose has a short attention span, so he often changes things he is doing

Family Issues. Both of Jose's parents work during the day, when Jose is at a babysitter's house until 3pm. When Jose's parents are at home, it is necessary for them to complete daily tasks of simple household chores, such as washing dishes, preparing for dinner, cooking, doing laundry, paying bills, etc. Jose's constant need of supervision, makes completion of these tasks very difficult. Additionally, Jose has an older sister, Veronica, with whom he rarely spends time. His parents would like to see Jose and Veronica play together, more like other brothers and sisters do in other families.

Program Essentials

Target Skill: Uses Simple Toys Independently

Teaching Tool: Shaping and Fading

Comments: Shaping will be used to teach Jose to play independently with more than one toy. Initially, imitation will be used to teach Jose how to play appropriately with a toy. Fading will be implemented to decrease Jose's dependence on imitation, as his independent play skills increase.

Clear Definition: Jose will initiate and maintain play for 30 seconds without adult assistance or prompts

The goal of this teaching program is to increase Jose's ability to use toys appropriately and independently.

Reinforcers: Social Praise and Hugs

Schedule of Reinforcement: Every correct response will receive a reinforcer.

Data Recording: What I will record: Both correct and incorrect responses will be recorded for this program. Schedule for data collection: Data will be collected on a continuous schedule.

Plan for Maintenance of Skills After Acquisition: After step 5, Jose's parents will continue with the same procedure in step 5, however, they will increase the time Jose needs to play independently with the toys. Jose's parents will also increase the range of toys that Jose has to choose from to play with.

Plan for Transferring Skills to New Settings: Jose's parents will use the basic methods of this teaching program to generalize his play skills to play with his siblings, play in different rooms in the house and to play with more complex toys.

Preparation: Toys should be available for Jose to use.

Schedule: Sunday at 9am; Tuesday at 4pm; Thursday at 4pm

One of Jose's mother's requests was that she be able to do laundry on Sundays and prepare for dinner without having to occupy Jose. Therefore, the schedule reflects these times. Initially, Jose's father and mother will implement the program. This will help to allow Jose's mother/father to do the necessary household chores, while the other parent teaches Jose this program. When Jose becomes more independent and requires less supervision with toy play, one of the parents can decrease his/her assistance in teaching this program.

Skill: Uses Simple Toys Independently   Start Date:　　　　Schedule: Sunday at 9am; Tues 4pm; Thur 4pm

Step #	Teaching Step	How do I know if s(he)'s right?	What do I do if s(he)'s wrong?	When do I move to the next step?
1 Use a toy car	Say, "Jose, let's play with the cars." Then say, "Watch me" as you demonstrate playing with a car for 5 seconds. Then say, "Now you try" while handing Jose the toy car.	Jose must play with the car appropriately for 5 seconds. Say "nice playing, keep going" as he plays. When he finishes playing, give Jose a hug and say "I love the way you are playing!" Score this as a correct response on your data sheet.	If Jose does not imitate playing with the car, say "this is how to play with the car" as you gently take his hand and prompt him to play with the car. Repeat the initial teaching step. If Jose plays appropriately, score a √ in the prompted correct row. If he still does not play with the car, repeat the prompt (as described above) and score this response as incorrect (a √ in the incorrect row).	When Jose has 80% correct responses for 3 play sessions in a row.
2 Use a toy car & race track	Say, "Jose, let's play with the cars." Then say, "Watch me" as you demonstrate playing with a car on the racetrack for 5-10 seconds. Then say, "Now you try" while handing Jose the toy car.	Jose must play with the car appropriately for 10 seconds. Say "nice playing, keep going" as he plays. When he finishes playing, give Jose a hug and say "I love the way you are playing!" Score this as a correct response on your data sheet.	If Jose does not imitate playing with the car, say "this is how to play with the car" as you gently take his hand and prompt him to play with the car & the racetrack. Repeat the initial teaching step. If Jose plays appropriately, score a √ in the prompted correct row. If he still does not play with the car, repeat the prompt (as described above) and score this response as incorrect (a √ in the incorrect row).	When Jose has 80% correct responses for 3 play sessions in a row.
3 Use legos	Say, "Jose, let's play with the legos." Then say, "Watch me" as you demonstrate playing with the legos for 5 seconds. Then say, "Now you try" while handing Jose lego.	Jose must play with the lego appropriately for 5 seconds. Say "nice playing, keep going" as he plays. When he finishes playing, give Jose a hug and say "I love the way you are playing!" Score this as a correct response on your data sheet.	If Jose does not imitate playing with the legos, say "this is how to play with the legos," as you gently take his hand and prompt him to play with the legos. Repeat the initial teaching step. If Jose plays appropriately, score a √ in the prompted correct row. If he still does not play with the car, repeat the prompt (as described above) and score this response as incorrect (a √ in the incorrect row).	When Jose has 80% correct responses for 3 play sessions in a row.
4 Use all toys	Say, "Jose, which toy do you want to play with?" (Give Jose a choice between both toys.) After Jose chooses a toy, say "Play with the ____ (toy)."	Jose must play with the selected toy for 15 seconds. Remember to say "Nice job, keep going" as he plays. When he finishes playing, give Jose a hug and say "I love the way you are playing!" Score this as a correct response on your data sheet.	If Jose does not imitate playing with the toys, say "Remember to play with the toys." Repeat the initial teaching step. If Jose plays appropriately, score a √ in the prompted correct row. If he still does not play with the car, repeat the prompt (as described above) and score this response as incorrect (a √ in the incorrect row).	When Jose has 80% correct responses for 3 play sessions in a row.
5 Use all toys	Say, "Jose, which toy do you want to play with?" (Give Jose a choice between both toys.) After Jose chooses a toy, say "Play with the ____ (toy)."	Jose must play with the selected toy for 30seconds. Remember to say "Nice job, keep going" as he plays. When he finishes playing, give Jose a hug and say "I love the way you are playing!" Score this as a correct response on your data sheet.	If Jose does not imitate playing with the toys, say "Remember to play with the toys." Repeat the initial teaching step. If Jose plays appropriately, score a √ in the prompted correct row. If he still does not play with the car, repeat the prompt (as described above) and score this response as incorrect (a √ in the incorrect row).	When Jose has 80% correct responses for 3 play sessions in a row.

After step 5, Jose's parents will continue with the same procedure in step 5, however, they will increase the time Jose needs to play independently with the toys. Jose's parents will also increase the range of toys that Jose has to choose from to play with.

Notes:

Beth - The Child Need addressed in this teaching program is: Communicating Wants & Needs.

General Description. Beth is an 8 year old girl just below average receptive and expressive language abilities. Beth is good at reading and spelling, but has difficulty with conversations, especially within the social context. Beth's parents would like Beth to engage in more age-appropriate activities, such as Girl Scouts, horseback riding, etc. in order to make friends. Currently, Beth's interactions with her same-age peers is limited to simple greetings, which precludes her from getting to know her peers.

Strengths	Weaknesses
Beth has grade level reading skills	Only uses one-word answers to questions
Beth has completed a "plays in a group of children" program	Limited repertoire of expressive vocabulary
Beth is interested in age-appropriate activities	Difficulty staying on topic of conversation

Family Issues. Beth's parents feel that it is important for Beth to have normal, age appropriate interactions so that she can participate in activities and interests for her age. When asked if Beth would like to participate in Girl Scouts or horseback riding, Beth says, "Yes". However, her parents are concerned, that while Beth will be able to do the activities, she will not have the skills to make friends, since she has difficulty with simple conversation skills. Teaching Beth to answer questions with more detail and to stay on topic, will increase Beth's ability to hold conversations with others and decrease her parents' feelings of guilt and level of stress when in those situations and watching Beth fail.

Program Essentials

Target Skill: Provides the listener with descriptive details spontaneously

Teaching Tool: Written Scripts and Fading

Comments: Given Beth's ability to read, scripts were chosen to assist Beth in providing answers from script cards, rather than imitating her parents' responses. This also gave Beth more independence in learning the scripts. Fading was chosen to decrease Beth's reliance on the script cards.

Clear Definition: When presented with an opportunity to describe a stimulus (e.g., specific event, picture, experience, etc), Beth will provide the listener with spontaneous verbal descriptive details in a full sentence about the stimulus.

Reinforcers: Social praise

Schedule of Reinforcement: A continuous reinforcement schedule will be used by Beth's parents. Thus, each time Beth says a correct response, she will receive social praise.

Data Recording: What I will record: For data, correct responses, prompted correct responses, incorrect responses, and no responses (that is, Beth does not speak).

Plan for Maintenance of Skills after Acquisition: All scripted questions will be asked of Beth after she has reached criterion on the last step of the program. Beth's parents will ask scripted questions every other day, at different times during the day. Beth should maintain 80% correct responses each time a set of questions are asked.

Plan for Transferring Skills to New Settings: Depending on Beth's performance with this program new script cards will be created and taught in the same manner as the script cards for this program, or Beth will be asked novel questions (not practiced) throughout the day and by different individuals to increase her ability to communicate with others. Other situations where they may teach Beth to more appropriately converse would be at a store, at a restaurant, in the synagogue, etc.

Preparation: For Steps 1 & 2: parent will set up specific conversational situation(s) and use scripted flashcards as cues.

Example of Script Cards:

Parent Question to Beth	Beth's answer
1. Beth, what color shirt do you want to wear?	1. I want to wear a (color) shirt.
2. Beth, what kind of fruit do you want to have with your lunch today?	2. I want a/an (fruit) with lunch.
3. Beth, what do you need to buy at the store?	3. I need to buy stickers at the store.

OR

Beth, what color shirt do you want to wear? (Front of card)	*I want to wear a (color) shirt.* (Back of card)

For Steps 3 & 4: parent will ask Beth a specific question where she will need to respond verbally in a full sentence.

Schedule: This program will be practiced five times a week; Monday through Friday at 6:30pm or after dinnertime.

Skill: Provides listener with descriptive details spontaneously   **Start Date:**   **Schedule:**

Step #	Teaching Step	How do I know if s(he)'s right?	What do I do if s(he)'s wrong?	When do I move to the next step?
1	Parent will ask a question on one side of the script card. (One side of the script card has parent questions, the other side has Beth's answers). Be sure to ask all of the questions on the card within a teaching session.	Beth should respond within 5 seconds of the question and answer using a full sentence on the back of the card. Reinforce Beth with praise and say, "OK Beth, you can wear a blue shirt today!"	If Beth does not answer within 5 seconds, or says something incorrect, repeat the question on the card. If she responds correctly, put a √ in the prompted correct row. If not, provide the answer to Beth (Say, "I want to wear a blue shirt."	Move to the next step when Beth has said 80% correct responses for three teaching sessions in a row.
2 Use two script cards	Parent will randomly ask the questions on the new script card as well as the questions on the script card used in Step 1.	Same as Step 1.	Same as Step 1.	Move to the next step when Beth has said 80% correct responses for three teaching sessions in a row.
3 Do not use script cards	Parent will ask questions (from script cards) throughout Beth's morning routine.	Beth should respond within 5 seconds of the question and answer using a full sentence (without using the script card). Reinforce Beth with praise and say, "OK Beth, you can wear a blue shirt today!"	Same as Step 1.	Move to the next step when Beth has said 80% correct responses for four teaching sessions in a row.
4	Parent will ask questions (from script cards) throughout Beth's afternoon routine.	Same as Step 3.	Same as Step 1.	Move to the next step when Beth has said 80% correct responses for four teaching sessions in a row.
5	Parent will ask questions (from script cards) to Beth throughout the day.	Same as Step 3.	Same as Step 1.	This step is considered as complete when Beth has said 80% correct responses for four teaching session in a row.

Notes:

► Create Your Own Program

Now it's time to try your hand at writing your own program. Just follow the steps below and refer back to Chapter 4 and earlier parts of this chapter to review information (definitions, issues, and choice points) on specific topics as needed. The following lists will help you with choices for selecting teaching tools, settings for instruction, instructional formats, and criteria for success is presented below.

Teaching Tools	Teaching Setting	Instructional Format	Criteria for Success	Degree of Stability
Shaping	Quiet, distraction free room	Discrete trial, massed practice	90% correct	Over 3 consecutive sessions
Fading	Within the home	Discrete trial, distributed practice	85% correct	Over 5 consecutive sessions
Type of prompt: • Verbal • Physical • Gestural • Visual	Within other highly familiar environments (e.g. homes of friend's and family)	Teaching within the natural environment	80% correct	Over 2 consecutive days
Method of prompting: • Most to least • Least to most	Within the community	Incidental teaching	75% correct	Over 3 consecutive days
			3 consecutive correct responses	Over 7 consecutive days
			5 consecutive correct responses	Over 2 weeks
				Over 3 weeks

Next, you need to decide what type of reinforcement that you will be using to motivate your child and the frequency of reinforcement. Remember, if you are using primary reinforcers, you need to have a plan for how to shift to more naturally occurring reinforcers so that the skills, once learned, will be maintained by environmental events e.g., social praise, preferred events, Here are some suggestions to help you select reinforcers for your teaching program and to determine the frequency of reinforcement and for fading the frequency of reinforcement.

Types of Reinforcement	Frequency of Reinforcement
Primary	<ul><li>Individual responses</li><li>Every correct response</li><li>Every 3rd correct response</li><li>Every 5th correct response</li></ul>
Activity or tangibles	<ul><li>Duration</li><li>Every 30 seconds</li><li>Every 60 seconds</li><li>Every 5 minutes</li><li>Every 10 minutes</li><li>Every 15 minutes</li><li>Every 30 minutes</li><li>At the end of each morning</li><li>At the end of each day</li><li>Every third day</li><li>Every 7 days</li></ul>
Symbolic or conditioned reinforcers (points, stars, coins)	<ul><li>Individual responses</li><li>Every correct response</li><li>Every 3rd correct response</li><li>Every 5th correct response</li><li>Duration</li><li>Every 30 seconds</li><li>Every 60 seconds</li><li>Every 5 minutes</li></ul>

	• Every 10 minutes
	• Every 15 minutes
	• Every 30 minutes
	• At the end of each morning
	• At the end of each day

Now it's time to decide what data you need to collect on your child's performance. As a general rule, do not collect more data than you need to determine whether or not your child is making adequate progress. The table, below, provides some guidelines to help you with decision-making about what type of data to collect.

Type of Data	Definition	Specific Examples
Frequency	Counting every instance of the behavior	Spontaneous speech: Record a plus each time your child says a word. This will give you a total number of words per observation session
Duration	The total amount of time exhibits a behavior. Timing begins with the onset of the behavior and ends when the behavior ceases.	• Length of tantrums. • Amount of time your child spends on homework. • Amount of time your child spends occupying his free time playing appropriately with toys. • Amount of time spent in the proximity of peers. • Amount of time your child engages in self-stimulatory behavior. • Amount of time your child watches a movie with the family before the first interruption. • Amount of time it takes your child to get dressed for school. • Amount of time your child remains seated at the dinner table.

Interval	Recording the presence or absence of a given behavior within a specified interval (e.g., one minute, five minutes, ten minutes, 30 minutes, etc.)	Interval recording is generally when the rates of behavior are high making it difficult to count each instance of the behavior. The number of intervals can be summarized and change measured by comparisons of the % of intervals scored within each observation (providing the observation intervals are equal in duration). Examples: • High frequency of disruptive noises • High frequency of self-stimulation Interval recording can also be used to measure behaviors that would ideally occur for extended time periods as follows: • Plays appropriately with peers • Remains on task with household chores or homework.

The last task is to determine the schedule for data collection. While performance data does not have to be recorded for every response your child makes, you need to have an adequate amount of data to allow you to determine whether or not your child is making progress (i.e., the program is adequate for teaching the skill to your child). Several options are available for data collection.

Continuous. All the time. Performance data is collected for every response that your child makes and every instance of behavior that you are monitoring is recorded.

Sampling. Data is recorded only intermittently as specified in a predetermined schedule. For example, you may only want to record performance data every third session, every third day, or even once a week. Sampling reduces the amount of data that you need to collect. When selecting sampling as a method, you need to be certain that you will not need trial by trial data to determine when to make changes in your teaching program. For example, you might be conducting a prompt fading program in which you have decided to decrease the level of prompt after your child makes three consecutive correct responses. In addition, you have decided that if your child makes 10 consecutive errors you will increase the degree of prompts until your child has again made three consecutive correct responses. If changes in your program require that you have to evaluate performance data to proceed, sampling is not the method of choice.

Pre-Post tests. This is the type of data collection that is well-suited for tasks involving accumulation of knowledge (i.e., labeling objects, answering specific questions about personal/biographical information, spelling and reading words, etc.). Pre-post tests could also be used to measure behaviors like number of social exchanges between your child and a peer. Pre-tests are completed before teaching and post-tests after teaching is completed. Post tests can be given intermittently to assess skill maintenance.

Many of the parents we work with prefer the sampling methods of data collection to the continuous data collection methods and you may as well. However, it is important to think about the cost-benefit (i.e., "What important data will I lose if I choose the sampling format?"). If the cost is low, then carry on!

Program Essential Worksheet

Target Skill: _____

Teaching Tool: _____

   Comments: _____

   _____

   _____

   _____

   _____

Clear Definition:

_____

_____

_____

_____

_____

Reinforcers: _____

Schedule of Reinforcement: _____

Data Recording: _____

   What I will record _____

   _____

   Schedule for data collection _____

   _____

Plan for Maintenance of Skills after Acquisition:

_____

_____

_____

_____

_____

Plan for Transferring Skills to New Settings:

_____

_____

_____

_____

_____

Preparation:

_____

_____

_____

_____

_____

Skill:		Start Date:	Schedule:	
Step #	Teaching Step	How do I know if s(he)'s right?	What do I do if s(he)'s wrong?	When do I move to the next step?

Notes:

7

Measurement

► What do We Mean by Measurement?

Measuring behavior simply means quantifying people's actions. We will be concerned with four basic methods of measuring behavior - counting how many times a behavior occurs (frequency), keeping track of the amount of time your child engages in the behavior (the duration of the behavior), seeing how accurately your child engages in the desired behavior or behavior you are trying to teach (percent correct), and looking at the presence or absence of behavior in a specific interval of time (interval recording). These methods are presented below along with examples:

Method 1. If your goal is to increase or decrease a behavior, measure the behavior by counting the number of times the behavior occurs. Again, this is called frequency. The example below demonstrates how to take a frequency count of the behavior, pinching.

Day	Behavior	Frequency	Total
Monday	pinching	///////	7
Tuesday	pinching	//////////	10
Wednesday	pinching	/////	5
Thursday	pinching	////////	8
Friday	pinching	/////////////	13

This mother measured pinching simply by using a chart on her refrigerator. Each time her child pinched someone, the mother wrote a tally mark under the frequency column. At the end of the day, the mother counted the total number of tally marks.

Method 2. If your goal is to change the amount of time a particular behavior lasts, write down the time that the behavior starts and the time the behavior ends. Then, calculate the total amount of time the behavior has occurred. This provides you with the duration of the behavior.

The example below demonstrates how to record the duration of a behavior, remaining in seat during dinner.

Day of the week	Start Time	End Time (when Jose was no longer sitting)	Duration of Sitting
Monday	5:05 PM	5:08 PM	3 minutes
Tuesday	5:14 PM	5:20 PM	6 minutes
Wednesday	5:09 PM	5:13 PM	4 minutes
Thursday	5:10 PM	5:15 PM	5 minutes
Friday	5:05 PM	5:12 PM	7 minutes

From this chart, you can calculate the average duration of sitting for this week to be 5 minutes (25 total minutes ÷ 5 days). The two tables you've seen so far would be considered Baseline Data because the data are collected before designing the teaching program. Additionally, these data provide us with an excellent starting point for developing a teaching program.

Method 3. If your goal is to determine the proportion a behavior is occurring in a desired way (i.e., learning is occurring on specific teaching programs that have right and wrong responses) you would use percent correct. This type of measurement is typically used in teaching programs, particularly for academic content. You are most likely familiar yourself with this measurement method, since throughout your school experience you received a percent correct (90%, 75%, 82%, etc) on tests, quizzes and the like.

To calculate percent correct, simply divide the number of times your child engaged in the correct behavior into the total number of times you presented the direction. If you use the data sheets provided, it should be relatively easy to calculate. Let's try a few examples:

Here is the formula that you can use:

To find out percent correct:

1) Number of Correct Responses: <u># A</u>

2) Number of trials (i.e., number of times you presented the directions): <u>#B</u>

3) <u>#A</u> ÷ <u>#B</u> = <u>#C</u>

4) Now take <u>#C</u> and multiply it by 100: <u>#C</u> x 100 = _____%.

Date: <u>10/13/03</u>
Teacher/Parent: <u>Mom</u>   Percent Correct: _____

	1	2	3	4	5	6	7	8	9	10
Correct			✓	✓			✓	✓	✓	✓
Prompted Correct		✓				✓				
Incorrect	✓				✓					
No Response										
Non Compliant										

1) Number of Correct Responses: 6

2) Number of trials (i.e., number of times you presented the directions): 10

3) 6 ÷ 10 = .6

4) Now take .6 and multiply it by 100: .6 x 100 = 60%.

60% is the percent correct.

Now you try the next example:

Date: <u>10/20/03</u>
Teacher/Parent: <u>Dad</u>   Percent Correct: _____

	1	2	3	4	5	6	7	8	9	10
Correct			✓	✓	✓		✓	✓	✓	✓
Prompted Correct		✓				✓				
Incorrect	✓									
No Response										
Non Compliant										

1) Number of Correct Responses: _____

2) Number of trials (i.e., number of times you presented the directions): _____

3) _____ ÷ _____ = _____

4) Now take _____ and multiply it by 100: _____ x 100 = _____%.

Did you come up with 70%? If not, try it again!

Method 4. Interval data is typically used when you want to measure a behavior that sometimes occurs so rapidly that it is difficult to count and it is simply important to know whether this behavior occurred or not (e.g., cursing). Also, it is used for behaviors that have unclear start and stop points, but it is easy to detect that the behavior is occurring (e.g., the transition between asking for something and then whining about it). Most often interval recording is used when frequency or duration recording is impractical because the components of the behavior are less important than the simple fact that it occurred (e.g., is it important that your child pinched a friend three discrete times in ten seconds, or rather simply that he pinched a friend?).

Interval	Cursing	Whining	Pinching
7:30 a.m. – 8:00 a.m.	✓	✓	
8:00 a.m. – 8:30 a.m.			
8:30 a.m. – 9:00 a.m.		✓	
9:00 a.m. – 9:30 a.m.	✓	✓	✓
Etc.			

When you use interval recording, summarizing the data are similar to that of percent correct, in that we now summarize percent of intervals in which the behavior occurred. To do this, you can use the following formula:

$$\frac{\textbf{\textit{Number of Intervals In Which the Behavior Occurred}}}{\textbf{\textit{The Total Number of Intervals Observed}}} \quad \textbf{\textit{x 100}}$$

Here is an example of how you would calculate the percent of intervals for the above table. Because we observed 4 half hour intervals, the denominator for the formula is 4.:

$$\textit{Cursing} = 2 \div 4 = .5 \text{ x } 100 = 50\%$$

$$\textit{Whining} = 3 \div 4 = .75 \text{ x } 100 = 75\%$$

$$\textit{Pinching} = 1 \div 4 = .5 \text{ x } 100 = 25\%$$

Why should you measure behavior? Measuring your child's behavior tells you if your child is making progress on the teaching programs that you implement. Without measurement, it might be possible to continue working on a teaching program that is "going nowhere" for too long. Measuring behavior can also give you information about the speed of your child's learning on specific teaching programs. Given all of the skills that you want to teach, it is crucial that time is not wasted! Also, measurement of behavior is critical in order to understand behavior problems, as discussed in chapter 5.

When should you start to measure behavior? It is important to measure your child's ability or performance on the teaching skills before you implement a teaching program. Measurement at this point gives you information about what your child is capable of doing and serves as a yardstick for measuring change.

When we measure behavior before we begin a teaching program, we refer to this period of initial data collection as a baseline. Below are two examples of baseline. In the first example, Mr. and Mrs. Juarez measured the amount of time that Jose sat at the dinner table after being called for dinner.

Day of the week	Start Time	End Time (when Jose was no longer sitting)	Duration of Sitting
Monday	5:05 PM	5:08 PM	3 minutes
Tuesday	5:14 PM	5:20 PM	6 minutes
Wednesday	5:09 PM	5:13 PM	4 minutes
Thursday	5:10 PM	5:15 PM	5 minutes
Friday	5:05 PM	5:12 PM	7 minutes

Over the course of five days, you can see that Jose did not sit for very long. While there were some day to day differences, his best time was nowhere near the duration of time that the family wanted him to remain at the table so that they could have dinner as a family. The family had set their teaching goal for 20 minutes. The baseline data they collected told them several things as follows:

- This is an appropriate goal as Jose is not able to sit with the family at dinner -time.

- Most likely, Jose's parents would start by having him sit for 5 minutes a day, because given the data in the table, 5 minutes would be within his current ability but not too low as to provide no challenge. Jose's parents might then use the teaching method of shaping, to gradually increase the duration of Jose's sitting during dinner-time.

- They will write a teaching procedure that gradually increases the duration of sitting by one-minute intervals as Jose succeeds at each step of the teaching program.

- It is important to point out that when Jose's parents design the teaching program, they will most likely use duration as a measurement of Jose's behavior.

Collecting data using data forms and examples. One of the most important things you can do to improve your implementation of the teaching programs you create, is to collect data accurately! You may want to read this section twice! The reason for this is that if you are not collecting data accurately, you may be over-teaching a skill, not teaching a skill for enough time, or not teaching a skill in the best way possible. The bottom line is that if you are not collecting performance data or you are collecting data ineffectively, you and others will not be sure of how well (or poorly) your child is performing on each step of your teaching program. While it is tempting to believe that it is easy to "have a feel" for how a child is learning, it is not precise enough to assist a child who has difficulty in learning. In our experience, parents and teachers who rely on their memory and impressions of how a child is learning, are far less effective than those who use systematic and consistent data recording.

There are many simple ways to collect data. We will discuss how to collect data using the data sheets provided in this book. The important thing to remember is: You need to have confidence that what and how you are teaching is effective for your child. Measuring behavior and collecting data are ways to increase your confidence and increase the effectiveness of each teaching program.

We have provided you with an example data sheet that you can use with the teaching programs described in chapter 6. Using this data sheet allows you to keep track of your child's responses throughout the session. Then, in a later section in this chapter, you will be able to take the data you collect and transfer it to a graph. Let's look at an example of what the data sheet will look like for one of the teaching programs.

Name: Lilia   **Schedule**: Monday @ 6:30pm; Saturday @ Noon

Goal: Answers Phone Appropriately

Current Step: Step 1   **Current Set**: Set 1   **Notes**: _____

Date: 10/13/03

Teacher/Parent: Mom   Percent Correct: 60%

	1	2	3	4	5	6	7	8	9	10
Correct		✓	✓	✓			✓		✓	✓
Prompted Correct										
Incorrect	✓				✓	✓		✓		
No Response										
Non Compliant										

Date: 10/18/03

Teacher/Parent: Mom   Percent Correct: 29%

	1	2	3	4	5	6	7	8	9	10
Correct						✓	✓			
Prompted Correct										
Incorrect	✓	✓	✓	✓	✓					
No Response										
Non Compliant										

Date: 10/20/03

Teacher/Parent: Dad   Percent Correct: 60%

	1	2	3	4	5	6	7	8	9	10
Correct			✓		✓		✓	✓	✓	✓
Prompted Correct										
Incorrect	✓	✓		✓		✓				
No Response										
Non Compliant										

Date: 10/25/03

Teacher/Parent: Mom   Percent Correct: 56%

	1	2	3	4	5	6	7	8	9	10
Correct					✓	✓	✓	✓	✓	
Prompted Correct	✓			✓						
Incorrect		✓	✓							
No Response										
Non Compliant										

Date: 10/27/03

Teacher/Parent: Dad   Percent Correct: 80%

	1	2	3	4	5	6	7	8	9	10
Correct	✓	✓	✓	✓	✓			✓	✓	✓
Prompted Correct						✓	✓			
Incorrect										
No Response										
Non Compliant										

On the next page is a blank template for you to copy and use for your own programs.

Name: _____   **Schedule:** _____

Goal: _____

Current Step: _____   **Current Set:** _____   **Notes:** _____

Date: _____
Teacher/Parent: _____   Percent Correct: _____

	1	2	3	4	5	6	7	8	9	10
Correct										
Prompted Correct										
Incorrect										
No Response										
Non Compliant										

Date: _____
Teacher/Parent: _____   Percent Correct: _____

	1	2	3	4	5	6	7	8	9	10
Correct										
Prompted Correct										
Incorrect										
No Response										
Non Compliant										

Date: _____
Teacher/Parent: _____   Percent Correct: _____

	1	2	3	4	5	6	7	8	9	10
Correct										
Prompted Correct										
Incorrect										
No Response										
Non Compliant										

Date: _____
Teacher/Parent: _____   Percent Correct: _____

	1	2	3	4	5	6	7	8	9	10
Correct										
Prompted Correct										
Incorrect										
No Response										
Non Compliant										

Date: _____
Teacher/Parent: _____   Percent Correct: _____

	1	2	3	4	5	6	7	8	9	10
Correct										
Prompted Correct										
Incorrect										
No Response										
Non Compliant										

► Visually Displaying Information for Ease of Interpretation

One of the first steps in organizing your data is to create a table. A table is a series of columns and rows that allows you to see all of the data at once. A summary table contains the important information from the teaching program data sheets that is necessary for graphing your data (to be explained below). For most of your teaching programs you will want to create a table that has two columns. However, it is possible to have more than two columns. You may have a column for "teacher/parent," "Prompted correct responses," or "Incorrect responses," or "time of day." In Chapter 8, Modification, we discuss hypothesis testing, which is used when a clear picture of your child's performance has not emerged from using only the percent correct data from your teaching programs. When you hypothesis test, you might add these columns to your table if you think they are significantly influencing your child's performance.

You have seen a few examples of tables above. Below is another example of a table and two templates that you can use for your data programs.

This example illustrates how to organize your data at the end of a teaching program. This type of table is helpful in evaluation because it summarizes a teaching program in a small area.

Step	Start Date	End Date	Total Days	Average Percent Correct
1	9/27/03	10/15/03	18	82%
2	10/16/03	10/22/03	6	88%
3	10/23/03	11/1/03	8	87%
4	11/2/03	11/18/03	16	83%
5	11/18/03	11/25/03	7	88%

Here is a template to organize your data before you graph performance. This table comes in handy a little later on in the chapter.

Session	Step	Teacher/Parent	Percent Correct

Here is a template if you are calculating duration:

Session	Start Time	End Time	Duration

Graphs. Once baseline data are collected, it is important to graph the data. Then, as you implement your teaching program, the data collected can be added to the graph. Graphing data allows you to look at the pattern of behavior over time. You are able to tell if the behavior or skill you are teaching is getting better, staying the same or getting worse. Since our memory for how our children perform is not accurate and precise enough, data graphing helps us remain objective in our decision making.

There are two basic types of graphs. The more commonly used graph is called a line graph. This type of graph is typically used when you are monitoring the progress of a teaching program or monitoring the behavior of someone. The important thing to remember about line graphs is that the data it displays are collected over time, and are continuous. Below is an example of a line graph of baseline data.

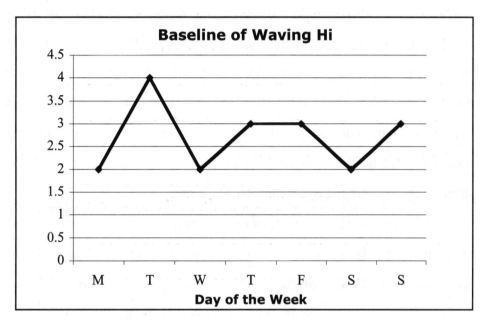

The next graph is the same, except we have added labels of the important features of a graph described below.

Let's use this graph to point out some important features of a graph.

1. X-axis. These are the dates, times, sessions, that you collect data.

2. Y-axis. This represents the amount, frequency or duration, of what you are measuring. So, if you are counting the number of times someone waved hi, you would use this axis as your scale. You want to make sure that the scale starts at zero and that the highest point of the scale is at least the highest measure that you have (or expect) to count. For instance, the highest number of times the child waved hi was 4, so our scale reads 0-4.5. If you scale has too large a range, (e.g., 0 to 100), it may be difficult to look at the minor changes in the data.

3. Data path. This is the line you draw that connects each point of data. The data points come from the data you collected. By looking at the graph you can tell that on Tuesday, the child waved hi 4 times, but on Sunday the child waved hi 3 times.

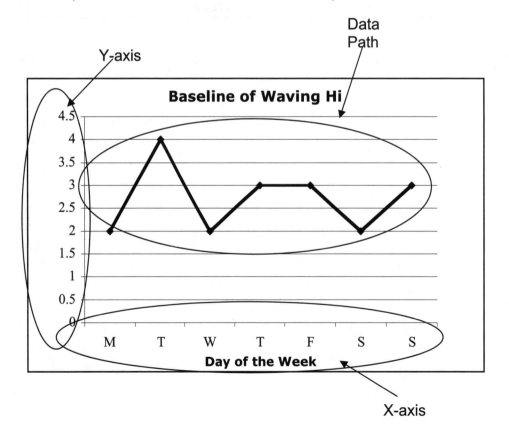

It is also helpful to determine an estimated trend of the data or performance trend. What we mean is, can you tell if the behavior is increasing, decreasing or staying the same? A simple way to estimate this is by drawing a line (diagonal or horizontal) along the average path of the data points. Take a look at these examples:

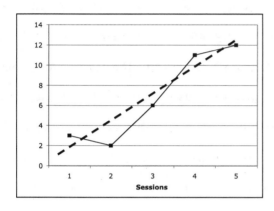

This graph shows an upward, or increasing trend. If this is a behavior that we want to increase, then our teaching program is working.

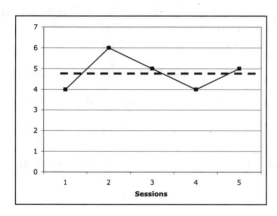

This graph shows an unchanging trend. A graph that looks like this tells us that the behavior has stayed the same. This is typical when you are collecting baseline data. However, if this graph shows data after you have started a teaching program, then your teaching program may not be effective in changing behavior, or there may be something that needs modifying in your teaching program.

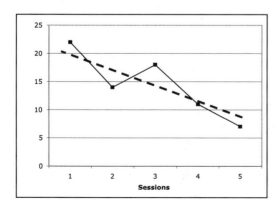

This graph shows a downward or decreasing trend. If this is a behavior that we want to increase, for example, tantrums, then our teaching program is working.

Scaling. One of the most important things that affect the interpretation of a graph, is the scale. Choosing the range for both the x-axis and y-axis can be difficult. A good rule of thumb is to make the values of your y-axis high enough to include all of the possible values. For example, if the y-axis is "percent correct," then the y-axis should range from 0 to 100. Using this example brings us to the next important point; you need to choose appropriate intervals for your y-axis. So, for percent correct, you may use 10 unit intervals, 25 unit intervals or even 2 unit intervals. When would you use each one? That depends on your data points and the detail you would like your graph to provide. If you want to easily look at your graph and know the exact number that a data point represents, then use 2 unit intervals. Sometimes using 2 unit intervals can look messy and may make your graph huge, since it takes up a lot of space to have 2 unit intervals (50 intervals) for a percent correct graph.

The same principles apply for the x-axis. Typically, you can plot each session or day, etc, on the x-axis.

Bar graphs. The other type of graph that you may use is the bar graph. A bar graph, or histogram. A good example of when you would use a histogram is when you are deciding on what type of reward to use in a program. Let's say that you have assessed your child's preference for 5 different items. A simple way to do this is to present two of the items at a time and record which item the child reaches for first. You would randomly present all of the possible pairs of items until all of the items have been presented with one another at least once. So, for 5 items, the order you present the item pairs might be:

1,5; 2,4; 3,1; 2,5; 4,3; 1,2; 4,5; 3,2; 5,3; 1,4; etc.

Here is an example of what your results might be:

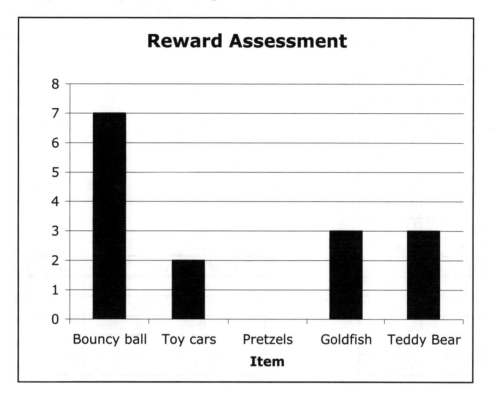

By displaying the data using this type of graph, you can easily detect which reward is most preferred. Another example of using a histogram is when you are comparing your child's performance across different family members or teachers. This will help you troubleshoot for problems when the trend of your child's performance is unchanging. As an aside, remember from chapter 6 that reinforcers may not be very stable. Like all of us, our preferred rewards (e.g., toys, food, stickers, TV shows, etc) tend to change every so often. That being said, it is important that we assess for reward preference often for children with ASD.

Below, on the left, is a table that organizes all of the teaching sessions conducted by the child's parents, and on the right is a summary of the data from the left table. By reorganizing the data this way, it is easier to graph.

Percent Correct	Parent
80	Dad
70	Mom
80	Mom
90	Dad
70	Mom
71	Mom
72	Mom
73	Mom
74	Mom
75	Mom
76	Mom
77	Mom
78	Mom
79	Mom
80	Mom

Percent Correct	Mom	Dad
60	/	
70	////	
80	//	///
90		////
100		/

Below is the graph from using the data from the right-hand table. After a quick glance at this table, you can easily tell that the Dad conducted the majority of sessions where the child emitted the highest percentages of correct responses.

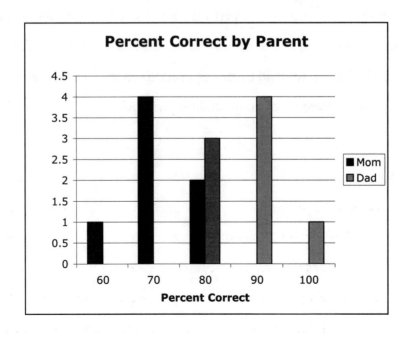

▶ Examples from Lilia's and Ricky's Programs

Remember Lilia's program, to teach her to appropriately answer the phone? Lilia's parents decided to give directions ten times in a row for each session. This way, it was easier for her parents to know whether or not Lilia had learned a step. Having 10 repetitions of directions also allowed for Lilia's parents to calculate the percent correct very easily. For example, if Lilia answered the phone correctly 6 times, the percent correct would be 60%. However, there were some sessions where more than or less than 10 directions were given. Using percent correct as a dependent variable still allowed Lilia's parents to compare her performance across sessions. To create the graph more easily, Lilia's parents summarized the data for each session in a table. One column listed the session number (note: Lilia's parents could have also used the date of the session also, which actually is more useful) and the other column listed the percent correct.

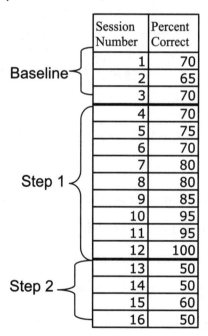

	Session Number	Percent Correct
Baseline	1	70
	2	65
	3	70
Step 1	4	70
	5	75
	6	70
	7	80
	8	80
	9	85
	10	95
	11	95
	12	100
Step 2	13	50
	14	50
	15	60
	16	50

The graph on the next page shows Lilia's performance so far. You can see that during the baseline phase, Lilia answered the phone correctly approximately 70% of the time. Step 1 was in progress for 9 sessions. During the 9th session, Lilia reached criterion and was able to advance to step 2. Notice the vertical lines that the parents drew on the graph. These vertical lines indicate step changes. In step 2 Lilia's performance declines to approximately 50%, which is at chance level. Draw a trend line for this step. Notice that the trend line can be described as unchanging.

This is worrisome, because her performance now is below baseline performance. In chapter 8 we will discuss what factors to consider if you see a drop in performance such as this.

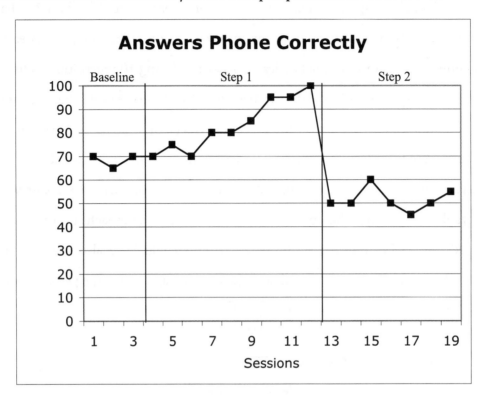

Let's take a look at the data from Ricky's Follows Functional Directions program. Percent correct data from Ricky's program are plotted on the graph below. By graphing the data, we can make some important observations. First, we can see that Ricky hardly ever followed functional directions, such as stop, sit down, or come here, as he only followed directions 40% of the time in the baseline phase. Soon after the teaching program began, Ricky's performance improved. Ricky's mother conducted most of the teaching sessions with Ricky. Even though he improved slowly, he continued to do better each time his parents taught this program. After the 22nd session, Ricky was ready to move to the next step, step 2. Notice the change in Ricky's performance at step 2. Typically, a child's performance does decrease when you move to the next step, because it is usually more complex than the preview step. However, as you will read in chapter 8, variability in the data path of your graph, as seen in Step 2 of Ricki's program, may indicate that there is a problem with the teaching program or the way the child is learning may be different for this particular step.

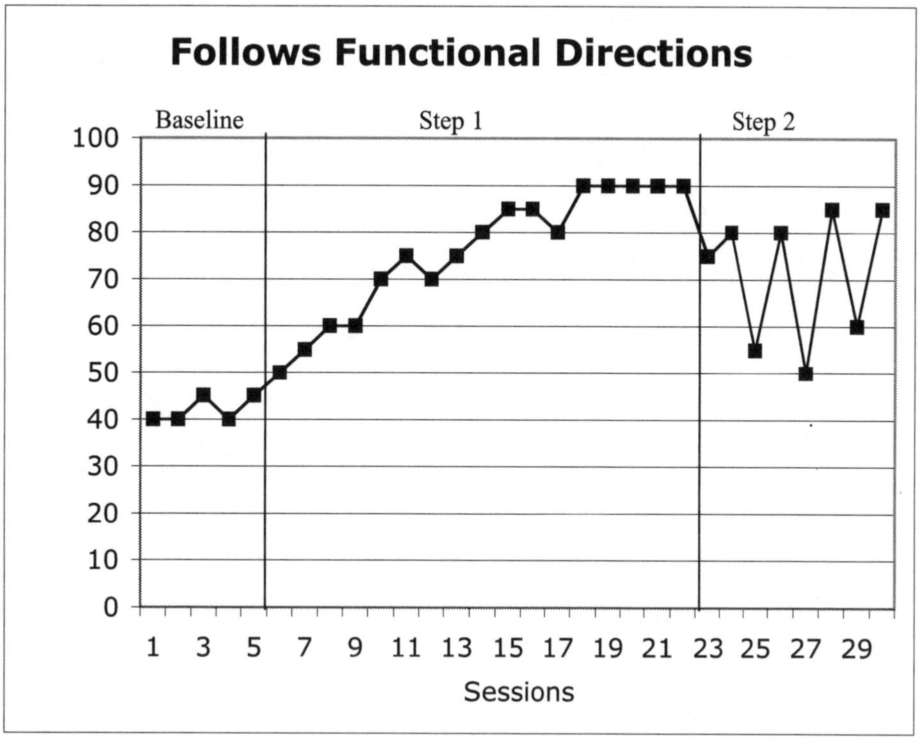
Follows Functional Directions
Baseline
Step 1
Step 2
100
90
80
70
60
50
40
30
20
10
0
1 3 5 7 9 11 13 15 17 19 21 23 25 27 29
Sessions

A note to computer users. You may have recognized that many of the graphs and tables throughout this chapter can be created using a spreadsheet program such as Microsoft® Excel®. If you feel comfortable using such programs, then we encourage you to use them as they can greatly speed up the process and easily store all of your child's records. However, if you are using such programs, there are a few cautionary statements. First, be careful, as many of the scaling functions of graphs are automatic and may distort the data displayed on your graph. Second, try not to recreate the wheel each time you do a table. Make templates in your spreadsheet program so that you have consistency in your data tables and graphs. And finally, fancy is not the point. We create graphs and tables for clarity of presentation of important information. Don't worry about how "pretty" they look!

8

Modification

This chapter is the logical follow-up to the measurement chapter. It addresses the question of what to do if your teaching program is not having the desired outcome and the steps that you can follow to identify the "culprit" (i.e., what is going wrong). It will also provide you with information about how to proceed if you are exceeding your goals.

Our rule of thumb is that when a child does not make progress on a specific program, it is not the child that is at fault, but rather the program or the teaching plan. Similarly, if your child does not make progress on a particular program, it does not mean that you should "give up the quest". If you recall, earlier in the book we stated that there is no right or wrong way to teach a skill or set of skills and that the beauty of using the A.I.M.M. model is that is has a built-in, method for self-correction. Thus, the measurement phase of the model tells you "how" you are doing (i.e., child progress), the modification phase of the A.I.M.M. model is designed to help you identify obstacles that stand in the way of child's progress. Once the potential "culprits" are identified, you can test plausible solutions until you conquer the obstacle and bask in your child's success. We refer to this process as hypothesis testing where the hypotheses are components of the teaching program that are "suspects" and the "test" is collecting information to see if your change effects a positive change in performance by altering the suspects in specific ways. This process can be likened to conducting mini-experiments that are intended to tell you whether or not the suspected culprit is playing a role in impeding your child's progress.

By way of example, suppose that you are trying to teach your child to sit at the dinner table for the duration of the family meal. You write a teaching procedure that says that you will systematically increases the amount of time that your child is required to stay at the dinner table (e.g., 5 minutes, 10 minutes, 15 minutes, etc.) in order to earn a powerful reinforcer. When you implement the program, you find that your child is not able to sit for even half the time required in the first step of the program (e.g., 5 minutes). What is the problem?

▶ Overcoming Obstacles

Not surprisingly, there are many different obstacles that can hinder progress. In the discussion below, we will examine a variety of "culprits" and then demonstrate how the hypothesis testing process works.

Possible "culprits" include the pragmatics associated with conducting the teaching program, the specific elements of the teaching program, your child's emotional/biological status at the time that teaching is scheduled, and the wrong kind of family support. Each of these categories will be elaborated upon, below.

The term "pragmatics", as used here, refers to the practical aspects of program implementation. These include the following:

- There is adequate teaching time allotted to a specific program.

  — Not surprisingly, the number of learning opportunities that are available for your child, will affect the rate (speed) of your child's learning. This is especially true if the skill is challenging or if your child tends to learn new skills slowly.

  — The general rule of thumb is that progress will be more rapid if your child has more opportunities to practice the skill.

- The skill is taught within the context of the optimal setting for learning.

  — In the early stages of teaching new skills, particularly challenging skills, it is usually best to minimize distracters.

  — If there is too much commotion or too many activities that compete for your child's attention, there will be less attention directed to the teaching task.

  — If, in order to be functional, the skill needs to be learned in a busy, distracting environment, you can teach your child to perform the skill in increasingly complex environments once the skill has been firmly established into your child's repertoire (i.e., generalization).

For example, few would argue that teaching your child to follow instructions in an isolated teaching environment is not functional skill because how often would you ask your child to do something in a quiet, distraction free setting? In our school setting, we typically address this issue by incorporating progressively more complex settings into the teaching program. The chart below illustrates the concept.

Follows an individual instruction within a one-to-one setting, e.g., "Johnny, go get your lunchbox".
Follows an individual instruction in a small group setting. Teacher says: "Johnny, go get your lunchbox" when Johnny is working within a group of 2-3 students.
Follows a group instruction in a small group setting. Teacher say: I want everyone to go and get your lunchboxes".

Other possible "culprits" may be related to the teaching program itself. Are you sure that …

- The target skill is broken down into appropriate units for teaching?

  — If they are not, your child may become frustrated when (s)he is unable to meet your expectations and earn reinforcement. Imagine the frustration your child would experience if (s)he were required to fasten buttons and did not have an adequate, prerequisite repertoire.

- Your first performance goal should not exceed the baseline by too much?

- Your child has a sufficient repertoire of prerequisite skill?

- Reinforcers selected for the program are effective?

- You have designed the program so that child has the opportunity to experience the reinforcer within the teaching context during the early phases of the teaching program?

- The program contains procedures for prompting the desired response?

- The environmental cues or antecedent events (i.e., those that signal that the behavior is expected) are clear?

Example 1		
Teaching Target	**Prerequisites**	**Is the skill present in your child's repertoire?**
Fastens the buttons on a front opening garment	Attends to task materials	Yes	No
	Exhibits pincer grasp	Yes	No
	Places small items into others	Yes	No
Example 2		
Follows simple, functional directions	Orients to speaker when name is called	Yes	No
	Associates spoken words with objects/events (e.g., points to objects or pictures on request or performs actions on request)	Yes	No

Your child's emotional/biological status at the time that teaching is scheduled can also impact upon the success of your teaching program. Poor performance may occur if you are routinely...

- Scheduling instructional sessions for challenging tasks when your child is typically fatigued (i.e., before nap time, just prior to going to bed, etc.).

- Using food reinforcement to motivate attention and task performance shortly after your child has eaten.

- Scheduling instructional sessions at times when medication effects are dissipating.

- Interrupting highly preferred activities to conduct teaching trials. Planning ahead and planning activities prior to the teaching sessions is recommended.

Poor task performance may also result if your child continues to resist teaching sessions despite your efforts to provide adequate motivation. In these cases, it may be necessary to address the behavioral issues first or concurrently with targeted teaching programs.

The wrong kind of family support can affect the success of a teaching program in the following ways:

- Allowing your child to have access to reinforcers used during teaching session any time of day

- Conducting teaching programs, but using a different teaching method

- Providing too much assistance on tasks that you are in the process of fading prompts to achieve more independent functioning

- Giving attention for unwanted behaviors and not giving attention for appropriate behavior

▶ Hypothesis Testing

Returning to our example of encountering difficulty when trying to teach your child to sit at the dinner table, we begin the hypothesis testing process by brainstorming a list of possible culprits. Several, come to mind. In the table below we have listed several hypotheses and procedures that could be used to "test" whether the hypothesis explains the performance problems.

Hypotheses	**How to Test?**
The 5 minute time period required in the first step of the teaching program, exceeded your child's ability to sit at the dinner table during baseline measures.	Redo the baseline. If baseline data are recorded on three separate occasions, use the average of the three durations for the initial step in the program. Run the teaching program with this new criteria for sitting duration and measure the results.
Your child is a picky eater and sitting at the dinner table for the purpose of consuming food, is not reinforcing.	Invite your child to play with preferred toys at the table while the family eats. Measure duration of sitting and see if this makes a difference. You can always feed your child before or after the family dinner or begin to slowly introduce preferred foods and dinner time along with sedentary activities to keep your child busy. Reimplement the program with this change and record the results.
Your child likes to snack in between meals.	Eliminate snacks and reimplement the program. Measure duration of sitting under these conditions.

Your child has a good appetite and eats very quickly. Once the food is gone, there is little motivation to remain at the table since participating in conversational exchanges is very challenging.	After your child has completed his/her meal, give your child the opportunity to engage in sedentary activities at the kitchen table. If the goal is to increase the family's ability to have dinner together, this might be a good compromise.

Select one of the hypotheses and put it to the test. Continue to record performance data for several days. If changes in the performance data occur after making the change, there is a good chance that you found a solution. If there are not changes in the performance data, select another hypothesis to test. Remember, make only one change at a time so you can reasonably conclude that the change in program implementation that you made and the change in the performance data are somehow related.

▶ Practice

Now we will apply the process to some of the examples you encountered in Chapter 7 by revisiting the programs that were developed and implemented for Lilia.

Lilia Revisited. Do you remember Lilia's home teaching program that targeted teaching her to appropriately answer the phone? The graph of her performance, below, showed a decline in the percent of correct responses made. During the 9th session, Lilia had reached criterion and was able to advance to Step 2. However, in Step 2 Lilia's performance declined to approximately 50%, which is at chance level. What happened? What is the culprit?

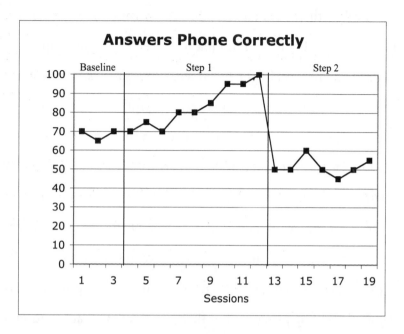

Hypothesis Testing. The first step in the process is to use the hypothesis testing worksheet. Lilia's parents reviewed the possible culprits outlined at the beginning of the chapter to help them generate hypotheses to test. Recall that in the first Step of the teaching program, Lilia was required to answer the phone and say "Hello" and then to ask, "Who is calling?". After the caller gave their name, Lilia was required to say, "Wait one minute."

The table shows the hypothesis testing process that Lilia's parents completed.

Hypotheses	How to Test?
1. Insufficient # of teaching trials	Review the data you have collected and count the actual number of trials. If the number seems low, increase the number of teaching trials.
2. Lilia did not appear to understand what she was supposed to do after saying, "Wait a minute". Her parents thought that maybe changing the "script" to "I'll get my mom (dad, etc.) might work better.	Write a script for Lilia to follow. This change in the teaching format would actually be a reasonable solution for hypotheses 3 and 4 as well.
3. Prompts are inadequate for the task	Same as #2.
4. Inadequate attention/concentration	Same as #2.

Lilia's parents checked their data and felt that the number of teaching trials was adequate. They were more interested in whether or not Lilia could remember the sequence of her telephone questions and responses and her dislike for sustained conversations. Therefore they opted to test hypothesis 2, first. They made a "telephone answering script" for Lilia and they showed her how to use via role-playing. Then, they left copies of the telephone script by each of the telephones at home. The graph below shows the change in Lilia's performance once the script card was added.

After Lilia's performance was "back on track", her parents had a decision to make. Should they continue to use the script card and add in other written cues to assist Lilia with task completion or should they fade out the use script prior to continuing with the program.

Ricky Revisited. Ricky made good progress on the first step of the "Follows functional directions upon request" teaching program, but then struggled with acquisition of Step 2. In Step 2 of the program, Ricky was required to follow the direction to "Sit" when the distance between him and his parents was increased by 2 feet. Massed practice and verbal prompting were used as the teaching methods and a continuous schedule of reinforcement was used. Every time Ricky responded correctly, he received both hugs and social praise. Both mom and dad conducted the teaching program.

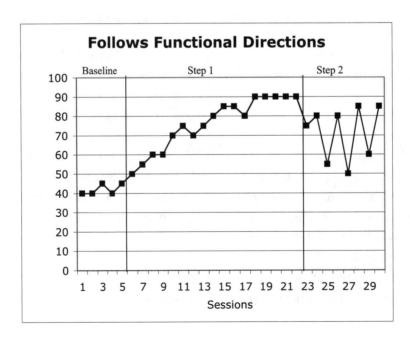

Hypothesis Testing. As above, the first step in the process is to use the hypothesis testing worksheet. Ricky's parents chose the following "possible culprits" to put to the test. The table also includes how they decided to test their hypotheses.

Hypotheses	How to Test?
Since mom and dad were both conducting the teaching program, it was possible that they were using a different teaching	Compare performance in sessions conducted only by mom to performance in sessions collected only by dad. If there is a difference, mom and dad should agree on how to conduct the program and then, collect and compare data.
The target skill is broken down into inappropriate units for teaching. It may be too much to expect Ricky to respond to his parents when they are 3 feet away.	Back up in the program and see what happens when Ricky is given the direction to "Sit" when his parents are only 2 feet away.
The reinforcers selected for the program were ineffective for motivating compliance.	Select a different reinforcer and continue to collect data. See if the change in reinforcer is associated with a change in performance.

Ricky's parents decided to try to test the first hypothesis since it was easy for them to regraph the data. Graphing the data in this way, shows real differences between Ricky's performance with mom and with dad.

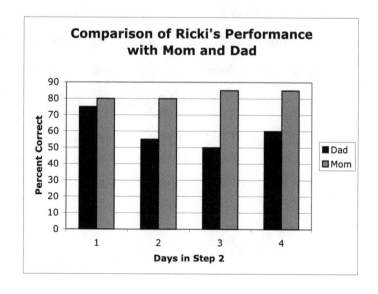

Ricky's parents were careful not to interpret the data to mean that one of them was "wrong" and the other, "right". Instead they concluded that they were likely doing something different. They proceeded to review the program, role-played the teaching interaction(s) outlined, and agreed on how they would conduct the program. The result was that Ricky began to make progress on Step 2 that was comparable to that made in Step 1.

▶ Other Considerations

Evaluation of progress on the home teaching plan. Another aspect of measurement is more global and relates to your child's progress on the entirety of the home teaching plan. That is, let's suppose that during your initial planning you have selected 10 teaching goals. In addition to measuring progress on each of the individual teaching programs, it is important to evaluate how many of the goals selected are being achieved. This is important for several reasons. First, if your child's progress is slow, looking at the extensive goal list may be disheartening. Evaluation of your child's rate of success on teaching programs can provide you with useful information for future home program planning and help you to reevaluate limits for short-term goal selection (e.g., how many teaching goals to select). On the other hand, if your child is quickly mastering the goals selected, then you may have underestimated the number of goals that you could accomplish within a specific time frame. The following Home Teaching Plan Evaluation Form, completed with information taken from Joey's home teaching plan (Chapter 9), shows how you can keep track of your child's progress on the goals selected.

Teaching goals	Program Start Date	Program End Date	Duration of Program	Outcome	Status
Follows pictorial directions in sequence	11/3/00	12/31/00	8.3 weeks	Successfully completed.	Maintenance
Maintains high levels of appropriate behavior to access reinforcers	8/3/01	9/30/01	9.7 weeks	Successfully completed.	Maintenance
Completes simple readiness worksheets independently	11/3/00	7/9/01	35.4 weeks (mastered 8 levels of difficulty	Excellent progress. New skills continuously added	Ongoing
Follows written directions	1/16/01	10/28/01	40.7 weeks (learned all words and used them functionally in the schedule	Successfully completed	Maintenance

The table above illustrates a successful home teaching plan. Although some of the teaching programs took longer to complete than others, throughout, there was steady progress and in the end, all goals were achieved. The end result was acquisition of a set of functional behaviors that made a significant difference on Joey's behavior at home and decreased stress for his mother.

The second example, that shows the program Home Teaching Plan Evaluation Form for Sean (also discussed in Chapter 9), illustrates a somewhat different outcome.

Teaching goals	Program Start Date	Program End Date	Duration of Program	Outcome	Status
Follows pictorial directions in sequence	2/6/00	6/9/00	17.7 weeks	Partially completed.	Suspended
Decrease aggression	8/1/99	7/21/00	44 weeks	Partially completed.	Suspended
Waits appropriately					Not Implemented
Plays in a small group using common toys	8/20/99	10/20/99	10 weeks	Partially completed	Suspended

Review of the completed form indicates that while there was some progress made on some of the programs, Sean's parents had difficulty implemented all of the programs included in the home teaching plan. Based on the review of the plan, it was advised that they re-evaluate their original time allocation to home teaching programs and to re-evaluate their priorities in order to focus their efforts.

Here's a blank Home Teaching Plan Evaluation Form for your use.

Teaching Goals	Program Start Date	Program End Date	Duration of Program	Outcome	Status

Is it realistic to think that I can address all behaviors/skills on my own? The intervention strategies contained in this book have focused mainly on the use of behavioral techniques designed to teach new skills/behaviors. In the examples provided, management of difficult behaviors have been addressed via positive approaches, that is, teaching pro-social skills that are incompatible with unwanted behaviors. This approach has tremendous merit since we cannot expect behavior change in a vacuum. In other words, it is important to teach children what you would like them to do instead of the unwanted behaviors. This strategy has several beneficial outcomes as follows:

By teaching positive alternatives to unwanted behavior…

- You help your child develop adaptive responses to situations that previously resulted in emotional distress.

- You teach your child responses that are valued by others. This, in turn, enables your child to engage in behaviors that are naturally reinforced by others and thus, maintained.

- Your child develops a repertoire of pro-social skills that enable them to participate in a variety of age-appropriate activities that they may have been previously unable to enjoy.

Nevertheless, there are some behaviors associated with ASD that are extremely recalcitrant to change. These include, but are not restricted to severe behavior problems, feeding problems, and sleep problems. If these are problems you are facing, and they do not respond quickly to positive approaches to intervention we have discussed, then we strongly recommend you seek competent professional consultation.

80 ✠ 03

9

Sharing Family Successes

In this chapter, we will use real examples of home teaching programs to demonstrate the process of developing and implementing in-home teaching programs that focus on addressing both child and family needs. We included these examples to demonstrate how all of the steps that we have been talking about can result in clinically significant changes that impact on child and family functioning. It is important to emphasize that in each of the examples presented, family members were active participants in all phases of the process (i.e., assessment, goal selection, prioritization, program development, data collection, and problem-solving/trouble shooting). For the sake of uniformity, each example will begin with description of the child that will contain the following information:

- Age
- Classification or diagnosis
- Standardized test results (administered around the time that program planning was initiated)
- Strengths and weaknesses as they related to child and family goals

Each example will also contain information about family circumstances, the goals identified by the child's parents, related curriculum tasks, and the status of the prerequisite skills needed prior to addressing the skills specified. When appropriate, the information will be provided in the worksheets that you have been using for program planning. Specific programs used in the interventions will be provided for a select group of the home teaching programs along with graphic summaries of the data collected on child performance. We will also identify issues that arose during program implementation (when applicable). Each example will conclude with a summary of successes, shortcomings, and recommendations for subsequent teaching programs.

Interestingly, the three examples selected demonstrate the use of child activity schedules as an integral part of the treatment plan. The applications of activity schedules you will read about demonstrate how this tool can assist you with managing behavior problems, decreasing your child's anxiety by improving the ability to anticipate events, increasing age-appropriate levels of independence, and helping children "share" their parents with other siblings and teaching them to wait appropriately for their parents to have completed essential household or personal tasks.

▶ Sam and The Mommy Schedule

About Sam...

Age	6 years, 5 months
Diagnosis	Autism
Standardized Test Results	
Receptive language	No standard score obtained
Expressive language	No standard score obtained
Overall communication	1 year, 6 months
Daily living skills	1 year, 8 months
Socialization	< 1 year

At the time of the intervention, Sam was extremely demanding of his mother's time; there was little he would do without her support. Moreover, Sam's play skills were limited; he spent the majority of his free time engaged in self-stimulatory behavior. Sam was using a picture communication book for expressive language. He was able to follow simple, verbal directions, but was not always eager to comply. Crying and tantrums were high frequency behaviors that occurred most often when Sam had to delay gratification (i.e., waiting), when he was ineffective in making his wants and needs known, when asked to stop preferred activities, and when demands were placed upon him.

About Sam's family…

- Sam lived with both parents and one older sibling, Jenny.

- Sam's sibling had developmental delays, but was not diagnosed with ASD.

- Sam's father worked the night shift and slept during day. Sam's mother also worked full-time, but was able to provide most of the childcare.

- Sam's parents were strongly committed to working at home to improve Sam's skills.

- The family had a limited support network for assistance with childcare.

- The family had a modest income and could not afford to hire "extra hands".

- Sam's mother had little time for herself and expressed the desire to spend more, quality individual time with each of her children.

- Sam's parents were strongly committed to increasing Sam's repertoire of age-appropriate skills.

Rationale for the Program(s). When reviewing parental concerns and Sam's strengths and weaknesses, a plan began to emerge. Our intent was to use and expand upon skills already in Sam's repertoire and to teach him to use his recognition of pictures to help him organize his time. In addition, we targeted the development of play skills as this was not only an age-appropriate skill, but it was also a target that would impact upon Sam's ability to interact with peers in a multitude of other settings.

Goals Selected

- ✓ Give Sam's mother a method for organizing time at home with an emphasis on increasing personal time and increasing 1:1 time with each of her children.

- ✓ Minimize interruptions from each child when mom is busy (help them to wait appropriately).

- ✓ Improve Sam's ability to use toys appropriately.

- ✓ Improve Sam's ability to wait for mom's attention (i.e., play appropriately when mom is unavailable).

- ✓ Reduce tantrums.

- ✓ Improve Sam's ability to follow a schedule to occupy his free time.

<u>Teaching Tasks</u>

- ✓ Follows a sequence of events displayed in pictures (i.e., a picture schedule)

- ✓ Uses toys appropriately.

- ✓ Takes turns (with sibling)

- ✓ Waits for parent's attention

<u>Prerequisite Skills Present in Sam's Repertoire</u>

- ✓ Made eye contact upon request

- ✓ Imitated a wide range of behaviors upon request

- ✓ Followed simple verbal directions

- ✓ Recognized pictures of familiar objects

- ✓ Pointed to pictures to communicate preferences

Two programs were run concurrently to achieve the skills. These included "Uses simple toys appropriately" and "Follows pictorial directions in sequence" (Individualized Goal Selection Curriculum, 1996).

The program essentials and the teaching method are specified for each program on the next page.

Program 1: Program Essentials Worksheet

<u>Target Skill:</u> Uses simple toys independently.

<u>Teaching Tool:</u> Shaping and fading.

<u>Clear Definition:</u> Sam will initiate and maintain play without assistance or prompts from his parents. Play is defined as appropriate toy usage for the time specified.

<u>Reinforcers:</u> Enthusiastic praise, physical stimulation in the form of "high fives" or pats on the back.

<u>Schedule of Reinforcement:</u> Sam will be reinforced for each interval in which his behavior meets the requirements for reinforcement. He will be reinforced for staying on task using a variable time schedule of 1-2 minutes.

<u>Data Recording</u>
What I will record: For each play session record a (+) for correct responses a P+ (responses that are correct following a single prompt, a (-) for incorrect responses, NR for no response, and NC for noncompliance (i.e., refusal to comply with parental request).

Schedule for data collection: Continuous data recording.

<u>Plan for Maintenance of Skills after Acquisition:</u> Following acquisition of the individual play skills, the skills will be incorporated into a picture schedule that specifies play routines so that Sam is able to occupy his free time at home with limited parental supervision. Additional programs will also address using the play skills mastered to encourage social play with his sibling, family members, and guests.

<u>Plan for Transferring Skills to New Settings:</u>
- ✓ Once the skills are mastered, staff will consult with mom regarding how to assist staff working in community-based settings (e.g., Sunday school) with scheduling and reinforcement of play activities with peers in these settings.
- ✓ Parents will also schedule outings to places in the community where Sam can apply his skills (e.g., a bowling alley).

<u>Preparation:</u> All toys that will be used for instruction should be kept in the teaching/play area. For the bowling activity, a piece of masking tape should be placed on the floor indicating where Sam should stand prior to rolling the ball.

Program 2: Program Essentials Worksheet

Target Skill: Follows pictorial directions in sequence

Teaching Tool: Verbal prompting and modeling.

Comments: In the early steps of the teaching program, the focus will be on teaching Sam to use a picture schedule to determine his mother's availability. Once he has demonstrated the ability to use toys independently, the schedule will also include pictures of toys that he should be using in order to productively occupy his time when his mother is unavailable. Next, a social component, playing with his sister, will be added.

Clear Definition:

- ✓ Throughout the day, Sam will be required to check his schedule when the kitchen time signals that it is time check. Sam will read the schedule to determine his mother's availability. If his mother is not scheduled to interact with him, he will occupy himself appropriately and will not interrupt his mother more than one time during the intervals during which she is not available for him.

- ✓ Sam will use his schedule to determine his mother's availability and to identify what he should be doing during that interval. Specifically, Sam will either play with the toy designated for that interval or play with his sister using the designated toy(s).

Reinforcers: Praise and preferred snacks.

Schedule of Reinforcement: Each correct response. Every time Sam reads the schedule, begins the activity designated, and occupies himself appropriately with only one interruption during intervals that he is scheduled to play on his own or with his sister.

Data Recording
What I will record: For each play session, record a (+) for correct responses and a (-) for incorrect responses.

Schedule for data collection: Event recording (i.e., each time there is an opportunity for the behavior to occur).

Plan for Maintenance of Skills after Acquisition: Once Sam has mastered the ability to follow the picture schedule for designated times at home, the schedule will be extended to include additional time and activities at home.

<u>Plan for Transferring Skills to New Settings</u>: Specialized schedules will be generated to help Sam cope with family outings (e.g., a schedule of chores that his parents need to complete in the community, schedules to help him cope with visiting friends or relatives, etc.).

<u>Preparation:</u> Arrange picture schedule on Sam's communication board that represent activities that he will participate in during the teaching session. Have kitchen time available.

Mommy Schedule 1: What's Mommy Doing?

In the second step of the teaching program, children were given a choice of activity so that they could occupy their time independently while Mom was busy. Accompanying changes in the picture schedule are depicted below. As you can see, there were times scheduled for each child to play alone as well as time for cooperative play.

Mommy Schedule 2: What Should I Be Doing When Mommy's Busy?

6:00 - 6:05			
6:05 - 6:10			
6:10 - 6:15			

Progress. The number of interruptions was graphed to evaluate Sam's progress. The graph, below, shows the number of interruptions during the course of the initial teaching phase.

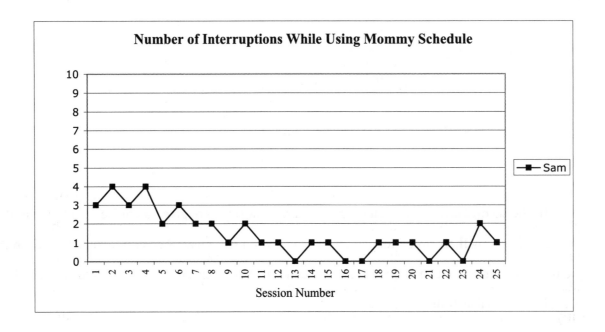

The performance data tells us that the program was reasonably effective in reducing the number of interruptions. The line indicates number of intervals with interruptions by Sam out of a total of 10 intervals. Because we were not able to determine the baseline number of interruptions while using the "Mommy schedule" without first implementing the schedule, session 1 serves as the baseline. Out of ten, 5-minute intervals, Sam interrupted during 3 of the intervals in the first session. Over sessions, the number of intervals with interruptions reduced to 1 or none. Measurement of Sam's performance indicated that the program was having a positive effect on Sam's behavior. However, his mother was not getting much relief because his sister continued to demand her time at very high rates. We offered to include Sam's sister in the program and Sam's mother was very receptive. The graph, below, shows Sam's and Jenny's performance on Step 1 of the program.

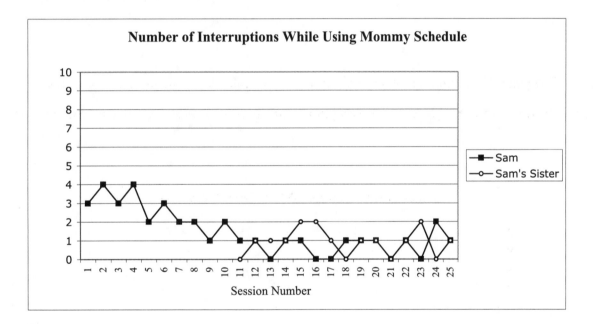

Recap. Comparing Sam's performance on the first four and the last four sessions on the graph, it is possible to see that the program was having a positive impact. Specifically, his average number of interruptions during the first four sessions was 3.5 and his average number of interruptions over the last four sessions was .75. A similar comparison of Jenny's performance early in the program and later in the sequence of program implementation (i.e., the line with the open circle) indicated that there was a slight increase in her average number of interruptions .75 -

1.0. The limited change in Jenny's behavior may have been due to the fact that the program had been implemented for a shorter amount of time than Sam's. Perhaps she needed more practice with the schedule. The other possibility is that at the beginning of the program, the frequency of Jenny's interruptions was fairly low.

▶ Joey's Household Chores and More

About Joey…

Age	10 years old
Diagnosis	Autistic Disorder and Fragile X Syndrome
Standardized Test Results	
Receptive language	Standard score = 64
Expressive language	Standard score = 40
Overall communication	Standard score = 59
Daily living skills	Standard score = 55
Socialization	Standard score = 76

About Joey's family…

- Joey's father, who was the primary caregiver, had recently passed away after a protracted illness.

- One younger sibling resided at home. This sibling was also diagnosed with autism, but had more intense care giving needs due to his level of cognitive functioning, limited ability to communicate, limited repertoire of adaptive behaviors, and high rates of behavioral excesses.

- Limited support network, locally.

- Extended family members were giving Joey's mother "advice" that she did not find helpful (i.e., considering residential placement for at least one of her boys).

- Joey's mother was committed to keeping both boys at home for as long as possible.

- Joey's mother had difficulty asking for or accepting help from others. She insisted that it was important for her to be able to raise her children without the help of others.

During our initial meetings, it was clear that Joey's mother was under considerable stress due to the recent death of her husband and the challenge of parenting two children diagnosed with ASD. At the time of the intervention, mom was having a difficult time getting Joey to follow her directions. She was also struggling with how to limit the physical "wrestling" that the boys engaged in because it was getting dangerous with increased size and strength of both boys. She reported that these management issues were increasing her stress levels and that she found, at times, she was not handling her emotional reactions well.

The primary issues/concerns identified during the initial consultation interview included the following:

- ✓ Keeping Joey productively occupied
- ✓ Minimizing instigation of physical activity with his brother (e.g., wrestling)
- ✓ Increasing compliance
- ✓ Improving Joey's academic skills.

Rationale for the Program(s). When reviewing parental concerns and Joey's strengths and weaknesses, a plan began to emerge. As in our description of Sam, our intent was use and expand skills already in Joey's repertoire and to teach him to use his recognition of pictures to help him organize his time.

Given the difficulties with child management that mom was encountering and the related stress, a strategy of "divide and conquer" was adopted. Looking at Joey's strengths, we felt that with only a little effort on mom's part, she could teach Joey to follow a picture schedule and increase his compliance with her requests. By increasing Joey's independence and compliance, our intent was that she would receive help with some (albeit minor) household chores and she would gain extra time to either attend to her other son or to personal or household tasks that needed to be addressed. Also by increasing Joey's repertoire of productive, age-appropriate behavior at home, we hoped to create an environment where mom could increase her attention on positive instead of negative (unwanted) behaviors. Moreover, if Joey was productively busy, we hoped that there would be less time for him to be instigating his brother.

We targeted household tasks and homework as the activities to be scheduled. Joey loved to help his parent(s) with household tasks and was very good at completing chores competently. Since our focus was to increase Joey's compliance with parental requests and increase his ability to complete sequences of tasks with limited parental supervision, only skills that were already in his repertoire were included.

In order to satisfy Joey's mother's interest in "boosting" Joey's academic skills, homework was also incorporated into the activity schedule. At first, the tasks sent home were only those that Joey had mastered in the school setting. Use of the maintenance tasks was seen as preferable to sending home worksheet involving new skills as the intent was to have Joey function as independently as possible at home. By using only maintenance tasks when we introduced the picture schedule, we were hoping that Joey would enjoy doing homework (i.e., getting reinforced for relatively easy work and having an opportunity to "show off" his skills) thereby increasing the likelihood that he would actually do his homework. The intent was to increase the difficulty of the homework content once Joey was successfully completing assigned tasks at home.

Goals selected

- ✓ Assist Joey's mother with dividing her time between her two children so that she could meet their individual needs.

- ✓ Heighten maternal awareness of the importance of establishing expectations for the performance of age-appropriate tasks at home.

- ✓ Capitalize on child's strengths and reinforce age-appropriate independence.

- ✓ Decrease maternal stress.

- ✓ Improve Joey's academic skills.

- ✓ Involve Joey in community-based extracurricular activities

Prerequisite skills present in Joey's repertoire

- ✓ Made eye contact upon request

- ✓ Able to follow one and two-part directions for familiar activities

- ✓ Able to carry out complex, procedures involving motivating and familiar tasks (i.e., dressing, cooking). In other words, he had good procedural memory.

- ✓ Good visual recognition skills (e.g., recognized pictures of familiar objects).

- ✓ Verbal: spoke in phrases and sentences

- ✓ Limited, but emerging sight word vocabulary (word recognition)

- ✓ Prior experience with token reinforcement in school. He had demonstrated the ability to manage behavior within acceptable limits using highly structured reinforcement programs.

- ✓ Basic awareness of contingencies (i.e., If you do this, then _____ will happen).

- ✓ Basic repertoire of readiness skills (matching, sorting, writing letters, copying words, etc.).

✓ Joey's visual and spatial abilities were stronger than his verbal abilities.

✓ Enjoyed helping others (i.e., a natural reinforcer)

Teaching Tasks

✓ Follows a sequence of events displayed in pictures (i.e., a picture schedule)

✓ Completes daily homework assignments. At first the worksheets addressed maintenance of skills learned at school and later reinforced new learning of sight words needed to transition his picture schedule to a written schedule of activities.

✓ Learns new sight words (schedule-related)

Other recommendations

✓ Involving Joey in age-appropriate, after school or extra curricular activities

✓ Stress management for Joey's mother

✓ Medication consult for sibling

✓ Exploration of respite services (i.e., center-based or in-home) to provide mom with assistance on an "as needed basis".

Three programs were run concurrently to achieve the skills. These included "Maintains high levels of appropriate behavior to access reinforcers", "Completes simple readiness worksheets", and "Follows pictorial directions in sequence" (Individualized Goal Selection Curriculum, 2000). A fourth program, "Follows written directions" was added later in the sequence of program implementation.

The program essentials and the teaching method are specified for each program on the next page.

Program 1: Program Essentials Worksheet

<u>Target Skill:</u> Maintains high levels of appropriate behavior to access reinforcers

<u>Teaching Tool:</u> Shaping and consequence alteration

Comments: The program was designed to gradually increase the number of intervals required for reinforcement. That is, in order to earn the reinforcer, Joey needed to improve his behavior during each successive step in the teaching program.

- ✓ The shaping procedure used in this program involved gradually increasing the criteria for reinforcement. In the early teaching steps, Joey was only required to behave appropriately for 71% of the opportunities provided daily. Once he demonstrated the ability to accomplish this goal, he was required to behave appropriately during 86% and then, during 100% of the daily opportunities.

- ✓ Consequence alteration referred to changing mom's response to Joey's behavior. Instead of nagging or coaxing him to follow through with task directions, she simply stated the contingencies for earning reinforcement. Hence, appropriate behavior was reinforced and inappropriate behavior was not reinforced.

<u>Clear Definition:</u> When prosocial behaviors (Following mother's directions promptly and ceasing unwanted behaviors when asked to "Stop") are included in a token reinforcement program, Joey will engage in high rates of the target behaviors to earn points that can be exchanged for reinforcers at a later time.

<u>Reinforcers:</u>

- ✓ Joey will earn points that can be exchanged for the following reinforcers: tangibles, special activities, riding in the front seat of the car…, verbal praise for compliance.

- ✓ Joey will also be able to earn the privilege of being a "special helper" every morning in school if he earns the required number of points at home on the previous night.

<u>Schedule of Reinforcement:</u> Points and verbal praise will be earned for each interval in which the target behaviors occur. Tokens/points may be exchanged at home at specific times as indicated on Schedule for Token Exchange. Being a "special helper" at school will be earned daily at school if Joey has earned his points at home on the previous day.

<u>Data Recording</u>
What I will record: If Joey earns his points for the interval without requiring a prompt, record a (+) for the interval. If he requires a prompt, record a (P+). Record a (-) for all instances of noncompliance. If Joey responds to mom's requests to cease an unwanted behavior, record a (+). If he requires a prompt, record a (P+). If he does not comply, record a (-). If mom does not need

to ask Joey to "Stop" an unwanted behavior or if there is no chore scheduled in an interval when data is recorded, record NO for no opportunity.

Schedule for data collection: From 2 P.M. to 9 P.M., daily, on weekdays.

<u>Plan for Maintenance of Skills after Acquisition</u>: Once criterion has been reached on the program, mom will continue to have Joey perform the chores on his schedule and will continue reinforcement for compliance with task and behavioral requests.

<u>Plan for Transferring Skills to New Settings</u>: Once Joey has met criteria on the current program, mom will identify other settings where she would like to implement the compliance and chore compliance program (e.g., completing specific chores/tasks when helping mom, run errands in the community as in the grocery store and ceasing unwanted behaviors in community settings (e.g., church, playground, the homes of friend's and relatives, etc.)).

<u>Preparation</u>:

- ✓ Have picture schedule available.
- ✓ Have point card available for token reinforcement.

Prototype of Joey's Picture Schedule

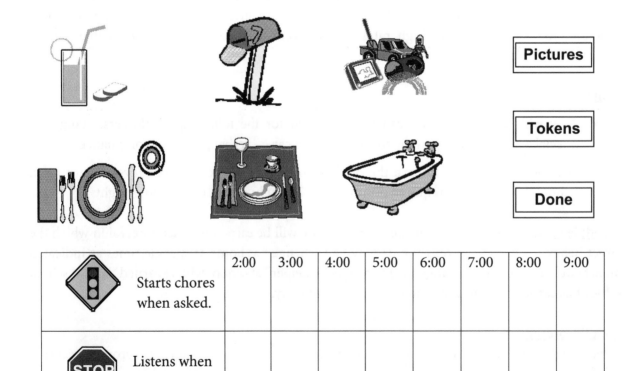

		2:00	3:00	4:00	5:00	6:00	7:00	8:00	9:00
	Starts chores when asked.								
	Listens when mom says "Stop".								

Skill: Maintains high levels of prosocial behaviors to access reinforcment Start Date:				Schedule: All day
Step #	Teaching Step	How do I know if s(he)'s right?	What do I do if s(he)'s wrong?	When do I move to the next step?
1	In the P.M. upon return from school, review the rules for earning tokens and the reinforcers. Post the rules in a visible place at home. After explaining the rules to Joey, have him repeat them back to you so you have some indication about his comprehension. Set the timer to signal the end of the 60 minute interval. Each time Joey requires a warning for starting his chores or to cease unwanted behavior, say," If you want to earn your points, you need to ..."	For each of the chore intervals, record a (+) if Joey begins the tasks when asked (within 10 seconds). Also, for each interval record a (+) if Joey responds to your requests to cease unwanted behavior within 10 seconds.	If Joey requires a prompt, say, "Joey, this is a warning. If you want to earn your points, you need to ____". After the warning, remind Joey that he needs to follow your directions if he wants to earn his points.	When Joey earns 5/7 points, i.e., combined (+'s and P+'s) over the course of three consecutive days, go on to Step 2.
2	Same as Step 1.	Same as Step 1.	Same as Step 1.	When Joey earns 6/7 points, i.e., combined (+'s and P+'s) over the course of three consecutive days, go on to Step 3.
3	Same as Step 1.	Same as Step 1.	Same as Step 1.	When Joey earns 7/7 points, i.e., combined (+'s and P+'s) over the course of three consecutive days, go on to Step 3.
4	Maintenance. Same as Step 1.	Same as Step 1.	Same as Step 1.	When Joey earns 7/7 points, i.e., combined (+'s and P+'s) over the course of 4 consectuive weeks, the program has been successfully completed. Continue to reinforce Joey's compliance for continued maintenance.

Notes:

Program 2: Program Essentials Worksheet

Target Skill: Follows pictorial directions in sequence

Teaching Tool: Shaping

Comments: *The shaping procedure in this program focused on systematically increasing the number of chores that Joey completed. In other words, as Joey mastered simple schedules, the schedule became progressively more complex.*

Clear Definition(s):

✓ Using pictures to sequentially depict activities, Joey will identify each task by carrying out the activities in the picture.

✓ Using words to identify a sequence of activities on a schedule, Joey will complete the designated tasks.

✓ Using a picture schedule indicating his mother's availability, Joey will regulate his activity based on his mother's schedule (i.e., he will occupy himself appropriately and not interrupt his mother more than one time during the intervals that she designates as being unavailable for him)

Reinforcers: Token reinforcement for each activity completed. Backup reinforcers will be preferred snacks that are assigned different point values. Joey's most preferred snacks will cost the most (a price list will be available at exchange times).

Schedule of Reinforcement: Joey will earn tokens for each task completed. However, to increase his ability to wait for reinforcement, the number of chores required prior to earning his snack will be systematically increased as follows:

# of Tokens	Reward
3 tokens	1 snack
6 tokens	1 snack
8 tokens	1 snack
10 tokens	1 snack

Data Recording

What I will record: Mom will record a (+) for correct responses, a (P+) for prompted responses, a (-) for incorrect responses, and (NR) for no response.

Schedule for data collection: Event recording. Each time there is an opportunity to complete a task or chore.

<u>Plan for Maintenance of Skills after Acquisition</u>: After Joey demonstrates mastery of the current schedule, mom will maintain his chore/task schedule at home. During maintenance, she will reinforce independent completion of all items scheduled.

<u>Plan for Transferring Skills to New Settings</u>: To be determined.
Preparation: Arrange picture or word schedule prior to initiating the program. Also have the token point card available for use during the program.

Program 3: Program Essentials Worksheet

<u>Target Skill:</u> Completes simple readiness worksheets independently

<u>Teaching Tool:</u> Verbal prompting and modeling

Comments: Anytime Joey makes an incorrect response, mom will verbally prompt a correct response. If the response remains incorrect, mom will model the correct response (i.e., demonstrate via example).

<u>Clear Definition(s)</u>: When presented with simple readiness worksheets in an individual work setting, Joey will complete the worksheet independently. Independently is defined as not requiring parental assistance to remain on task and responding appropriately (not necessarily accurately).

<u>Reinforcers</u>: Enthusiastic praise and a token for beginning work when instructed to "Do your homework" and completing assignment(s).

<u>Schedule of Reinforcement</u>: Joey will earn a token for each assignment completed.

Data Recording
What I will record: Record a (+) for correct responses and a (-) for incorrect responses after Joey has completed the worksheet.

Schedule for data collection: Event recording for each item included on the homework worksheet.

<u>Plan for Maintenance of Skills after Acquisition</u>: After Joey demonstrates mastery of readiness skills, more challenging assignments, commensurate with his abilities, will be sent home.

<u>Plan for Transferring Skills to New Settings</u>: If there are opportunities for Joey to participate in an after school or respite program, skills will be transferred to that setting.

<u>Preparation</u>: Arrange a quiet location where Joey can complete his homework.

Program 4: Program Essentials Worksheet

<u>Target Skill:</u> Follows written directions

<u>Teaching Tool:</u> Verbal prompting and massed practice

Comments: Joey will acquire sight words via drill and practice.

<u>Clear Definition(s):</u> Joey will independently complete a list of activities written on a schedule at home. When he has completed 10 activities, he will earn a snack.

<u>Reinforcers:</u> Social praise.

<u>Schedule of Reinforcement:</u>

- ✓ For the sight words drills, reinforce each correct response.
- ✓ When written words replace pictures on the schedule, use a fixed ratio schedule of reinforcement. Joey will earn a snack after completing 10 chores/activities.

<u>Data Recording:</u>
What I will record: Mom will record a (+) for correct responses, a (P+) for prompted responses, a (-) for incorrect responses, and (NR) for no response.

Schedule for data collection: Event recording.

<u>Plan for Maintenance of Skills after Acquisition</u>: Continued use of written activity schedule that will be reinforced as specified in the program.

<u>Plan for Transferring Skills to New Settings</u>: Expanding sight vocabulary to include items that might be found on a shopping list, a "to do" list, etc.

<u>Preparation</u>: Have sight words available. Arrange activity schedule using sight words acquired at each step of the program and pictures for sight words not yet acquired.

Sight Words	
lunch	story
coat	dishes
sneakers	trains
mail	toys
homework	TV
cook	dishes
table (represents "set table")	ball
dinner	pillow
bath	to road (represents "trash cans to road")
bed	to house (represents "trash cans to house")

Also have the token point card available for use during the program.

Skill:Follows written instructions in sequence Start Date:		Schedule: Daily		
Step #	Teaching Step	How do I know if s(he)'s right?	What do I do if s(he)'s wrong?	When do I move to the next step?
1	Prior to beginning a teaching trial, Joey should be sitting quietly at the table. Hold up an index card with the written direction. Say, "What does this say?" Continue the procedure for each of the five word cards selected for this step of the program.	If Joey correctly identifies the word on the card, reinforce with social praise. Record a (+).	If Joey responds incorrectly, record a (-). Model the correct response and immediately re-ask the question. Present up to three models before ending the teaching trial.	When Joey responds with 90% accuracy on the first set of word cards over three consecutive days, replace the pictures on his schedule with the word cards. Proceed to Step 2.
2	Same as Step 1 with second set of 5 word cards.	Same as Step 1.	Same as Step 1.	When Joey responds with 90% accuracy on the second set of word cards over three consecutive days, replace the pictures on his schedule with the word cards. Proceed to Step 3.
3	Same as Step 1 with third set of 5 word cards.	Same as Step 1.	Same as Step 1.	When Joey responds with 90% accuracy on the third set of word cards over three consecutive days, replace the pictures on his schedule with the word cards. Proceed to Step 4.
4	Same as Step 1 with fourth set of 5 word cards.	Same as Step 1.	Same as Step 1.	When Joey responds with 90% accuracy on the fourth set of word cards over three consecutive days, replace the pictures on his schedule with the word cards. Proceed to Step 5.
5	Maintenance. Only word cards will be used on Joey's activity schedule.	If Joey begins the activity specified on the word card within 20 seconds and completes the activity, record a (+). When 10 points are earned, Joey may trade his points for a preferred snack.	If Joey does not comply with the written direction, physically prompt the response using a least to most prompting procedure. Record a (-)	When Joey completes his chores using the written directions only with 100% accuracy, the program is officially completed. Continue to reinforce compliance with tasks on his activity schedule.

Notes:

Progress. The graph below shows the average percent correct for the number of chores that Joey completed during each step of the program (i.e., indicated by number of chores completed). While the data are not dramatic, they demonstrate the ease with which new skills can be learned when teaching programs adequately break complex tasks into simpler components.

Acquisition of Picture Schedule

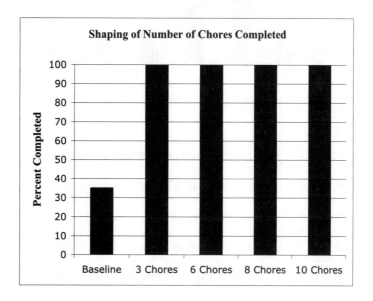

The next graph shows the number of trials that it took Joey to learn to follow the written directions. The large number of sessions required to master Step 2 indicates that Joey had difficulty making the transition from pictures to words. However, his mother persevered and after he "caught on", he quickly met criteria on other steps that required him to use words instead of pictures.

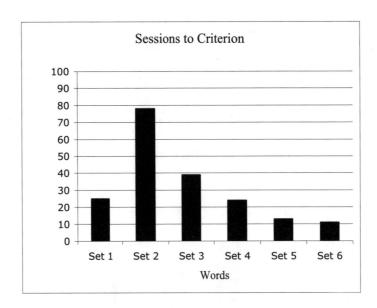

Recap. The home teaching plan that was implemented for Joey was effective in increasing compliance with parent requests (i.e., both task and behavior-related instructions), increasing his ability to occupy his free time appropriately, and increasing his ability to perform age-appropriate household tasks. In addition, the plan focused on a positive approach to reducing unwanted behaviors at home (i.e., instigating his sibling and potentially dangerous rough housing). Finally, mom's desire to increase Joey's reading skills (i.e., increase sight vocabulary) was addressed within the context of the daily schedule.

The individual teaching programs were designed to effect behavior change in a gradual fashion. That is, each of the teaching targets was broken down into small steps that could be easily achieved. The effect, visible in graphs of Joey's performance, was high rates of correct or appropriate responding and little experience with frustration for both mom and Joey. Thus, Joey did not resist participation in the home teaching programs and mom continued to implement the programs because they were mutually satisfying.

Joey's mother did seek out and receive some in-home support that she utilized for only a short time. She also enrolled Joey in an after school social skills group that met weekly and other seasonal activities (e.g., soccer).

Perhaps the most important outcome achieved was the reduction of parental stress. Mom reported feeling like she was becoming more effective with limit setting and felt much better about how she was parenting her boys. Moreover, she reported feeling as if there was more structure and order in her home and that she had more individual time to devote to each of her boys.

► Sean's Aggression: Using Assessment to Create an Effective Intervention

About Sean...

Age	3 years, 3 months
Diagnosis	Autistic Disorder
Standardized test results	
Receptive language	Below 1 year, 9 month level
Expressive language	No standard score obtained
Overall communication	1 year, 1 month
Daily living skills	1 year, 5 months
Socialization	< 1 year
Motor skills	3 years, 5 months

About Sean's family...

- Sean's parents had recently relocated to a suburban area and his father was still living and working out of town except on weekends.

- One other sibling, a brother (age 5), resides at home.

- The family had a limited support network, locally.

At the time of the intervention, Sean was nonverbal and had begun to use a picture communication system to indicate his needs and wants. Although he had some ability to express his needs/wants, he had difficulty waiting for his needs and wants to be satisfied. Also, Sean was very resistant to completing or participating in activities of daily living. This made completion of daily routines very difficult for his mother. Sean's aggression was creating problems in that his brother had begun to avoid him and his mother was sustaining bruises. The aggressive behavior was a source of significant stress in the household.

Primary parental issues/concerns were as follows:

✓ Reducing aggression

✓ Improving Sean's ability to wait for preferred activities

✓ Increasing appropriate social interaction with family members (particularly with his brother).

✓ Increasing Sean's ability to transition from one activity to another (and tolerating interruption of preferred activities).

Descriptive Assessment of Sean's behavior

Step 1: Collecting information

In order to better understand the factors that precipitated and maintained Sean's behavior, we had his parents record the frequency of aggressive behaviors and the settings and circumstances in which the aggressive behaviors occurred. We asked Sean's parents to collect data separately for each type of aggression identified (hitting and kicking, biting, and throwing). Clear definitions for each of the target behaviors were provided in the teaching programs that were written to address the target behaviors. Parents were asked to record the frequency of each of the behaviors, the duration of the behaviors, the length of the observation sample, the antecedent or setting events, the consequences, and the intensity of the behavior on a 1-3 scale (i.e., 1=mild, 2=moderate, 3=severe) using a record sheet similar to the one below.

Date: _____ Observation Period Start: _____ End _____							
Behavior	Frequency	Intensity 1-3	Time (Duration)	Setting	Antecedent	Consequence	Notes / Comments

Step 2: Interpretation of the Information Collected

Once the information was collected, it was summarized in several ways. First, we categorized the situations that were most frequently associated with aggressive behavior and looked at the relative amount of aggression by situations. Nine categories of antecedents were identified when reviewing the data collected by Sean's parents. These included the following:

1. Toileting
2. Dressing (Sean was dependent for dressing)
3. Undressing: (Sean was dependent for undressing)
4. Access to preferred activities denied
5. Access to preferred foods denied
6. Access to preferred toys denied
7. Expectations unmet
8. Cessation of preferred activities
9. Specific fear inducing activities

The proportion of aggressive behaviors in each of the categories is shown in the pie chart, below.

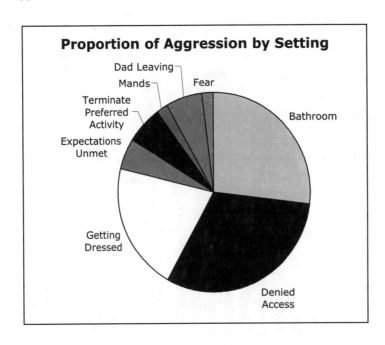

The chart indicated that the antecedent associated with the most aggression was when Sean was asked to terminate a preferred activity. The antecedent associated with the second highest frequency of aggression was getting dressed and so on. The graph below shows the intensity of aggression associated with specific antecedent events.

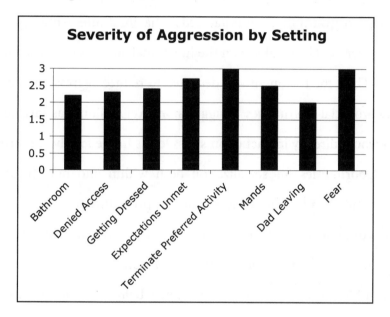

Finally, the graph, below, shows the combined frequency of aggression over a 20-day period. Although there was a considerable amount of variation in the number of aggressive behaviors that occurred daily, the emotional consequences for the family, the impact the behavior had on completion of age-appropriate tasks, and the social consequences of the behavior, resulted in a decision to intervene in an effort to reduce aggression.

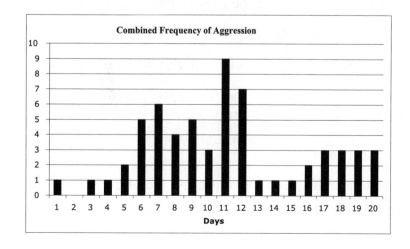

Review of the consequences that followed aggression was not as informative as there was no consistent parental response. Sean's parents reported that they had been using a time-out procedure to manage the aggression. However, the information that they collected indicated that they did not use the time-out procedure consistently.

Rationale for Program(s). A multifaceted, behavioral intervention plan was developed to address family concerns. The results from the functional analysis were used to select the target behaviors of focus. Thus, the treatment was designed to reduce aggression and at the same time teach appropriate, prosocial alternatives to aggression. Aggression was targeted because it was felt that reduction would directly impact upon stress levels in the family and provide Sean with a greater range of opportunities for socialization both within and outside of the family. In addition, the family had already been using a time out procedure to reduce aggressive behavior and they wanted to continue using this intervention strategy. When developing the intervention, every effort was made to maximize the resources available in the family and to capitalize on existing resources within the school setting to teach new behaviors and to assist parents with the generalization of skills acquired at school to the home setting.

Goals Selected

- ✓ Decrease aggression
- ✓ Increase Sean's ability to manage toileting needs independently
- ✓ Increase Sean's ability to dress himself
- ✓ Improve Sean's ability to transition between activities without incident
- ✓ Increase Sean's tolerance for delaying gratification
- ✓ Increase Sean's ability to engage in family social activities without aggression

Prerequisite Skills Present in Sean's Repertoire

- ✓ Made eye contact upon request
- ✓ Sean was able to identify pictures and use and recognize pictures within the context of communication exchanges.
- ✓ Imitated a wide range of behaviors upon request

✓ Followed simple verbal directions

✓ Sean was knowledgeable about contingencies (simple cause-effect relationships) as the result of having participated in behavioral interventions in the school setting. Sean worked well for preferred tasks/snacks and had a wide variety of interests (i.e., potential reinforcers).

✓ Sean had a history of rapid learning rate if the teaching programs adequately simplified the teaching steps and the steps were appropriately sequenced.

Teaching Tasks

✓ Since toileting was a trigger for aggression at home, parents were advised to refrain from toilet training. Two school programs were targeted to address the toileting issues namely, "Remains dry and unsoiled between scheduled toileting" and "Indicates need to toilet when reminded". Generalization of skills to the home setting was planned following acquisition in school. This "division of labor" is an example of how parents can utilize other agencies to help and decrease the stress/burden on families.

✓ Since dressing and undressing were also identified as antecedents to aggression, a dressing task, "Puts on front opening garment", was targeted. It was felt that this would be a good task to begin with since going outdoors after putting on his coat was predicted to be a naturally occurring reinforcer for Sean. The goal was initially implemented at school with the intent of generalizing the skill to the home setting following acquisition.

✓ "Follows pictorial directions in sequence" was targeted as a home program. The focus of this program was to provide a structure to help Sean adhere to a schedule of activities and to anticipate events. This goal was included to address aggression associated with the need to terminate preferred activities and to help Sean cope with unmet expectations. Specifically, it was thought that by showing Sean that more preferred activities would occur after less preferred activities, he might be more motivated to complete the less preferred activity. The logic for using the schedule to help Sean cope with unmet expectations was that although he might not be able to engage in preferred activities when he wanted to, they would appear somewhere on the schedule. Thus, this program was intended to be run with the "Waits appropriately program, below.

✓ Once the ability to use a basic picture schedule was acquired, the plan was to modify the program to teach Sean to tolerate variations in the schedule.

✓ "Waits appropriately" was also targeted as part of the solution for aggression that occurred when Sean's "expectations were unmet". During discussions with Sean's parents, they described situations that required Sean to wait (i.e., delay gratification). Specific examples included wanting to leave his brother's swimming lesson, waiting for food at a restaurant, etc.

✓ "Plays in a small group using common toys" was targeted in an effort to increase Sean's ability to socialize with family members, particularly his brother. The goal was also selected for the purpose of increasing Sean's range of interests.

Program 1: Program Essentials Worksheet

<u>Target Skill:</u> Waits appropriately

<u>Teaching Tool:</u> Stimulus control procedures and shaping.

Comments: During the implementation of this program, Sean was taught to use age-appropriate toys and activities that his mother carried in a tote bag. The bag and a kitchen timer set for the duration of the "waiting" period and the verbal instruction, "Sean, you have to wait. Find something in your bag to keep yourself busy" were the environmental events that informed Sean that he needed to wait appropriately.

<u>Clear Definition:</u> When informed that he needs to wait patiently, Sean will occupy his time using age-appropriate toys/activities included in a tote bag of playthings without engaging in disruptive behaviors (i.e., crying or screaming) and aggressive behaviors.

<u>Reinforcers:</u> Verbal praise, tickles and hugs, preferred toy/activity

<u>Schedule of Reinforcement:</u> Reinforcement is scheduled to occur after Sean has waited appropriately for the specified period.

<u>Data Recording:</u>
What I will record: Record a (+) for correct responses (i.e., Sean waits appropriately for the designated time period) on the first trial. Record a (P+) if Sean waits appropriately on the second trial. Record a (-) if Sean does not wait appropriately on either trial.

Schedule for data collection: During every teaching opportunity.

<u>Plan for Maintenance of Skills after Acquisition:</u> Once Sean has reached mastery levels of performance, his parents will continue to use the waiting strategy during routine daily activities. In order to ensure that Sean maintains the skill learned, collect data on use of the skill on two days during the week. If the behavior is maintained for three consecutive weeks, discontinue data collection, but continue to use the program.

<u>Plan for Transferring Skills to New Settings:</u> Following mastery, select one regularly attended, public setting in which you will implement the program. Once Sean demonstrates the ability to use his skills in this setting, select another setting and so on.

<u>Preparation:</u> Prepare the toys/activities for the tote bag. Toys should be those that are minimally disruptive to others (e.g., electronic games, music with headset, etc.). Activities may include developmentally appropriate worksheets (e.g., dot to dot, matching, coloring, etc.). In order to maintain Sean's interest and motivation, frequently change the toys/activities in the tote bag. Also, be sure to always have Sean's preferred toy/activity available for reinforcement.

Skill: Waits appropriately Start Date: Schedule: Throughout the day				
Step #	Teaching Step	How do I know if s(he)'s right?	What do I do if s(he)'s wrong?	When do I move to the next step?
1	Acquisition at home: Intermittently during the course of the day when Sean requests an item or an activity, tell him that he has to "Wait" and "Play with your toys" while presenting him with a tote bag filled with age-appropriate games, toys, puzzles, etc. Set a digital kitchen timer for 30 seconds. Demonstrate (model) for Sean what you expect him to do and when the timer goes off, say, "That's the way we wait!"	If Sean imitates toy play and keeps himself busy for 30 seconds, reinforce him with verbal praise, tickles, and/or a preferred toy. Record a (+).	If Sean does not imitate your behavior, physically prompt him to select a toy or activity from the tote bag and using a least to most prompting sequence, prompt appropriate play. Immediately reset the timer and repeat the task instructions "You have to wait"; "Play with your toys". Record a (P+) if Sean complies. Record a (-) if he does not. If tantrums or aggression occur, terminate the teaching trial. Record a (T).	Continue to conduct trials in this manner until Sean receives (+'s) on 80% of the teaching trials on at least 10 trials each day. Then proceed to the next step. If Sean does not earn (P+)'s or (+'s) on 80% of the trials presented over 3 days, consider decreasing the duration of play to 15 seconds. When Sean achieves 80% correct responses over 3 consecutive days, continue with Step 2.
2	Same as Step 1 except that Sean must occupy himself for 90 seconds.	If Sean occupies himself appropriately for 90 seconds, reinforce him with verbal praise, tickles, and/or a preferred toy. Record a (+).	If Sean does not occupy himself appropriately for 90 seconds, physically prompt him to select a toy or activity from the tote bag and using a least to most prompting sequence, prompt appropriate play. Immediately reset the timer and repeat the task instructions "You have to wait"; "Play with your toys".	Same as Step 1 except that if the number of (P+'s) and (+'s) fall below 80%, decrease the time interval to 60 seconds until the criteria is reached. Then proceed.
3	Same as Step 1 except that Sean must occupy himself for 3 minutes.	If Sean occupies himself appropriately for 3 minutes, reinforce him with verbal praise, tickles, and/or a preferred toy. Record a (+).	If Sean does not occupy himself appropriately for 3 minutes, physically prompt him to select a toy or activity from the tote bag and using a least to most prompting sequence, prompt appropriate play. Immediately reset the timer and repeat the task instructions, "You have to wait"; "Play with your toys".	Same as Step 1 except that if the number of(P+'s) and (+'s) fall below 80%, decrease the time interval to 2 minutes until the criteria is reached. Then proceed.
4	Same as Step 1 except that Sean must occupy himself for 4 minutes.	If Sean occupies himself appropriately for 4 minutes, reinforce him with verbal praise, tickles, and/or a preferred toy. Record a (+).	If Sean does not occupy himself appropriately for 4 minutes, physically prompt him to select a toy or activity from the tote bag and using a least to most prompting sequence, prompt appropriate play. Immediately reset the timer and repeat the task instructions, "You have to wait"; "Play with your toys".	Same as Step 1 except that if the number of(P+'s) and (+'s) fall below 80%, decrease the time interval to 2 minute, thirty seconds until the criteria is reached. Then proceed.
5	Same as Step 1 except that Sean must occupy himself for between 4 and 8 minutes. The duration required should vary.	If Sean occupies himself appropriately for the specified time period, reinforce him with verbal praise, tickles, and/or a preferred toy. Record a (+).	If Sean does not occupy himself appropriately for the specified time period, physically prompt him to select a toy or activity from the tote bag and using a least to most prompting sequence, prompt appropriate play. Immediately reset the timer and repeat the task instructions, "You have to wait"; "Play with your toys".	Same as Step 1 except that if the number of(P+'s) and (+'s) fall below 80%, decrease the time interval to 4 minutes until the criteria is reached. Then proceed.
6	Same as Step 1 except that Sean must occupy himself for between 8 and 12 minutes. The duration required should vary.	If Sean occupies himself appropriately for the specified time period, reinforce him with verbal praise, tickles, and/or a preferred toy. Record a (+).	If Sean does not occupy himself appropriately for the specified time period, physically prompt him to select a toy or activity from the tote bag and using a least to most prompting sequence, prompt appropriate play. Immediately reset the timer and repeat the task instructions, "You have to wait"; "Play with your toys"	When Sean is able to occupy himself appropriately for up to 12 minutes on 9/10 occasions over 3 consecutive days, the teaching program is completed. Implement maintenance and generalization programs.

Program 2: Program Essentials Worksheet

<u>Target Skill:</u> Decrease aggression

<u>Teaching Tool:</u> Consequence alteration and differential reinforcement of incompatible behaviors

Comments: Consequence alteration refers to a change in the consequences for unwanted behaviors. The time out procedure has been retained per your request. The change in the consequence involves the consistency with which the procedure is implemented. In order to be effective, time out should be used after each instance of aggressive behavior. The differential reinforcement procedure requires that you give Sean positive attention for not engaging in aggressive behavior.

<u>Clear Definition:</u> Aggression includes hitting, kicking, biting, pinching, and throwing objects at others. It is defined as forceful contact with another person (i.e., arm, leg, mouth) or contact made with another person by an object that was thrown in their direction.

<u>Reinforcers:</u> verbal praise for behaviors that are incompatible with aggression. You should label the appropriate behavior (e.g., "Nice playing") with light tickles, and hugs.

<u>Schedule of Reinforcement:</u>
- ✓ at the end of every five minute interval for which there is no aggression
- ✓ at the end of every ten minute interval for which there is no aggression
- ✓ at the end of every twenty minute interval for which there is no aggression
- ✓ at the end of every thirty minute interval for which there is no aggression

<u>Data Recording:</u>

What I will record: for each of the behaviors identified above, record the time of day, duration of the behavior, the intensity, the consequence (including time out), whether or not time out is implemented, and the antecedent. Use the monitoring sheet to indicate intervals in which reinforcement was given for no aggression.

Interval Recording for Appropriate Behavior Circle Observation Interval: 5 10 20 30 minutes Mark a (+) if reinforcement was given and (–) if it was not												
Time:	1	2	3	4	5	6	7	8	9	10	11	12

Schedule for data collection: Event recording for each aggressive behavior; interval recording for appropriate behavior.

<u>Plan for Maintenance of Skills after Acquisition</u>: After Sean reaches the criteria for program completion, continue to reinforce appropriate behavior and to use time out for aggression. Consider introducing a token reinforcement program that may be easier to implement.

<u>Plan for Transferring Skills to New Settings</u>: Introduce program into the community with modifications, as needed.

<u>Preparation</u>: Arrange for a quiet space for time out. Have recording sheets available.

Program 3: Program Essentials Worksheet

<u>Target Skill:</u> Follows pictorial directions in sequence

<u>Teaching Tool:</u> Prompt fading and shaping

Comments: The program is designed to gradually increase the number of activities that Sean is required to complete on his schedule and to decrease the number of adult prompts needed to follow the schedule, find the task materials, and complete the activities. In the early steps of the program he will need to complete one and then two tasks that should be followed by preferred activities (i.e., the reinforcer). In the next step of the program, Sean will be required to leave a preferred activity to access another highly desirable task/activity. Preferred and nonpreferred activities are then intermixed and the number of tasks/activities to be completed are increased. Finally, household tasks and tasks related to daily routines will be added.

<u>Clear Definition</u>: At the sound of the kitchen timer, Sean will look at his picture schedule to identify the scheduled task/activity. He will then get the materials necessary, engage in the activity until it is completed or until the timer goes off, and will then return to the schedule board, place the completed activity in the "Done" pocket and will begin the next task.

<u>Reinforcers</u>: Primary reinforcement in the form of a preferred "snack" and preferred toys or activities.

<u>Schedule of Reinforcement</u>: The schedule of reinforcement is directly linked to the schedule. If there are two activities on the schedule (i.e., one task and a snack), the reinforcement schedule will be a Fixed Ratio 1. If there are three activities on the schedule, two activities and snack, the reinforcement schedule will be a Fixed Ratio 2 schedule.

<u>Data Recording</u>

What I will record: Record a (+) for each activity completed at each step of the program, a (P+) for activities needing prompts, and (T) if the program needs to be terminated because of problem behavior.

Schedule for data collection: Data should be collected during each teaching session.

<u>Plan for Maintenance of Skills after Acquisition</u>: Following mastery of the skills needed to follow a picture schedule, continue using the schedule at home to assist Sean in organizing and completing activities of daily living and leisure activities.

<u>Plan for Transferring Skills to New Settings</u>: After Sean demonstrates mastery of the skills needed to follow a picture schedule, schedules can be devised to provide a structure for Sean during outings in the community. Activities such as helping to gather specific groceries, getting

in line at the checkout counter, paying, and having the snack purchased will likely help Sean delay gratification and reduce problem behaviors while shopping.

Preparation: Have materials ready to make the schedule. Also have a kitchen timer available.

Step #	Teaching Step	How do I know if s(he)'s right?	What do I do if s(he)'s wrong?	When do I move to the next step?
Skill: Follows pictorial directions in sequence Start Date:			Schedule: After school daily.	
1	Prior to the start of the session, arrange the picture schedule for two activities: a moderately preferred play activity and a highly preferred activity. Set the kitchen timer. When the kitchen timer rings, tell Sean that it is time to check his picture schedule, e.g.,"Did you hear the bell?" "Let's check your schedule". Show Sean his picture schedule and point to the first activity. Say, "Look! It's time to ____!" Assist Sean with getting the materials and bringing them to the designated task area. Place the activity card in the "Doing" section of the schedule. Set the kitchen time for 5 minutes. Tell Sean, "You can put your things away when the timer rings". When the timer rings, tell Sean that it's "Clean up time". Help him put the materials away, place the activity card on the schedule in the "Done" pocket, and direct his attention to the next activity. Say: "Look, it's time for snack". Throughout, follow a least to most prompting procedure.	Record a P + for each behavior that Sean completes with no more than three adult prompts on the data sheet as follows: Gets materials, places activity card in the "Doing" column, completes activity, puts materials away, places activity in the done column, looks for next activity, and gets materials for next activity. Record a "+" if Sean performs the task component without adult assistance.	If Sean requires more than three prompts to complete the task component, use hand-over-hand prompting and record a (-). If he refuses to participate in the activity, prompt up to three times. If he does not respond or engages in aggression or tantrum behavior, terminate the tria. Record a (T).l	When Sean has earned a minimum of 12/14 (+'s) and (P+'s) for each of the task components for the two tasks, on 3 consecutive days, go on to Step 2.
2	Same as in Step 1.	Same as in Step 1 except that you will only record a P+ if Sean requires no more than 2 adult prompts to complete each task component.	Same as in Step 1 except that hand-over-hand prompting is required when Sean requires more than two prompts.	When Sean has earned a minimum of 12/14 (+'s) and (P+'s) for each of the task components for the two tasks, on 3 consecutive days, go on to Step 3.
3	Same as in Step 1.	Same as in Step 1 except that you will only record a P+ if Sean requires only 1 adult prompt to complete each task component.	Same as in Step 1 except that hand-over-hand prompting is required when Sean requires more than one prompt.	When Sean has earned a minimum of 12/14 (+'s) and (P+'s) for each of the task components for the two tasks, on 3 consecutive days, go on to Step 4.
4	Same as in Step 1 except that the last task on the schedule should be a snack or a preferred activity.	Same as in Step 1 except that you will only record and reinforce correct responses.	Remind Sean that he needs to complete his tasks if he wants to earn preferred toys or activities (e.g., "tickle time").	When Sean has earned a 100% for each of the task components for each of the two tasks on 3 consecutive days, go on to Step 5.
5	Same as Step 1 except that three tasks sequenced from least preferred task to more preferred tasks. Snack or a preferred activity included as the third task.	Same as Step 4.	Same as Step 4.	When Sean has earned a 100% for each of the task components for each of the three task on 3 consecutive days, go on to Step 6.
6	Same as Step 1 except that four tasks are included on the schedule with snack or a highly preferred activity included as the fourth task.	Record a (+) if Sean transitions from one activity on the schedule to the next. Record a (-) if he does not. Record a (T) if the session is terminated due to refusal, tantrums, or aggression.	Same as Step 4.	When Sean has made 4/4 transitions (+'s) on 3 consecutive days, go on to Step 7.
7	Same as in Step 1 except four tasks should be sequenced as follows: preferred, less preferred, moderately preferred, highly preferred.	Same as Step 6.	Same as Step 4.	When Sean has made 4/4 transitions (+'s) on 3 consecutive days, go on to Step 8.
8	Same as in Step 1 except four tasks should be sequenced as follows: highly preferred, less preferred, moderately preferred, highly preferred.	Same as Step 6.	Same as Step 4.	When Sean has made 4/4 transitions (+'s) on 3 consecutive days, go on to Step 9.
9	Same as in Step 1 except three of the four tasks should be routine activities. Parents may want to continue using activity schedule during specific times of day.	Same as Step 6.	Same as Step 4.	When Sean has made 4/4 transitions (+'s) on 3 consecutive days, go on to Step 10.
10	Maintenance and generalization. Construct schedules for daily routines and schedules for community activities.	Same as Step 6.	Same as Step 4.	

Program 4: Program Essentials Worksheet

<u>Target Skill:</u> Plays in a small group using common toys

<u>Teaching Tool:</u> Fading and differential reinforcement

<u>Clear Definition:</u> When presented with familiar toys (i.e., those that Sean has learned to use appropriately) in a group of 1-3 other family members, Sean will remain in the play area and engage in appropriate play behaviors. That is, Sean will use toys appropriately, will refrain from taking toys from others or throwing toys, and will not wander away from the play area, tantrum, or aggress. Interactive play is not required, but should be encouraged.

<u>Reinforcers</u>: physical reinforcement (i.e., "tickle time")

<u>Schedule of Reinforcement</u>: Specified in the steps of the teaching program. Reinforcement will be delivered after successful completion of 5, 10, 15, or 20 minutes of appropriate play during each 30 minute teaching session.

<u>Data Recording</u>
What I will record: Record a (+) for intervals in which all of the behaviors defined above are observed and no aggressive or disruptive behaviors are present. Record a (P+) if Sean requires only one prompt to remain in the play area and play appropriately. Record a (-) if Sean engages in any unwanted behaviors or he requires multiple prompts to remain in the play area for the specified interval.

Schedule for data collection: Data recording will vary as a function of the step that you are working on in the teaching program. During Step 1, 5 minute intervals, you will record data for each 5 minute interval. During Step 2, you will record data for each 10 minute interval and so on.

<u>Plan for Maintenance of Skills after Acquisition</u>: Following mastery of the program, continue to set up play sessions with family members. New toys and activities may be introduced as Sean adds new skills to his repertoire.

<u>Plan for Transferring Skills to New Settings</u>: Once mastery of appropriate play within a small group is achieved, implement the program with other children or family members (i.e., cousins, neighbors, in a play group, etc.).

<u>Preparation</u>: Set up play area with some of Sean's favorite toys/activities. Also include items that are conducive to cooperative play, e.g., assembling floor puzzles, bowling pins, etc.

Skill: Plays in a small group Start Date:		Schedule: 30 minutes per day		
Step #	**Teaching Step**	**How do I know if s(he)'s right?**	**What do I do if s(he)'s wrong?**	**When do I move to the next step?**
1	Set kitchen timer for 5 minutes. Say, " Sean, let's play with toys". Remind Sean that if he wants to earn tickling, he needs to play nicely. Family member should play with toys of their choice (i.e., floor puzzle, building blocks, race cars, trains, etc.). Periodically invite Sean to play with your toys.	At the end of the 5 minute interval provide reinforcement for appropriate toy use and behavior (i.e., no aggression). Record a (+) and reinforce. Record a(P+) if Sean responds to prompts to remain in the play area or to play with toys (i.e., he stays in the play area or plays with toys for 1 minute following the prompt). Reset timer for another 5 minutes.	Provide verbal prompts to redirect Sean to the play area if he wanders off and provide verbal prompts to encourage toy play. If Sean stays outside of the play area for more than one minute, physically guide him back to the play area. If Sean needs more than three prompts to stay in the play area or if Sean becomes upset, discontinue the trial and record a (-). Wait 5 minutes and introduce another teaching trial. Implement the time-out procedure if aggression occurs.	When Sean's performance reaches 100% correct responses (which include (+)'s and (P+)'s) over 10 consecutive trials, move on to Step 2.
2	Same as above.	Same as above.	Same as above.	When Sean's performance reaches 100% on (+)'s only on three consecutive days, move on to Step 3.
3	Set kitchen timer for 10 minutes. Say, " Sean, let's play with toys". Remind Sean that if he wants to earn tickling, he needs to play nicely. Family member should play with toys of their choice (i.e., floor puzzle, building blocks, race cars, trains, etc.). Periodically invite Sean to play with your toys.	Same as above.	Same as above.	When Sean's performance reaches 100% on (+)'s only for three consecutive days, move on to Step 4.
4	Set kitchen timer for 15 minutes. Say, " Sean, let's play with toys". Remind Sean that if he wants to earn tickling, he needs to play nicely. Family member should play with toys of their choice (i.e., floor puzzle, building blocks, race cars, trains, etc.). Periodically invite Sean to play with your toys.	Same as above.	Same as above.	When Sean's performance reaches 100% correct responses over 3 conssecutive days, move on to Step 5.
5	Set kitchen timer for 20 minutes. Say, " Sean, let's play with toys". Remind Sean that if he wants to earn tickling, he needs to play nicely. Family member should play with toys of their choice (i.e., floor puzzle, building blocks, race cars, trains, etc.)	Same as above.	Same as above.	When Sean's performance reaches 100% correct responses over 3 conssecutive days, move on to Step 6.
6	Set kitchen timer for 30 minutes. Say, " Sean, let's play with toys". Remind Sean that if he wants to earn tickling, he needs to play nicely. Family member should play with toys of their choice (i.e., floor puzzle, building blocks, race cars, trains, etc.).	Same as above.	Same as above.	When Sean's performance reaches 100% correct responses over 3 conssecutive days, your program is successfully completed.

Notes:

Progress. Review of the progress on the goals targeted in the school setting indicated that Sean did successfully complete a toilet training program and the dressing program (i.e., "Puts on a front-opening garment"). Moreover, his mother participated in teaching sessions at school and the skills were easily transferred to the home setting.

The decrease in documented progress on the remaining home programs was largely due to the fact that Sean's parents stopped data recording. They reported that they continued program implementation at home and that they were highly satisfied with the behavioral changes that resulted. Unfortunately, we were no longer able to to consult on these home programs because there was no data to enable us to engage in the Measurement and Modification phases of the A.I.M.M. model. Therefore the programs were classified as "partially successful" and from a consulting standpoint suspended until Sean's parents provided us with adequate data so that we could resume the consultation process.

Recap. This example demonstrated the use of a functional analysis to guide goal selection. Based on the results of the assessment, the home teaching plan included teaching programs focused on reducing aggressive behavior and teaching incompatible, social responses including how to wait patiently, how to play near others without incident, and how to follow a picture schedule so that Sean could anticipate when events/activities would occur and so that he could learn to make transitions between activities smoothly.

In addition, Sean's example highlighted how to utilize resources outside of the home to achieve home goals. Remember the toileting and dressing skills that were taught in the school setting first to minimize the burden on the parents?

Although Sean's parents were highly motivated to implement the home teaching programs, this example also illustrates how families can be overzealous and try to implement too many programs at once. Nevertheless, the family was successful in effecting some degree of change in the behaviors of interest and their efforts paid off. Sean's behavior improved, he learned to play within an a play area with others without incident, and he learned to follow a picture schedule. Family stress was decreased because Sean's ability to transition from one activity to another improved, he was toilet trained and became more independent with dressing, and he could play with his brother for short periods of time.

▶ Summary

The examples included in this chapter were selected since they highlight the importance of considering the child as part of a larger unit and the positive impact that this type of planning and goal selection can have on both child behavior and family functioning. In all three examples, families reported decreased stress, better allocation of parent time, improved child behavior, and more satisfying relationships amongst family members.

It is important to note that in the example describing Sean, his parents seem to have overcommitted to the home intervention plan. Moreover, his mother had a difficult time with the structure of the behavioral interventions (i.e., the perceived rigidity and the need for data collection). Although she did not consistently implement the programs as written or routinely provide us with information about Sean's daily performance, she did report that she followed the procedures during the course of their daily activities. The data that we did receive, indicated that progress was made on each of the goals targeted. We can only imagine what the outcome would have been if she had been more consistent with program implementation and provided us with performance data so that we could have consulted on program modifications to help her troubleshoot problems that may have impeded progress.

ဆာ ✕ ಬ

10

Things to Remember

You have completed the "How to" part of the book and have read through several, real life examples of how the ideas about family focused intervention can be applied to select goals that benefit your child and your family. In this chapter we present you with lists of the basic ideas conveyed in the book to keep in mind when you embark on this journey.

As you begin the process of developing a family individualized enhancement plan, there are several guidelines to follow.

When creating the FIEP

- ✓ Be patient: Meeting the individual needs of family members is a process that takes time.

- ✓ Be judicious: be a good listener. If you want your family to participate, all family members must be heard.

- ✓ Mediate: balance individual and family needs – everyone gets something.

- ✓ Prioritize!

- ✓ Maintain balance: Contemplate overlapping needs when selecting goals

- ✓ Be creative: Think outside of the box. Using the examples in the book may be helpful. Also use the resources listed in Chapter 11.

- ✓ Don't ignore your own needs

- ✓ Be clear about the roles of family involvement in the home teaching process

When developing a home teaching plan for your child

- ✓ Be realistic

- ✓ Use examples in the book

- ✓ Use a curriculum guide

- ✓ Think in terms of sequence; simple to the complex

- ✓ Organize your wish list into functional sequences of behavior

<u>When developing home teaching programs</u>

- ✓ Use principles

- ✓ Break complex skills into manageable skill components

- ✓ Provide adequate reinforcement

- ✓ Set evaluation criteria

- ✓ Measure performance/progress

- ✓ Use performance data for decision-making

- ✓ Engage in the hypothesis testing process to figure out what might be hindering progress on programs. Remember that this is a process. You may not get it right the first time.

- ✓ Modify programs when the data inform you that something is not "quite right".

<u>How do I know when I am in trouble?</u>

- ✓ My child is not making adequate progress

- ✓ Challenging behaviors are exacerbated by the home teaching process

- ✓ The general atmosphere of the family has gotten more despondent.

- ✓ Stress levels are on the rise.

- ✓ Significant mood problems become visible in one or more family member(s)

<u>If you encounter difficulty</u>

- ✓ Seek professional consultation

- ✓ Be a good consumer. Evaluate the quality of the service. Be appropriately assertive; don't waste your time with unskilled service providers.

<u>Coping strategies you can use</u>

- ✓ Take breaks: Make sure that everyone in the family gets personal time.

- ✓ Use scheduling to maximize clarity of each family member's responsibility

- ✓ Start small; add more to your home program as you encounter success

- ✓ Take time to reinforce yourself and your family for their efforts

✓ Don't be a superhero

✓ Let others help

✓ Utilize available resources

✓ Think creatively about resources

✓ Make sure you don't forget family recreational activities. It is important to share fun activities together.

▶ Some Resources

Obviously this book cannot provide you with the all of the information you and your family will need to achieve all of your goals. Here are some of our favorite books that we recommend to parents and will provide you with important information to help in your continuing development of the skills discussed in this book.

- *Autism: Identification, Education and Treatment*, 3rd edition. Edited by D. E. B. Zager. Lawrence Erlbaum Associates, Publishers: Mahwah, NJ.

- *Autism: Teaching Does Make a Difference*. Written by B. Scheuerman and J. Webber. Wadsworth Thomson Learning: Belmont, CA.

- *Behavioral Intervention for Young Children with Autism: A manual for parents and professionals*. Edited by C. Maurice; Coedited by G. Green & S. C. Luce. Pro-ed: Autisn, TX.

- *Behavior Modification: What It Is and How to Do It*. Written by: G. Martin and J. Pear. Prentice Hall: Upper Saddle River, NJ.

- *Children with Autism: A Parent's Guide*. Edited by M. D. Powers. Woodbine House: Bethesda, MD.

- *Clinical Practice Guideline for Autism/Pervasive Developmental Disorders*. Sponsored by the New York State Department of Health. http://www.health.state.ny.us/nysdoh/eip/index.htm

- *Let Me Hear Your Voice: A Family's Triumph Over Autism*. Written by C. Maurice. Fawcett Columbine: New York.

- *Preschool Education Programs for Children with Autism*. Edited by J. S. Handleman & S. L. Harris.

- *Right from the Start: Behavioral Intervention for Young Children with Autism*. Written by S. L. Harris & M. J. Weiss. Woodbine House: Bethesda, MD.

- *The Autism Encyclopedia.* Edited by J. T. Neisworth and P. S. Wolfe. Brooks Publishing Co: Baltimore, MD.

- *Topics in Autism: Siblings of Children with Autism: A Guide for Families.* Written by S. Harris. Woodbine House: Bethesda, MD.

▶ Conclusion

Our purpose in creating this book was to assist families in the development, implementation, and evaluation of a Family Individualized Enhancement Plan, using the AIMM model. The topics and principles we presented may be new to you, and it may take some practice and re-reading until you feel comfortable with this strategy. But don't be discouraged! Remember, people we refer to as having expertise are skilled service providers who typically have spent four or five years in post-graduate study, several more years of internship and supervised practice, and many years of implementing complex intervention programs for children with ASD and their families. All skills take practice and time to learn for everyone. However, remember, you are not trying to acquire the skills of a professional in order to help the diversity of children with ASD and their families, but rather are focusing on your own family. If you do implement a FIEP, you will see change in your child with ASD, your family, and yourself. Before long you will be taking control of your child's development and family's functioning and your efforts will be rewarded!

৪০ ✠ ൦൪

References

American Psychiatric Association (June 15, 2000). *Diagnostic and Statistical Manual of Mental Disorders DSM-IV-TR* (Text Revision). Arlington, VA: American Psychiatric Press.

Anderson, S. and Romanczyk, R.G. (2000) "Early Intervention for Young Children with Autism: Continuum Based Behavioral Models." *The Journal of the Association for Persons with Severe Handicaps*, 24 (3),162-173.

Baker, B.L., Smithen, S.J., & Kashimal, K.J. (1991). "Effects of parent training on families of children with mental retardation: Increased burden or generalized benefit?" *American Journal on Mental Retardation*, 96, 127-136.

Bebko, J.M., Konstantareas, M.M., & Springer, J. (1987). "Parent and professional evaluations of family stress associated with characteristics of autism." *Journal of Autism and Developmental Disorders*, 17, 565-578.

Bentovim, A. (1972). "Emotional disturbances of handicapped preschool children and their families: Attitudes to the child." *British Medical Journal*, 3, 579-581.

Boyce, G., Behl, D., Mortensen, L. & Akers, J. (1991). "Child characteristics, demographics and family processes: Their effects on the stress experienced by families of children with disabilities." *Counseling Psychology Quarterly*, 4 (4) 273-288.

Braaten, E. & Felopulos, G. (2003). *Straight Talk about Psychological Testing for Kids*. NY: Guilford Press.

Breismeister, J.M. & Schaefer, C.E. (Eds.). (1998). *Parent training. Parents as co-therapists for children's behavior problems*. New York, NY: John Wiley and Sons.

Bristol, M.M. (1979). *Maternal coping with autistic children: The effect of child characteristics and interpersonal support*. Unpublished doctoral dissertation, University of North Carolina, Chapel Hill.

Bristol, M.M. & Schopler, E. (1983). "Stress and coping in families of autistic adolescents." In E. Schopler & G.B. Mesibov (Eds.), *Autism in adolescents and adults* (pp. 251-278).

Bristol, M.M. and Schopler, E. (1984). "A developmental perspective on stress and coping in families of autistic children." In J. Blacher (Ed.), *Severely handicapped children and their families* (pp.91-141). Orlando, FL: Academic Press.

Bromley, B. E. & Blatcher, J. (1992). "Parental reasons for out-of-home placement of children with severe handicaps." *Mental Retardation*, 29 (5) 275-280

Buoma, R. Schweitzer, R. (1990). "The impact of chronic childhood illness on family stress. A comparison between autism and cystic fibrosis." *Journal of Clinical Psychology*, 46, 722-730.

Constantine, L.L. (1986). *Family paradigms: The practice of theory in family therapy.* New York: Guilford Press.

DeMyer, M. (1979). *Parents and children in autism.* New York: Wiley.

DeMyer, M. & Goldberg, P. (1983). "Family needs of the autistic adolescent." In E. Schopler & G.B. Mesibov (Eds.). *Autism in adolescents and adults.* (pp. 225-250). New York: Plenum Press.

Eddy, D.M., and Hasselblad, V. (1994). "Analyzing evidence by the confidence and profile method." In *Clinical Practice Guideline Development: Methodology Perspectives.* McCormick KA, Moore SR and Siegel RA (eds.) Rockville, MD: Agency for Health Care Policy and Research, Public Health Service, US Department of Health and Human Services (AHCPR Publication No. 95-0009)

Goldenberg, I. & Goldenberg , H. (1998). *Counseling Today's Families.* Pacific Grove, CA: Brooks/Cole.

Goldenberg, I. & Goldenberg , H. (2000). *Family therapy: An overview.* Belmont, CA: Wadsworth/Thomson Learning.

Goldenberg, H. & Goldenberg, I. (2002). *Counseling today's families* (4th edition). Pacific Grove, CA: Brooks/Cole.

Hall, R.V. & Hall, M. (1980). *How to select reinforcers.* Lawrence, KS: H & H Enterprises, Inc.

Hawley, D.R. & DeHann, L. (1996). "Toward a definition of family resilience: Integrating life-span and family perspectives." *Family Process*, 35, 283-298.

Howard, J (1978). "The influence of children's developmental dysfunction on marital quality and family interaction." In R.M. Lerner and & G.B. Spanier (Eds.), *Child influences on marital and family interaction: A life-span perspective* (pp. 275-297). New York: Academic Press.

Howlin, P. (1988). "Living with impairment: The effects on children having an autistic sibling." *Child Care, Health and Development*, 14, 395-408.

Holland, J.P. (1995) "Development of a clinical practice guideline for acute low back pain." *Current opinion in orthopedics*, 6, 63-69.

Noyes-Grosser, D., Holland, J.P., Lyons, D., Romanczyk, R. G., & Gillis, J.M. (in press). New York State Clinical Practice Guidelines I: Rationale and Methodology for Developing Guidelines for Early Intervention Services for Young Children with Developmental Disabilities: Evidence-based clinical practice guidelines for infants and toddlers with disabilities and their families: Recommendations for finding children early and supporting parents in the intervention process. Submitted to: *Infants and Young Children*.

Kalachnik, J.E., Leventhal, B. L., James, D.H., Sovner, R., Kastner, T.A., Walsh, K., Weisblatt, S.A., & Klitzke (1998). "Guidelines for the Use of Psychotropic Medication." In Reiss, S. and Aman, M.G. (Eds.) *Psychotropic Medication and Developmental Disabilities: The International Consensus Handbook*. The Ohio State University Nisonger Center.

Koegel, R.L. & Koegel, L.K. (1995). *Teaching Children with Autism: Strategies for Initiating Positive Interactions and Improving Learning Opportunities*. Baltimore, MD: Paul H. Brookes.

Koegel, R.L. & Koegel, L.K., and Schreibman (1991). In R. Pranz (Ed.), *Advances in behavioral assessment of children and families*. London Jessica Kingsley Publishers.

Kohut, S. (1966). "The abnormal child: His impact on the family." *Journal of the American Physical Therapy Association*, 42, 160-167.

Kozloff, M.A. (1974). *Educating children with learning and behavior problems*. NY: John Wiley & Sons, Inc.

Kysela, G., McDonald, L., Reddon, J., & Gobeil-Dwyer, F. (1988). "Stress and supports to families with a handicapped child." In Marfo, K. (Ed.). *Parent-child interaction and developmental disabilities: Theory, research, and intervention*, NY: Praeger.

Lutzker, J.R. & Campbell, R.V. (1995). *Ecobehavioral family interventions in developmental disabilities*. Pacific Grove, CA: Brooks/Cole.

Maurice, C., Green, G., Foxx, R.M. (2001). *Making a Difference: Behavioral Intervention for Autism*. Austin, TX: Pro-Ed.

Maurice, C., Green, G., Luce, S.C. (1996). *Behavioral Intervention for Young Children with Autism: A Manual for Parents & Professionals*. Austin, TX: Pro-Ed.

Maurice, C. (1993). *Let Me Hear Your Voice: A Family's Triumph over Autism*. New York: Fawcett Columbia.

Milgrim, N.A. & Atzil, M. (1988). "Parenting stress in raising autistic children." *Journal of Autism and Developmental Disorders*, 18, 425-424.

Minuchin, S., Lee, Y.W., & Simon, G.M. (1966). *Mastering family therapy: Journeys of growth and transformation*. NY: Wiley.

Moes, D., Koegel, R.L., Schreibman, L., & Loos, L.M. (1992). "Stress profiles for mothers and fathers of children with autism." *Psychological Reports*, 71, 1272-1274.

Morgan, S.B (1988). "The autistic child and family functioning: A developmental family systems perspective." *Journal of Autism and Developmental Disabilities*, 18, 263-280.

Minuchin, S., Lee, Y.W., & Simon, G.M. (1966). *Mastering family therapy: Journeys of growth and transformation*. NY: Wiley.

National Research Council (2001). "Educating Children with Autism." Committee on Educational Interventions for Children with Autism. Division of Behavioral and Social Sciences and Education. Washington, DC: *National Academy Press*.

Newson, E. & Hipgrave, T. (1982). *Getting Through to Your Handicapped Child*. Cambridge, MA: Cambridge University Press.

New York State Department of Health Clinical Practice Guideline: The Guideline Technical Report. – *Autism/Pervasive Developmental Disorders, Assessment, and Intervention for Young Children (Age 0-3 Years)*. Publication No. 4217. New York State Department of Health, 1999.

New York State Department of Health Clinical Practice Guideline: The Guideline Technical Report. – *Communication Disorders, Assessment, and Intervention for Young Children (Age 0-3 Years)*. Publication No. 4220. New York State Department of Health, 1999.

Powers, M. (1989), (Ed). *Children with Autism. A Parent's Guide*. Bethesda, MD: Woodbine House.

Rice, E.P. (1993). *Intimate relationships, marriages, and families*. Mountain View, CA: Mayfield.

Ritvo, E.R., Freemen, B.J., Geller, E., and Yiwiler, A. (1983). "Effects of fenflouramine on 14 outpatients with the syndrome of autism." *Journal of the American Academy of Child Psychiatry*, 22, 549-558.

Rodrigue, J. R., Morgan, S.B., & Gefkin, G. (1990). "Families of autistic children: Psychological functioning of mothers." *Journal of Clinical Child Psychology*, 19, 371-379.

Romanczyk, R.G., Lockshin, S.B. & Matey, L. (2000). *The Individualized Goal Selection Curriculum*. Apalachin, NY: CBT Associates.

Romanczyk, R.G., Arnstein, L.. Soorya, L and Gillis, J. (2002). "The Myriad of Controversial Treatments for Autism: A Critical Evaluation of Efficacy." In Lilienfeld, Lohr, and Lynn (Eds.), *Science and Pseudoscience in Contemporary Clinical Psychology*.

Romanczyk, R.G. and Gillis, J.M. (2004). "Treatment Approaches for Autism: Evaluating Options and Making Informed Choices." In D. Zager (Ed.), Autism: *Identification, Education, and Treatment* (3rd Edition). Hillsdale, N.J: Lawrence Erlbaum Associates.

Scheuerman, B. & Webber, J. (2002). *Autism: Teaching does make a difference*. Belmont, CA: Wadsworth Thomson Learning.

Schriger, D.L. (1995) "Training panels in methodology." In *Clinical Practice Guideline Development: Methodology Perspectives*. McCormick, K.A., Moore, S.R. and Siegel, R.A. (eds.) Rockville, MD: Agency for Health Care Policy and Research, Public Health Service, US Department of Health and Human Services (AHCPR Publication No. 95-0009).

Shermer, M. (September 2002), *Smart People Believe Weird Things*. NY, NY: Scientific American, Inc.

Trute, B. & Hauch, C. (1988). "Social network attributes of families with positive adaptation to the birth of a developmentally disabled child." *Canadian Journal of Community Mental Health*, 7, 5-11.

U.S. Department of Health and Human Services. *Mental Health: A Report of the Surgeon General—Executive Summary*. Rockville, MD: U.S. Department of Health and Human Services, Substance Abuse and Mental Health Services Administration, Center for Mental Health Services, National Institutes of Health, National Institute of Mental Health, 1999.

Van Hasselt, V.B., Sisson, L.A., & Aachi, S.R. (1989). "Parent training to increase compliance in a young multihandicapped child." *Journal of Behavior Therapy and Experimental Psychiatry*, 18, 275-283.

Walsh, F. (1966). "The concept of family resilience: Crisis and challenge." *Family Process*, 35, 261-281.

Wing. L. 1972 *Autistic children: A guide for parents*. New York: Brunner/Mazel

Wing, L. (1985). *Autistic Chidlren: A guide for parents and professionals.* New York, NY: Brunner/Mazel.

Wolf, L.C. & Goldberg, B.D. (1986). "Autisitic children grow up: An eight to twenty-four year follow up study." *Canadian Journal of Psychiatry,* 31, 550-556.

Wolf, L.C., Noh, S., Fisman, S.N., & Speechley, M. (1989). Brief Report: *Psychological Effects of Parenting Stress on Parents of Autistic Children.*

Woolf, S.H.. (1991) *AHCPR Interim Manual for Clinical Practice Guideline Development.* Rockville, MD: Agency for Health Care Policy and Research, Public Health Service, US Department of Health and Human Services, (AHCPR Publication No. 91-0018).

Woolf, S.H. (1994). "An organized analytic framework for practice guideline development: using the analytic logic as a guide for reviewing evidence, developing recommendations, and explaining the rationale." In *Clinical Practice Guideline Development: Methodology Perspectives.* McCormick, K.A., Moore, S.R. and Siegel, R.A. (eds.) Rockville, MD: Agency for Health Care Policy and Research, Public Health Service, US Department of Health and Human Services (AHCPR Publication No. 95-0009)

80 ✠ 03